A Century of College Humor

Norman
Rockwell

A Century of College Humor

Cartoons, Stories,
Poems, Jokes and
Assorted Foolishness from
Over 95 Campus Magazines,
Edited by Dan Carlinsky

RANDOM HOUSE/NEW YORK

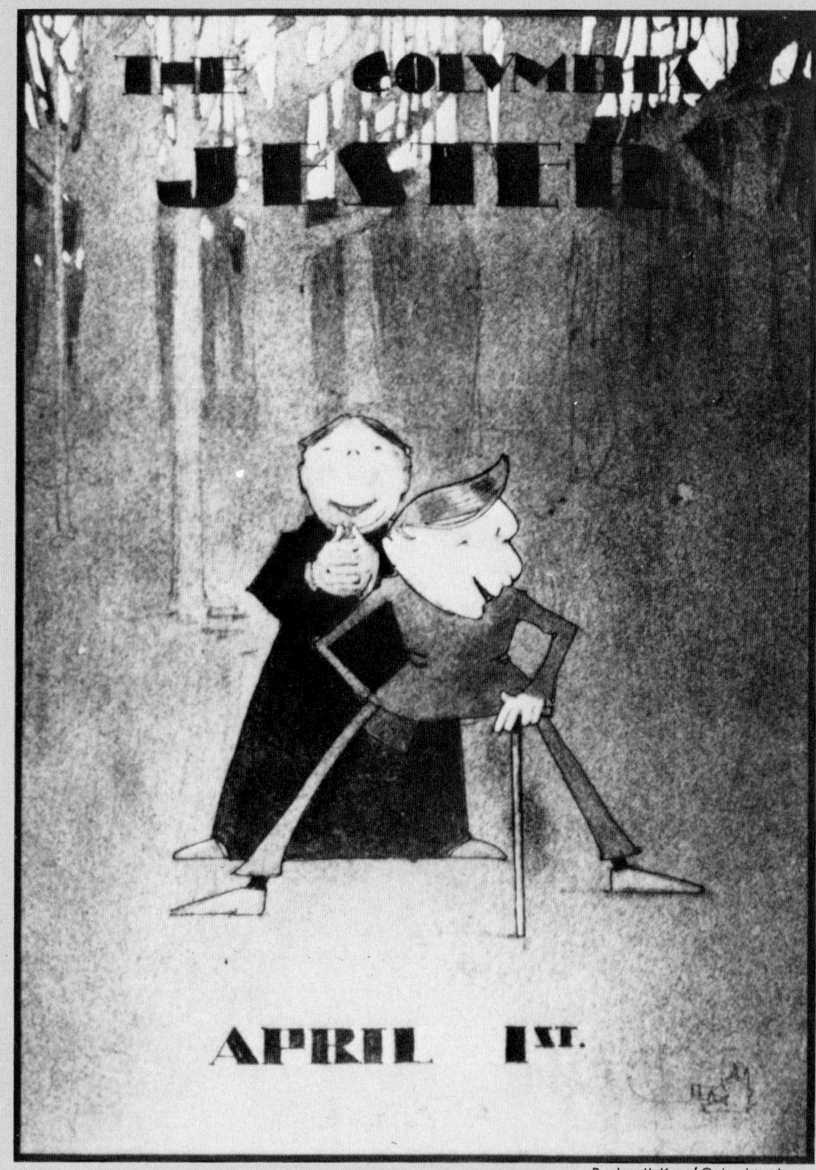

Rockwell Kent/*Columbia Jester*

 Published in the United States by Random House, Inc., New York, and simultaneously in Canada by Random House of Canada Limited, Toronto.

ISBN: 0-394-46002-2
Library of Congress Catalog Card Number: 95-117647

Manufactured in the United States of America

This book was composed at The Poole Clarinda Company, printed at Rae Publishing, Inc., Cedar Grove, New Jersey, and bound at Economy Bookbinding Corporation, Kearny, New Jersey.

Design: Charles Schmalz

98765432
First Edition

Princeton Tiger

Princeton Tiger

NYU Medley

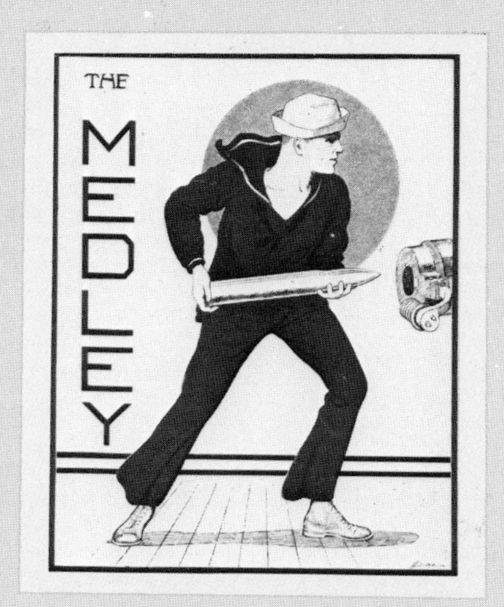

NYU Medley

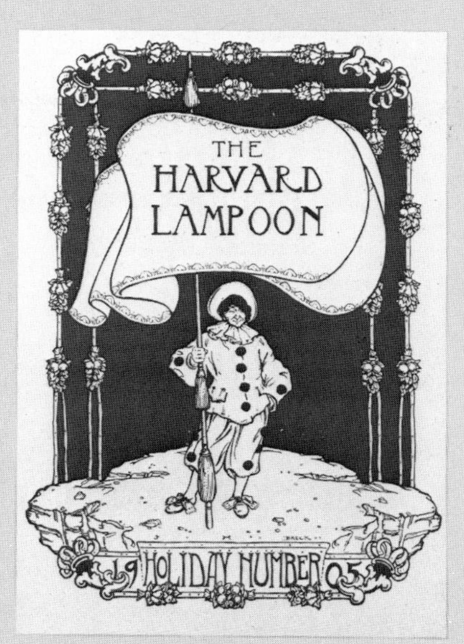

Joseph Breck/*Harvard Lampoon*

Robert C. Hallowell/*Harvard Lampoon*

Durr Friedley/*Harvard Lampoon*

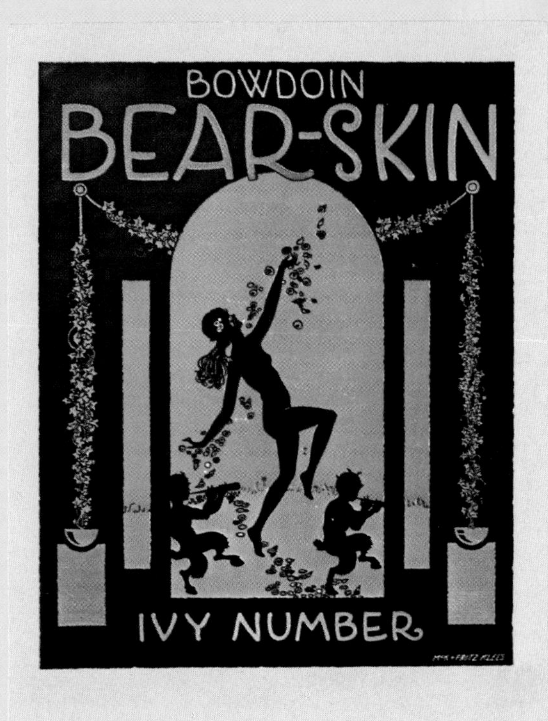

McK. and Frederic S. Klees/*Bowdoin Bear-Skin*

R. J. Holmgren/*Columbia Jester*

William B. Banks/*Johns Hopkins Black & Blue Jay*

Girard Meeks/ *Utah Humbug*

Bryan Quirk/ *Johns Hopkins Black & Blue Jay*

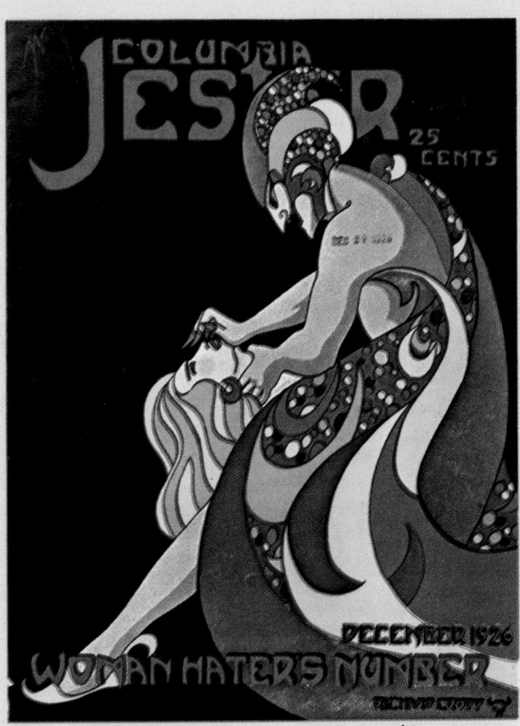

Richard Cropp/ *Columbia Jester*

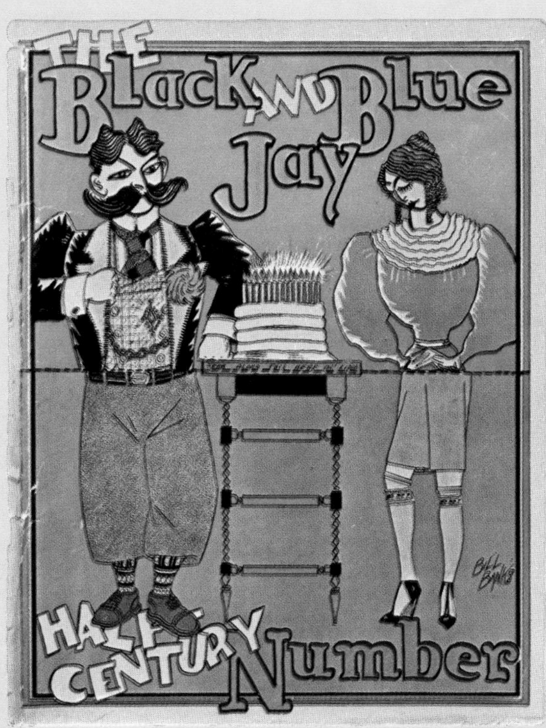

William B. Banks/ *Johns Hopkins Black & Blue Jay*

Contents

Purdue Rivet

A FEW WORDS ABOUT IT ALL 12

THE EARLY YEARS 17
1876–1899

COMING OF AGE 35
1900–1919

PROSPEROUS & COLLEGIATE 61
1920–1929

SOPHISTICATED? GAWD! 91
1930–1939

THROUGH THE WAR 121
1940–1949

COASTING 149
1950–1959

FREEDOM & THE FADEOUT 177
1960–1969

THE NINETY-NINE MOST REPEATED (AND PROBABLY THE WORST) COLLEGE JOKES OF THE CENTURY 213

INDEX 220

GOTHAM Grads
Fine Soft Ribbed Knit Pullover Shirts
with Shorts Tailored Like Track Trunks

THE PRUDENTIAL INSURANCE CO. OF AMERICA, Home Office Newark, N.J.

GORDON a New
ARROW
form-fit
COLLAR

Slip into a Bradley
–and Out-of-Doors!
Bradley
KNIT WEAR

OMAR
A Combination unique of
Selected Turkish and Domestic
leaf, never used in any other
Cigarette, anywhere at any time
20 for 15¢

Coca-Cola
Youth Will Be Served
And Life, Liberty and the
Pursuit of Thirst just naturally
lead to a call for Coca-Cola's
happy, healthy refreshment.
IT HAD TO BE GOOD TO GET WHERE IT IS – 7 MILLION A DAY

"FRESH!!!"
"YOU SAID IT!"
Old Gold
PRIZE-CROP TOBACCOS
DOUBLE-MELLOW
2 JACKETS OF "CELLOPHANE"
FACTORY-FRESH

45 minutes' toasting develops
its aristocratic flavor—the
enormous production makes
possible its democratic price
LUCKY STRIKE
"IT'S TOASTED"

But only Time will Tell . . . .
HENRY WILL PROBABLY DISCOVER HOW TO MAKE GOLD FROM WATER!
HE'LL BE ANOTHER LOUIE PASTEUR!
HE EVEN LOOKS LIKE A GENIUS!
HOW CAN THEY TELL SO SOON? HE'S LIABLE TO WIND UP WITH FRENCH DRESSING!
ONLY TIME WILL TELL ABOUT A BUDDING SCIENTIST! AND ONLY TIME WILL TELL ABOUT A CIGARETTE! TAKE YOUR TIME...
Test CAMELS for 30 days
for Mildness and Flavor!
CAMEL leads all other brands by billions of cigarettes per year!

Chesterfield
CIGARETTES
MARION HUTTON
in Glenn Miller's Moonlight
Serenade, broadcasts . . .
Today's most
popular number
Chesterfield
There's a greater demand than ever for Chesterfields. Smokers who have tried them are asking for them again and again, and for the best of reasons...Chesterfields are cooler, better-tasting and definitely milder. Chesterfields are made for smokers like yourself . . . so tune in now for your 1941 smoking pleasure.
They Satisfy
Copyright 1941, Liggett & Myers Tobacco Co.

Gordon Ingram/ *Pomona Sage Hen*

Wayne Wood/ *Emory Phoenix*

MIT Voo Doo

A FEW WORDS ABOUT IT ALL

Late one Saturday night a couple of thousand years ago, in a secluded corner of the campus of Socrates State U, Plato snuggled up next to his blind date and whispered into her ear.

HE: Do you neck?

SHE: That's my business.

HE: How's business?

The pretty little thing shuddered.

HE: Come on—how's about a little kiss?

SHE: No, I have scruples.

HE: That's OK—I've been vaccinated.

The dainty coed stood up and grabbed Plato by the hand. "Let's go," she said, "I've got to get back or the house mother will have a fit. Call me a taxi."

"All right," Plato replied gently, with just a trace of a grin. "You're a taxi."

And thus was college humor born.

In the beginning there wasn't much. Two groups at Princeton tried publishing comic journals—*The Thistle* and *Chameleon*—in the 1830s; neither magazine survived more than a year. The real action didn't start until more than forty years later and most of it wasn't, by our standards, very amusing, consisting of heavy pen-and-ink sketches with irrelevant captions, and unpointed prose.

But after only a few years of the new century, every college worth its booze had a humor magazine. And by the twenties, there were well over a hundred, loosely bound in brotherhood by a national monthly, *College Humor*, which at its peak sold 800,000 copies an issue, and didn't die until 1943.

I really don't give a damn whether the *Harvard Lampoon* or the *Yale Record* deserves to call itself the first college humor magazine. I only think it's great that the current staffs, even though they may not publish as regularly as their predecessors, still care enough to fight about it.

The stuff of college humor magazines occasionally has been peculiar to college types, but more often has come, one way or another, from popular entertainment like vaudeville or from men standing around the cracker barrel—or their modern equivalents. Humor on campus, of course, has never been the sole property of the humor magazine staff: student laughter can be brought about as well by newspaper editors, fraternity men, band musicians, and—I suppose—chess players. But the humor magazine staff is a special family, dedicated to entertainment, ridicule, and shock. Its members room together, dine together, take classes together. And it is a very proud family at that.

Although generation after generation of campus humorists have learned quickly after graduation to be embarrassed by their collegiate creations, that lesson is rarely learned by those who follow them to power. Their work is, in their peculiar circle, the finest of sophistication, cleverness, and wit. (The only magazine that ever told the truth about itself is Berkeley's *Pelican*, which once admitted, "The *Pelican* isn't as good as it used to be. In fact it never was.")

The first rules learned by new college humor magazine

editors—even before they are introduced to the world of picas and halftones—concern plagiarism. The guidelines are simple: a) Don't copy long writings from other magazines, because student prose of more than five hundred words is invariably bad. b) When lifting a joke, cartoon, or short poem, give no credit, because chances are the source itself stole it from another magazine, possibly an old issue of yours.

Thus credit lines in this anthology are to be considered suspect. In the last chapter, "The Ninety-nine Most Repeated (and Probably the Worst) College Jokes of the Century," sources are ignored completely.

For convenience, I have arranged most of the material here by decade. Certainly, whatever trends can be found in college humor have never formed themselves into neat ten-year patterns, but I found few arguments for any other sort of arrangement. Plagiarism being what it is, and certain invariable collegiate interests being what *they* are, there are many instances of jokes and cartoons appearing in and across as many as six decades. One two-liner from a magazine of the late twenties ended up the other month—so help me—as a *Playboy* Party Joke.

In the decade of the sixties, there was a net decline in the number of college magazines devoted to humor. Those who talk about such things say it happened because the times became more serious and students more active; other traditional student pastimes also suffered. Yet the magazines that continued (and the few new ventures) came up with at least some drawings and writings that cause us of the television age to guffaw, while we can only murmur and smile at most earlier wit. And the magazines of the sixties, at least until the great freedom epidemic of the end of the decade, kept up the tradition of getting into trouble with the college administration.

No campus humor magazine of the seventies is without problems. The combination of politics, pot, and deficits doubtless will continue to take victims. The survivors will continue to be anachronisms. Though they may add timely targets to the standard fare of liquor, sex, and professors, there will continue to be an air of racoon-and-flask about them. But, true to their tradition, their editors will tell each other they are urbanely hilarious—and they will believe it.

You may notice, as you page through this book, a number of easily recognizable names. Since many of the items attributed to these well-known names are not particularly funny, it might be assumed that they are included because their creators later became famous. This is quite true.

But there is another, deeper reason for including so many college works by famous men. It is to demonstrate what college humor editors through the ages have told their disbelieving parents: it *is* possible to waste one's time writing dirty jokes with a bunch of sophomoric kids and still amount to something.

This, then, is a book of college humor, written and drawn, from its beginnings. A lot of it is funny. And a lot is good only for nostalgia. What's wrong with that?

Dan Carlinsky, New York City, August 1971

Princeton Tiger

Brown Jug

George Fuller/California Pelican

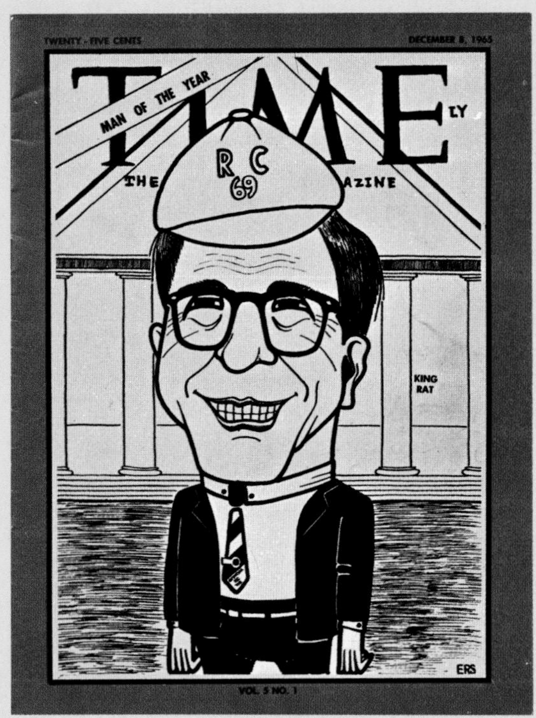

Edward R. Sala/ *Roanoke Expression*

Harvard Lampoon

Carol Nicklaus/ *Ohio State Sundial*

Wesley F. Moore/ *MIT Voo Doo*

George Barkentin/*Harvard Lampoon*

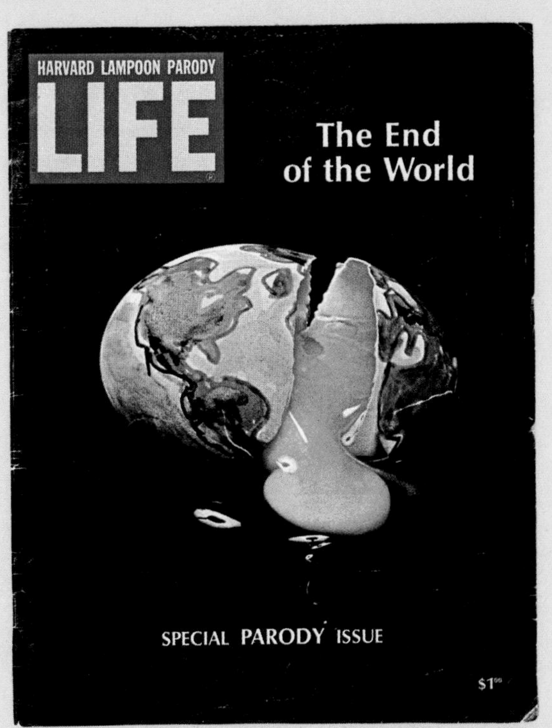

Al Freni/*Harvard Lampoon*

Harvard Lampoon

Columbia Jester

THE EARLY YEARS

(1876-1899)

Ye First Yale-Harvard Foot-Ball Game.

A MISTAKEN impression that Yale played her first game of foot-ball with Harvard in 1875 has gained credence because of its acceptance by all those who have written up the history of Yale athletics. This impression we desire to correct, having discovered manuscripts and other proofs to show that a game was played between the two colleges on November the 21st, 1791—by a remarkable coincidence, exactly one hundred years from the date of next Saturday's contest.

Previous to this date the game had existed in form crude but popular. It was often practiced between the sophomore and freshman classes, Common's Hall being the scene of action, and codfish being substituted for the later-developed pig-skin ball. The records of these games became mixed up with those of the famous "Bread and Butter Riots" of the same date, and it is hard to distinguish one from the other. Both of these athletic sports, however, soon fell under the disfavor of the faculty.

It was not until the year 1791 that the game assumed such importance as to become an inter-collegiate sport. Early in that year a secret communication was received from Harvard, containing the outlines of a dual-league proposition. Harvard urged that although no such sports were yet in existence, it would be well to provide, for the future, a plan of yearly contests between the two colleges, in foot-ball, base-ball, rowing, and track-athletics. It will be seen from this that the dual-league proposition is not a new one.

Eliphalet Pettibone, who was the major-bully at that time, called a meeting of the college in his bed-room in Lyceum, to take action on Harvard's proposition. Now Eliphalet, before coming to Yale, had held a position on the editorial staff of *Harpers' Weekly;* so he knew everything there was to know about foot-ball, and naturally favored that sport. "Gentlemen," he said, "I have called you here for the purpose of choosing a foot-ball team." Some, bolder than the rest, murmured that they did not know what a foot-ball team was. "Never mind!" said the college bully severely, "That is not the question!" and immediately he proceeded to choose an eleven. This eleven, to tell the truth, presented rather a motley appearance; for Eliphalet was much limited in his choice by the fact that most of the senior and junior classes were away on an Indian war.

Now all of this took place just one week before the date agreed upon for the game; so that it was necessary for the team to do some hard training in order to get into shape for the contest. Eliphalet immediately, therefore, got the men together, running them out as far as "Judges' Cave," and making each man hew down an elm tree before breakfast each morning. After breakfast he made them fall on the ball—a cannon-ball used in the Revolution, as the foot-ball he had sent to England for had not yet arrived. A few hours each day were spent in fencing, boxing and wrestling. By this process he hoped to get all the superfluous flesh off of his men, reducing them to sinew and bone. In this he succeeded.

The two end-rushers and the quarter-back died; but Eliphalet bore these disappointments with a courage worthy to be imitated by future captains.

On the morning of the 21st, Eliphalet gave his players their final instructions, and then made them run to Springfield; a foolish thing to do, as he did not arrive until dusk, and the owner of the foot-ball field, having decided that he would not come, was plowing it for sowing. After some delay an arrangement was made with the owner and with Cotton Smith, captain of the Harvard team. It was dusk when play began, and grew darker as play went on; so we have no reliable account of the details of the game. It is generally conceded, however, that neither side scored, and that the Yale eleven took advantage of the darkness to lay up Eliphalet Pettibone, who had run the team with such high-handed policy. They considered themselves treated harshly by Eliphalet. We quote an extract from a letter written by the umpire of the game to a friend, describing the contest:—

"It was now pitch dark, and the referee, Ephraim Daggett, with rare wisdom did call the game. Now as the maimed Yale captain was being borne from the field by his weary eleven, a dispute arose for the possession of the ball with which the game had been played. Forsooth, the wrangle was like to become another encounter of fists, my good William, when I took it upon myself to interfere between the disputants. First to Captain Cotton Smith, of Harvard, did I put the question, 'Sir, did you bring with you a foot-ball to the game?' For I suspected he had not, and indeed his answer approved my suspicion. Then I did turn to Captain Pettibone of Yale, and posed the same question. His answer did surprise me; for forsooth it was the same as the Harvard captain's. Further inquiry I made immediately, and found that no person had brought to Springfield town a foot-ball. Then did the disputants look at each other foolishly; for, Odd Zooks, my good William, the game had been fiercely contested for a full hour and a half, with varying success, and neither side had discovered that they were playing without a ball!"

William Stoutenborough Terriberry/*Yale Record*

THE game was won, and the cheering crowds surged toward the gates, drowning out all else with their maniacal shouts of joy. They fell back to make room for the grimy hero as he trod up the steps with the mud-bespattered ball nestling unconsciously in his strong right arm. Suddenly a beautiful maiden dashed out from the crowd and, seizing the pigskin from its bewildered bearer, pressed it fervently to her cherry lips.

"Alice," drawled her cold-blooded escort a moment later, as they passed on up the walk, "your mouth's dirty."

Princeton Tiger

HIAWATHA'S WOOING

Far away in Massichusix,
Where the winter's long and dreary.
Where the North Wind spends his fury,
Lived a maiden, Yuba Wanna—
Handsomest of all the women.
She, the dashing Poco's daughter;
She, the singer and the dancer,
Struck a mash on Hiawatha;
Hiawatha paid for soda,
Hiawatha paid for ice cream,
Hiawatha paid for eysters—
Everything the maiden wanted.
Often in the summer evening,
When the air was warm and balmy,
When the moon was soft and dreamy,
Hiawatha took his buggy—
Took his narrow side-bar buggy—
And went and sought his Yuba Wanna.
All around the village drove they
Seated on the soft-stuffed cushion.
When at last their ride was ended
And they reached the Poco's wigwam,
By the gate awhile they lingered,
Lingered long and talked together;
Talked of flowers and the springtime,
Of the crimson leaves of autumn,
Of the singing of the Cawcaw,
And the dingy snows of winter.
Hiawatha then waxed spoony,
Hiawatha's tones grew tender,
Hiawatha talked of lovers,
Talked of love to Yuba Wanna—
Handsomest of all the women.
And he grasped the maiden's fingers,
Grasped her hand with both of his'n.
Then he drew her softly to him,
And he whispered, "Yuba Wanna,
Fairest one of all the Portchucks,
Daughter of the noble Poco,
Will you come and share my wigwam,
Will you come and share my prayer cuts,
Share my summonses and term bills?"
Then the maiden Yuba Wanna,
Fairest one of all the Portchucks,
Answered him in tones of nickel—
"Betcher boots, my Hiawatha."

Harvard Lampoon

He—How beautiful she is as she stands there so unconsciously; under the mistletoe too, by Jove! If I only dance! Not a soul in the room either. But no, it would frighten her, dear little girl; she is so modest and shy.

She—I declare what fools men are. They don't deserve a tenth of the good things they get. I have been standing here now, ten minutes by the clock, and that silly Jack stands there like a calf. Tom didn't use to be so bashful.

Princeton Tiger

Newark doctor, visiting patient in the only hotel in the place, stands his umbrella in entry with following inscription pinned on:
This umbrella belongs to a man who strikes a 200 lb. blow. Will return in five minutes.

On his return finds umbrella gone and the following note in its stead:
Umbrella taken by a man who walks eight miles an hour. Will not return at all.

Yale Record

THE HISTORY OF YALE COLLEGE, III.

1892. First Day at the Commons. E. S. Oviatt/*Yale Record*

Blest be the tie that binds
The collar to my shirt.
With gorgeous silken front it hides
At least a week of dirt.

Yale Record

CHARLIE: It's funny, isn't it? We never hear of labor unions south of the Equator.
JOHNNIE: Well, you know, you're not allowed to strike below the belt.

Yale Record

MEDIEVAL HISTORY

[The historical accuracy of this is not guaranteed. It is merely a sample for the benefit of Sophomores, of the graceful, easy style of Dry-Your-Eyes text book.]

After the peace of Tritwagoldfingen in 1743, Charles the Thin came to the throne. He had two brothers, Charles the Good and Charles the Bad. Charles the Good was bad, and Charles the Bad was good. They both made war on the Pope, Clement XXXIII, who was a nephew of Leo XXXII, whose sister had golden hair and married Edward VI of England, who made war on the Picts and Scots, who were incensed at the Holefstauffen family because Charles VIII, of England, had married the deceased wife's sister of Petro, King of Italy, whose ancestors were Arthur and Mary, King and Queen of Bohemia, who were related by marriage to Ferdinand and Isabella of Spain. In Germany, about this time, the King of France was making war on the King of England, by the advice of the Czar of Russia and the Emperor of China, on account of the alliance of the Visigoths with Katherine of Aragon, whose brother was a Mohammedan, named Albizo, who was victorious at the battle of Bretagne-sur-mer, in Burgundy. In 1753 Charles the Thin died of embonpoint.*
[*Ed.'s Note.—The above paragraph is thought now not to be substantiated by facts.] *Yale Record*

ROMEO AND JULIET.

ALTHOUGH Juliet was of kittenish and tender years, she has often been put on the boards as quite an old stager. Juliet was not old enough to enter Bryn Mawr, and it is to be doubted if sufficient wisdom could have been tutored into her to fit her for the entrance exams. She was too much addicted to Romeo to have time for outside affairs. The Markee Capulet, her guv'ner, had a row with Romeo's father about a horse trade, and the Markee told Juliet if that young Mr. Montague came fooling around the house any more he would boil the little monkey alive. After that Juliet told Romeo he had better not call any more when her papa was at home.

There is nothing to indicate whether Romeo was a sport or a poller, but his friend and kinsman, Mercutio, was dead game. Juliet had a cousin Tybalt, who was originally from Texas. He and Mercutio had a difference, and Mercutio came out second best. In fact, he proved a grave subject.

The evening before this really painful affair occurred Rome called on Jule when the Markee was supposed to be in bed. Shakespeare knew how to get up a surreptitious love scene when he got at it.

Romeo says the usual thing in a different way. He does it almost as well as the Glee Club men do. He says he will swear off cigarettes for her and no one else, and she tells him to swear not at all, but just quit 'em. He says he thinks lots of her, and she says she thinks he is smooth. Then she interrupts herself suddenly as the old man drops the dog gently out of window. "Say, Rome," she whispers, "I think my folks are on to you," and Romeo starts to get away and the dog starts to get Romeo.

Romeo did not have his way, but Bigwilly (the canine) had Romeo and came home reminiscently chewing the remnants of young Montague's new Poole tights.

Soon after this Romeo utterly wrecked Tybalt, and had to leave town for a spell. This brought on that sad, last act where the girl in the next seat weeps her nose red, and Juliet gets a chance for a great fall when the play is staged. We have no words for Paris. He is only brought in to be incidentally killed in a casual sort of way by Romeo, and to make one more death at the end. The last act, as we have intimated, is real touching and gory. We have not the heart to speak of it.

Booth Tarkington/*Princeton Tiger*

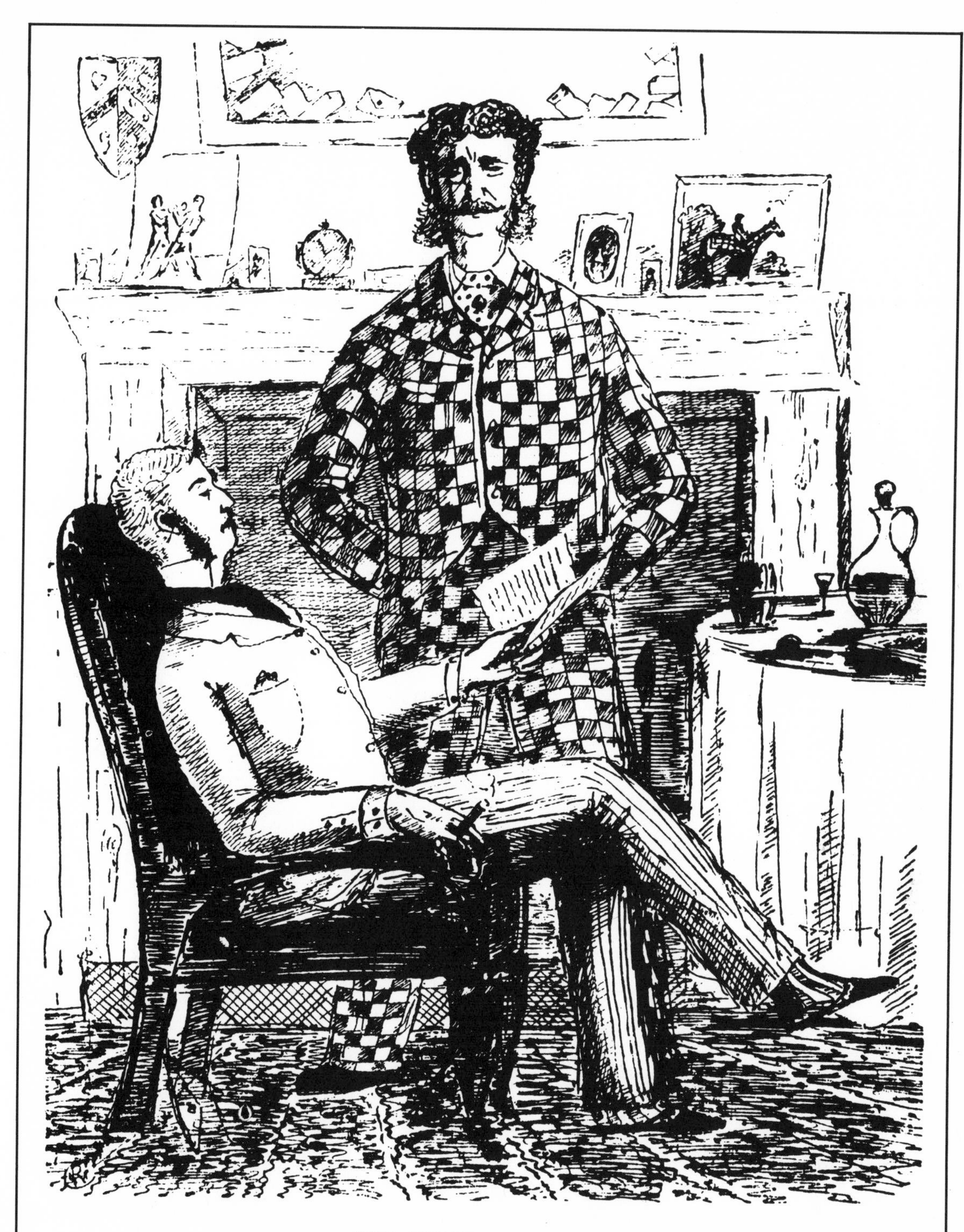

OUR ENGLISH COUSINS.

Oxford. I SAY, WHERE'S HARVARD?
Cambridge. O—AH—SOMEWHERE IN THE STATES, I BELIEVE.
Oxford. WHERE'S YALE?
Cambridge. THERE YOU HAVE ME, OLD BOY,—DON'T KNOW. WHY?
Oxford. THEY WANT US TO ROW AT A PLACE CALLED CENTENNIAL NEXT SUMMER.
Cambridge. O, INDEED! HA, HA!

Harvard Lampoon

A CHANGE OF MOOD

A youth of a Greek with very great cheek
Did jest at a sage on his way,
And when the wise man his hide tried to tan,
He promptly yelled "λεγω I say!"

But finding his wail was naught of avail,
The lad cried, "Politer I'll be";
So he ceased to be rude and altered his mood,
Saying, "Please, sir, will you λεγοιμι?"

Yale Record

IN PHYSICS

Prof. (lecturing on galvanism): What would be the effect, Mr. Broken, if you should hold a quantity of gold in one hand and of silver in the other?
Broken: I should experience a decided shock.

Yale Record

Two brothers there were in Sioux City;
Each thought the other tioux pretty.
So each took his knife
And the other one's life.
Now which of the tioux Sioux yioux pity?

Harvard Lampoon

INTERNATIONAL WEATHER

Our change climatic
We think acrobatic
And sigh for a land that is better—
But the German will say,
In a very dry way,
That the weather with him is still Wetter.

J. R. Joy/Yale Record

In the army once was a gay colonel,
Who wrote all he did in his jolonel.
His wife found it one day,
And loudly did say:
"I think this is simply infolonel!"

Yale Record

IN WETHER VESNE

Their was a fare made from Duquesne
Who dared not go fourth in the resne.
If her head once got wet
She'd again be brunette,
For her heir she'd have died all in vesne.

Princeton Tiger

Miss Sweetlie (who makes it a point never to say anything unkind). O MR. SNEERWELL, DO LOOK AT MR. GAWK AND HIS BRIDE! COULD THERE BE A MORE *perfect* MATCH?

Harvard Lampoon

DINING A-LA-CARTE.

Yale Record

CATECHISM MODERNIZED

Teacher: What is the difference between the body and the soul?
Johnny (vacantly): The body is mortal and material; the soul—
Teacher (impatiently): Yes, and the soul?
Johnny: The soul is immortal and immaterial.

George Santayana/*Harvard Lampoon*

"Why is a fossil like a cafeteria meal?"
"One's a fair trilobite, the other a trite bill o' fare."

Yale Record

A MEMORY OF THANKSGIVING

"What are we thankful for to-day, Jimmie boy?"
"Turkey."
"Yes, but before that?"
"Soup."

Harvard Lampoon

A LEAP-YEAR TALE

There once was a maiden didactical,
In appearance—well, somewhat stalactical,
Who said to her steady,
"I'm willing and ready"—
I leave it to you, was it tactical?

Princeton Tiger

TO A WATER-NYMPH

Dark is my loved one's witching face,
She cometh from far Spain,
Her skin is olive, like the race
On which the Moor has left his trace;
Her beauty makes her vain.

My lady's form is plump and fine;
She knows it, ah! too well;
She hides her 'mid the leavy vine—
This vine yields water and not wine—
Its leaves, her convent cell.

Dark maid, thy heart is known to me—
The red heart of a felon,
The *cholera morbus* there I see—
Its seeds are blackly sown in thee,
Thou art a water melon.

J. R. Joy/*Yale Record*

HIBERNIAN HUMOR.

Small Mucker. I SAY, MISTER, GET OFF AND LOOK AT YOURSELF RIDE.

Harvard Lampoon

AN ANECDOTE

"Jule," remarked Brutus as he strolled into the great Caesar's tent, "did I ever tell you of the fight I once had among the Allobroges?" Gets off a long windy tale involving the single-handed slaughter of eleven ferocious barbarians.

"Brute, my boy," remarked Caesar solemnly when he had finished, "I admire Gaul, especially Transalpine Gaul, but still I must say that you remind me of a harp shattered by the lightning of great Jove."

"How so?" inquired Brutus, unwarily.

"Because you're a blasted lyre," answered Caesar taking a long pull at a flask of Chian of the 754 vintage.

And from that day forth Brutus began to meditate on the Ides of March.

Yale Record

A DUET.

(One night, toward the close of last summer, the moon got in its fine work, and they became engaged. They are thirteen hundred miles apart as the scene opens. They are thinking.)

HE thinks: She is the dearest girl in the world—but what in the name of goodness I got engaged to her for, I don't know! I don't want to marry for *years*. Ass that I was! What am I going to do about it? I'd like to know that! How am I to let her down easy?

Just as like as not she'll go into a convent, or fade away. She might go into a decline and die.

I never could feel right about it afterward. I'd gamble the poor child is dreaming of me now. No doubt some dense friend is boring her to death, and she is saying to herself that she'd give the whole world to have him away and have me there in his place. Poor thing! poor thing! I can't write and tell her—I just *can't*. I'll wait and break it to her Christmas. It will break her all up. Poor thing! Poor thing!

SHE thinks: He is the dearest fellow in the world—but I was dreadfully foolish to make him think I meant to marry him. He will take to drink, I know he will! I wish I could think of some way to make the blow less hard.

He may shoot himself! I never could feel happy after that, as long as I lived. He is probably looking at my picture, this minute—far away from me, poor fellow—and worshipping it. It would kill him if he knew how I sit here wondering why Sidney has not come.

How am I to tell him? I cannot write it, and I feel guilty when I write him those terrible, false, tender letters. I'll have to tell him when he comes home for the holidays. It will break his heart. He won't care to live. It ruins all my hopes of having a pleasant winter. Poor, poor fellow!

CURTAIN WHILE THEY WAIT.

Booth Tarkington/*Princeton Tiger*

Astounding Instances—which have recently come to light—of Natural Selection, and Survival of the Fittest.

Abnormal development of the smelling and hearing faculties of the sunlight-bereft inhabitants of the North Pole.

Remarkable protective growth of the pediments of the colored race in the earthquake districts.

Other cases,—discovered in a German village,—the result of unusual musical proclivities.

Harvard Lampoon

ATTENTION, '98!

THE large number of men who wish to enter '98 has induced the faculty to raise the standard of admission, and it is through their courtesy that we are permitted to publish some sample questions. We would advise all who intend to enter '98 to study the extracts carefully, and if possible, to memorize them.

MATHEMATICS

Plot one of Carter's curves. If you can read a *Record* joke without laughing, what is the force of gravity? If a man weighing 150 lbs. leans against a lamp-post under the influence of ten beers, what is the tension on the post? Fifteen beers? Twenty? Calculate the circumference of his head the next morning. If a student gets sixty marks in two months, with what acceleration is he dropped? Is this plane? Can you dyne on a poundal of meat?

LATIN

Translate (Horace, Bk. I. Lat. 12), at sight:

Mea est amica
Suus sum amicus
Mea est Anna
Ejus sum Josephus.
Mox nos nubemus
Nunquam separare
Parva Anna Rooney
Dixit se me amare.

Divide into feet and show how the cæsura affects the sense. How often did he metre? Give a brief sketch of the characters.

Give the construction of the italicized words in the following sentences: (1) Dearsum ivit *Magintius* in imum mare; (2) Hia, *recens,* illam candelam extingue.

HISTORY

Give a brief sketch of Bob Cook's life. How many times has Yale won the quadruple championship? In what year did Yale beat Harvard at foot-ball 52-0? Draw a diagram of a foot-ball V, showing position of players.

Yale Record

"FRESHMAN CHEEK." (Examination, U. E. R)

Proctor (*to* SNODKINS, '82). WHAT QUESTION DID YOU ASK THAT GENTLEMAN?
Snodkins. I ASKED HIM IF HE WOULD BE KIND ENOUGH TO EXCUSE MY BACK.

Charles A. Coolidge/Harvard Lampoon

THE ART OF KISSING

KISSING is or should be made one of the fine arts. While there is no immediate danger of its becoming one of the lost arts, or even lapsing into innocuous desuetude, still it is just as well to do what we can to keep it up to an art standard. For heaven's sake don't make a business of it and don't jump at it with your hat in one hand and your overshoes in the other. Don't pounce down on a womans' lips as you would a piece of watermelon or a ripe tomato and bend her head back till you hear the bones crack in the back of her neck. Don't glue your face to hers and have a good time all to yourself while you're flattening her nose all over one of her cheeks. Don't take her by both ears and look into her eyes and then try to grab it quick, you are sure to bump noses. These are a few of the things to avoid. A few general rules will now be given which may at all times be safely observed. Stand a little bit behind her, just on the right side. Place your left arm diagonally about her form, extending from her right shoulder down to and partially around her waist, until the ends of your fingers touch her belt buckle. If she don't wear a belt buckle the arm will get there just the same. Take it easy, don't get excited. Take your right hand and gently brush the golden ringlets from the left side of her alabaster brow, looking meantime into the liquid depths of her azure eyes. Take it easy. Don't get excited. Let your hand rest gently for a moment on the warm velvet of her pink and white left cheek. Then gently work the muscles of the right arm until her right cheek rests firmly on your left shoulder, just over the watch pocket. Take it easy; don't be in a hurry, it'll keep. Send a little energy along the line of the left arm. Now stand still as long as you can. Then remove your right duke from her left cheek, letting it drop gently under her chin, work muscles of your right arm gently. Take it easy; don't hurry. As her chin rises, work neck muscles and let your head fall gently forward. Now a little more motion down the left arm, and as the ripe lips, like twin rose buds, part revealing pearly gates behind, through which there steals the warm sweet perfume of her fragrant breath, then—well, you know the rest as well as I do—only take it easy; don't hurry; it can't get away from you, and it would not if it could.

Emory Phoenix

VACATION MEMORIES.—A Turn In the Conversation.

Sentimental Youth (having screwed his courage to the sticking-point). YES, MISS JULIA, I FEEL MORE AND MORE THAT WITHOUT *Love* THE WORLD WERE BUT A WILDERNESS!

Cruel Fair. YES, MR. SAPPLETON; BUT JUST SEE WHAT A GREAT BIG FUZZY CATERPILLAR THERE IS ON YOUR RIGHT FOOT.

Harvard Lampoon

IN YE OLDEN DAYS
MISTRESS MARGARET HATH TWO LOVERS
AND, SHE NOT BEING ABLE TO CHOOSE BETWEEN THEM, YE TWO FIGHT (YS BEING YE CUSTOM WHEN A MAIDE IS UNDECIDED)
AND SHE WILL HAVE NAUGHT TO DO WITH YE SURVIVOR (IT BEING NOW CLEAR YT HE WHO WAS SLAIN WAS YE ONE YT SHE LOVED)
Tarkington
BUT, RATHER THAN NOT MARRY ANYBODY, SHE MARRYETH YE SURVIVOR'S SECOND (YE MAN ON YE RIGHT)
AND YE SURVIVOR MARRYETH A CERTAIN MAIDE
SO YT EVERYTHING IS WELL ENDED
AND CHEERFUL FOR ALL
(EXCEPT, MAYBE, FOR HIM WHO WAS SLAIN.)

Booth Tarkington/*Princeton Tiger*

WHAT WE ARE COMING TO

Miss Tottie Townley (four years, from Philadelphia, visiting her cousin): Does oo know Muver Goose?

Miss Amelie Bostonique (five years): I have sometimes amused myself with such repetitions.

Miss Tottie: Tan oo say 'was a 'ittle dirl an' see had a 'ittle turl?'

Miss Amelie: Perhaps not in the prescribed phraseology. If I remember, it runs about as follows: 'At a recent period in the annals of the human family, there existed a diminutive feminine specimen of humanity whose conspicuous decoration was a capillary spiral appendage of minute dimensions, descending perpendicularly upon her head. When she was amiably disposed, she produced the impression of being excessively agreeable, but when she abandoned herself to the natural inclinations of an unregenerate spirit, her deportment became—

Miss Tottie: Boo-hoo-hoo! Twit tallin' me names—hoo—!

Miss Bostonique: I never could endure children!

Princeton Tiger

Teacher: Can you name the four seasons?

Jimmie: They ain't but two; the football 'n' the baseball seasons.

Stanford Chaparral

LOVE THYSELF AS THY NEIGHBOR.

Poor Little Girl. O, WHAT A LOVELY DOLL! WON'T YOU GIVE IT TO ME?
Rich Little Girl. I WOULD, IF IT WASN'T MINE.

George Santayana/*Harvard Lampoon*

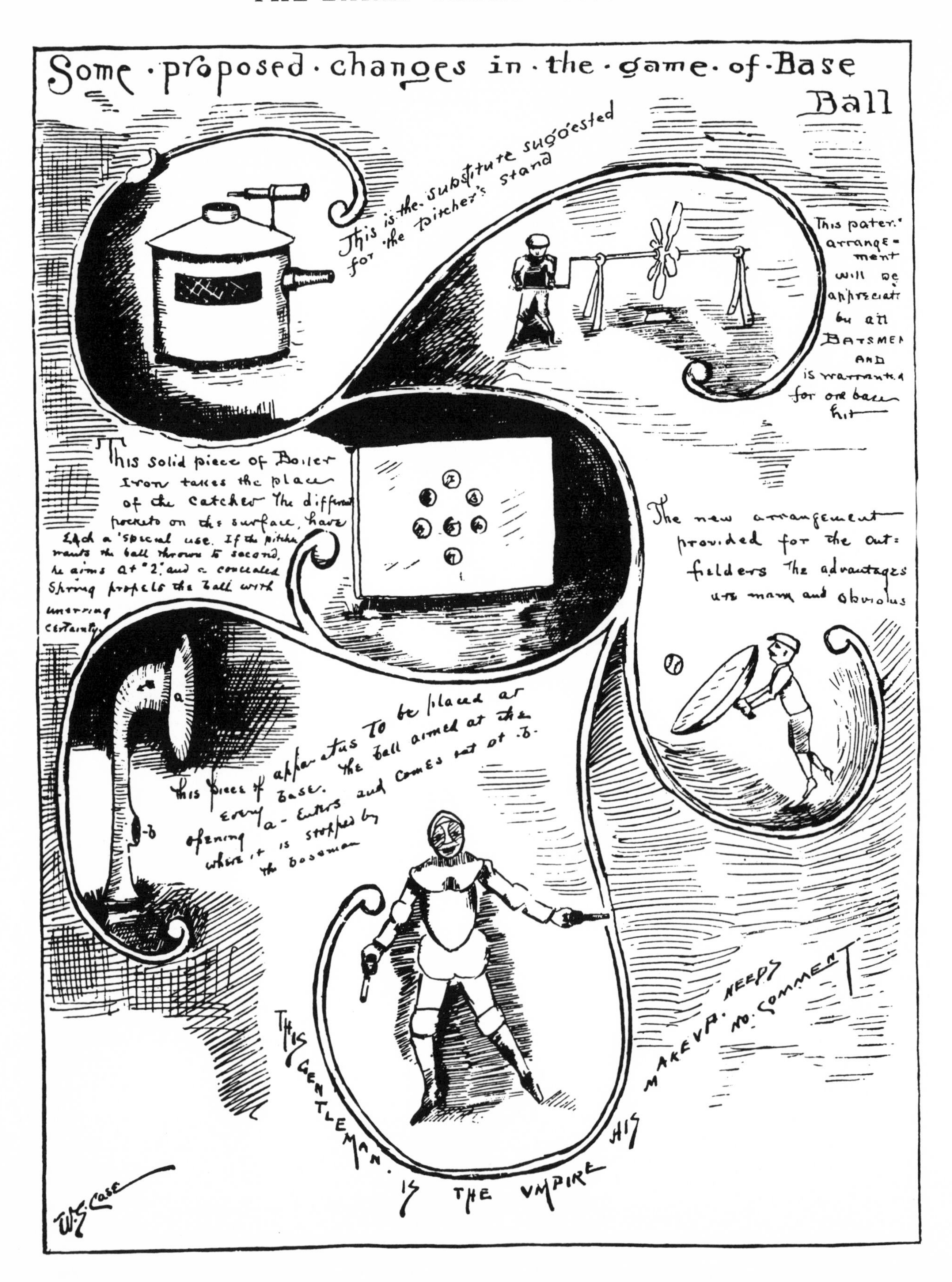

William S. Case/Yale Quip

Blucher Cut Shoes

FOR

COLLEGEMEN

SPORTSMEN

AND TOURISTS

FRENCH PATENT LEATHER
$6.50

ENG. ENAMEL LEATHER
$6.50

CALFSKIN $5.00

HEAVY RED "GRAIN"
$6.50

John P. Twaddell, 1210 and 1212 Market St., Philadelphia

Hotel Lafayette

PHILADELPHIA

TERMS

American Plan, $3, $3.50 and $4. (Baths extra.)
European Plan, $1, $1.50 and $2. (Baths extra.)

L. U. MALTBY

PACH BROTHERS

COLLEGE - CLASS - PHOTOGRAPHERS

MAIN OFFICE

935 BROADWAY, NEW YORK

Special rates to Students and family connection

The McKinley Bill has not hurt our prices or our trade. We have secured in our Spring Importations an elegant line of Suitings and Overcoatings for business and dress wear, and invite your attention to them at old time prices.

COLYER & CO.,
815 and 817 Broad St., Newark, N. J.

COLLEGE HEADQUARTERS

FOR

MUSICAL INSTRUMENTS

FINEST STOCK IN PHILADELPHIA

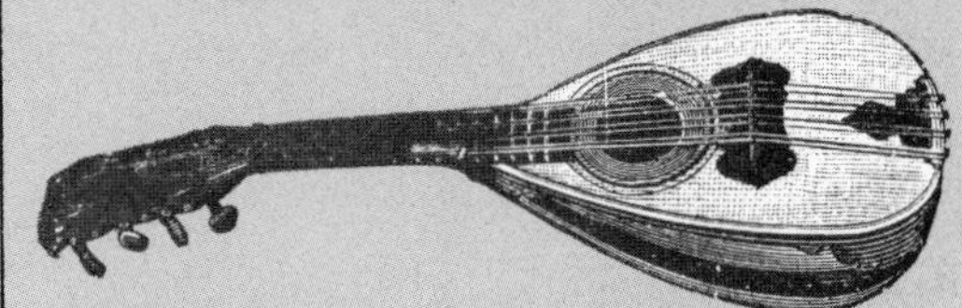

FINE STRINGS A SPECIALTY.

INSTRUMENTS SENT ON APPROVAL

F. H. Griffith & Co.

1102 Chestnut Street, Philadelphia.

Lawrenceville School

JOHN C. GREEN FOUNDATION

Early application for admission is advisable

REV. J. C. MACKENZIE, PH. D.
Headmaster

Are you ever puzzled to know what to buy for a pretty and inexpensive present? For a Souvenir, Birthday or Wedding? If so, spend a half hour with

COOK & JAQUES

FASHIONABLE ART JEWELERS OF TRENTON

and you will see more new ideas there than in any one jewelry store in large cities. It's their style

COMING OF AGE
1900-1919

WHITE Steam and Gasoline CARS
FOR 1911

Having disposed of our 1910 product, we now announce our steam and gasoline models for 1911.

Full details regarding the new models, dates of delivery, etc., may be obtained on application to any of the offices or agencies of the company.

The White Company

Broadway at 62d Street **New York**

QUAE ENIM VITA?

WHAT'S the Freshman here for, here for?
What's the Freshman here for?
To throw rocks unawares
At Professor's windairs,
Which crash o'er his head as he's saying his prayers,
And frighten his daughter a-going upstairs.
In short, to raise Hades—
This pleases the ladies—
Who are always surprised and think's it so queer
When the dear boy comes home with a flea in his ear.
That's what the Freshman's here for, here for,
That's what the Freshman's here for.

What's the Sophomore here for, here for?
What's the Sophomore here for?
Ah! nobody knows;
But wherever he goes
He wants you to notice the cut of his clothes,
The part of his hair and the grace of his pose.
He's a very tough lad—
Yes, most deucedly bad;
And always, you know, on a racket, by gad;
But a model young man when at home with his dad.
That's what the Sophomore's here for, here for,
That's what the Sophomore's here for.

What's the Junior here for, here for?
What's the Junior here for?
Why, for knowledge, of course,
From many a source;
To fall sick o'er the physics of matter and force;
To learn how to gracefully stick on a *horse*;
To learn to play poker,
To euchre the joker,
To raise a moustache, to put a plug hat on,
To mash on the train, and get awfully sat on.
That's what the Junior's here for, here for,
That's what the Junior's here for.

What's the Senior here for, here for?
What's the Senior here for?
To run up little bills
To pay for the frills
He has to put on when the maiden he kills;
While the tailor and hat man grow white round the gills.
It is only a "Dip,"
But there's many a slip;
For the sheriff may break up his neat little game
Before he can write the B. A. to his name.
That's what the Senior's here for, here for.
That's what the Senior's here for.

Princeton Tiger

THE DESERT ROSE

IT was summer on the desert. The little cowslips were just beginning to slip upon one another. From a grove of fir-trees came the clear, warbling note of a codfish. Just above the horizon, the classic dome of a gashouse was visible.

Across the rolling sand dashed Isshui ben Beaneri, on his ship of the desert, which was very fleet. Behind him, on the second hump, rode his newly-made bride, the shriek's daughter. Her puh-pah, with his tribesmen, pursued on their racing hippos, but they could not overtake the tuh, as Ish was a dead beat.

For weeks they fled; then, as their food gave out, they became weaker. They went so fast that they soon ran out of water. Omigawd! Finally, dying of thirst (even as you and I) they took a fond farewell—see Cos—and lay down to die. With a last feverish movement, Ish jerked out his trusty Ingersoll. His face lit up, perhaps because he was lantern-jawed. They were saved. He had found a spring in his watch.

Cornell Widow

COMING OF AGE 1900-1919

BE YE FOREWARNED.

Feed at Beck—half a wreck—
Crabbed maiden aunts;

Half-past nine—draw the line:
Aunties want to dance.

Richard Henry Dana, Jr./*Harvard Lampoon*

JOHN MASEFIELD EXTENDS THE EVERLASTING MERCY TO THE TIGER

From '96 to nineteen blank
My conduct was described as rank.
From nineteen blank to 1905
Men wondered why they let me live,
I cut my aged mother's throat,
I acted like a bloody goat;
And that I weren't no blooming parson
I showed by piracy and arson!
From 1905 to 1910
I roared 'round on the loose again!
All day I'd booze, or chew, or smoke
Heroin, hasheesh, hop and coke.
On to '15 I plunged in revel,
I sold my soul unto the devil—
And what I did, in slums and bars,
I mercifully show by stars!
* * * * * * *
By then I'd used up all my tricks,
"I'm bloody in a bloody fix!"
I said—and searched the law-books through
To find some final crime to do,
The one huge, unforgiven sin
That bloody rots the heart within!
The sin that like a steel-tight jersey
Removes you from eternal mercy!
I bloody shrank a bit at first
To crown my horrors with a worst!
But soon I yielded. Vileness filled me,
I went to Princeton—and it killed me!

Stephen Vincent Benét/*Yale Record*

COMING OF AGE 1900-1919

WHY SOME SHUN TOLSTOY

PRINCESS Sizzizyqqssihetch-hetchykoffski sat sipping her vodka. She was waiting for her lover, the gallant Count Cisibeo-leotweedledeedeeskirumpskitump-skishkiskivitchovitch, to call for her in his droski. What would her husband say? Probably "Wyzxxi-sizksizgghskizzski"; no more; he was *so* indifferent! Anyhow, the husband, or to call him by the pet name she had given him when they were wed, Alexnicholastom-dickharryheuvaheluvaskibumkukl-uxklandamtheinsurrectoevitchkoff-ski, was off snipe snaring at their country place on the Bugabugosi-zosizosizoziszkgzjgjsazxggxzsqq Steppes, with his quarter brother, little Sanisixtellwityalequff, who was called for short, Brrbrrxcvx-cvzexexevezxizzisxixszisvvccggkz-iz.

What was that? Lo! Harski! The Count was there with the droski. Hastily seizing a samovar of vodka and throwing on her robe of serf-skin, she leaped through the window. "Come, dear little Gedumpdeltrobridgeissajrw-skisolizziesez," he called softly through his whiskers. In a twinkling she had climbed into a pocket of his cossack-fur coat. They were off, guilty but gleeful, for the little town of Eatachelseasizki-heulavaheluvanameskirecrecrecre-crecrecrecrecvitchovitchoskiokoffo-damskioski.*

*Marks death of the linotyper.

Harvard Lampoon

EXAGGERATION?

SOPH: There must be at least twice as many good-looking co-eds in school this year as last.

JUNIOR: Yes, I met both of them at the prom last night.

Pittsburgh Panther

ILLUSTRATED VERSE

slow, But if it breaks it comes down
up
goes
elevator
The so.

Yale Record

There once was a man from Nantucket
Who kept all his cash in a bucket;
But his daughter named Nan
Ran away with a man,
And as for the bucket, Nantucket.

Princeton Tiger

Flo was fond of Ebenezer—
"Eb," for short, she called her beau.
Talk of "tide of love"—great Caesar!
You should see 'em, Eb and Flo.

Cornell Widow

Tobacco is a dirty weed; I like it.
It satisfies no normal need; I like it.
It makes you thin, it makes you lean;
It takes the hair right off your bean;
It's the worst darn stuff I've ever seen.
I like it.

G.L. Hemminger/Penn State Froth

There was once a young man named Otto
Who had more time for loaf than he'd otto.
He went for a spiel
In his ottomobile,
As you'd think Otto ot in his otto.

Princeton Tiger

He stood by his father's bier and wept.

Rube Goldberg/California Pelican

HOW TO BE HAPPY IN COLLEGE

HOWLS of anguish have been floating across the gently undulating hills of Broadway and One Hundred and Sixteenth Street, and in thru the windows of JESTER'S—or the exemption board's—office in East Hall. And the burden of the howls is this: "College takes all the joy out of life." The fact of the matter, old dears, is that nothing could be further from the truth. College is an unalloyed delight. We can prove it. Follow our carefully prepared manual for one glorious day, and we'll vouch for an ear-to-ear grin on your faces when you trek for home.

Your first class is in Journalism. Arrive at 8:08, and with a reasonable amount of luck, you may squeeze into the elevator by 8:59. Bestow a kiss upon the brow of Hamlet, the noblest elevator chauffeur extant, and sneer at the extension students that hem you in on all sides. You are now in a beatific mood for your

9 O'CLOCK CLASS. POLITICS.

Select a seat as far from the front of the room as possible. Fire a board rubber at the Prof. as he enters. Read "Judge." The Prof. will ask you, "If a man is discovered to be involved deeply in every form of corruption known, what becomes of him?" Answer: "They make him Mayor of New York." Eat Zu Zus, or other noisy crackers. This always appeals to Politics professors. You are now ready for your

10 O'CLOCK CLASS.
ENGLISH B.

Select a seat as far from the front of the room as possible. Read Loiseaux's Spectator papers. Be sure you laugh at every line of the "Religio Medici." It's meant to be funny. When the Prof. asks you to name eleven of Shakespeare's plays, look inspired, and reply " 'Ten Nights in a Bar Room' and 'Julius Caesar.' " Proceed, thereupon, to your

11 O'CLOCK CLASS.
ECONOMICS.

Select a seat as far from the front of the room as possible. Economics is a snap course. Read "Snappy Stories." The Prof. will say: "We will now turn to the laws of consumption." Cough loudly at this point: the Prof. is bound to appreciate the subtle and original humor of your action. He has been appreciating it now for eighteen years. Never stay longer than fifteen minutes in an Economics class; if you do, the Prof. will invariably take advantage of your good nature. You now are in a position to enjoy your

NOON RECESS.

Eat a regular lunch, or go over to the Commons. This is a good time to ask one of your instructors why you received only a "D–" on that last quiz; instructors, of course, care nothing about their lunch. Drop into Spec office, graft seven or eight cigarettes, and read all the mail on the rack. It's being done this year. By consulting your schedule, you will discover that the next act on the program is your

1 O'CLOCK CLASS. HYGIENE.

We can suggest no way in which you can be happy in a Hygiene class. Cut.

2 O'CLOCK CLASS. MATH.

Select a seat as far from the front of the room as possible. Read "Police Gazette." Very strong on figures. The Math Prof. is polite. He will say: "Mr. Blank, I should be indeed grateful if you would explain that theory to me." Answer—just as politely: "Sorry, Prof., but I never quite could understand that theory myself." At the eighth lecture, the Prof. will tell you about the man who entered an empty trolley car with seven policemen and a blind man, and found his watch gone when he came out. This is a joke. Laugh very heartily, and get an "A" for the course. Set your compass in a Southeasterly direction and navigate in the direction of your

3 O'CLOCK CLASS. FRENCH.

Select a seat as far from the front of the room as possible. Read "Parisienne." Smoke a French briar pipe; the Prof. will furnish the tobacco. It is advisable to avoid singing "Deutschland Über Alles" in this class. When the Prof. asks you how you decline "drink" in French, tell him gently, but firmly, that you don't decline drink in any language.

This is your last class of the day. Dash madly down to the Journalism library. (It is considered bad form to knock over more than two instructors on your way.) In the corner of the library—just beind the desk—you will find a glorious maiden with auburn locks and a light in her eyes that makes you feel like old Saint Peter strumming gaily on his golden ukulele.

Take her hand gently. Lead her cautiously from the building—and into the street. The sun is still shining. A fresh, crisp breeze puts a tingle in your blood and a sparkle in your eyes.

Oh, boy! "Happy" ain't the word for it!

Are we right?

Bennett Cerf/*Columbia Jester*

SHE: Are you an oarsman?
HE: No, miss, I'm a Swede.

Columbia Jester

PHIL: Got anything to smoke? I left my pipe at home and I want a smoke the worst way.
WILL: Here, try a stogie. That's the worst way you can smoke.

Cornell Widow

PRACTICE MAKES PERFECT

"Yes, Father, when I graduate I am going to follow my literary bent and write for money."
"Humph, John; you ought to be successful. That's all you did the four years you spent in college."

Pennsylvania Punch Bowl

DEAN: What is density?
HANSEN: I can't define it but I can give a good illustration.
DEAN: The illustration is good, sit down.

Nebraska Awgwan

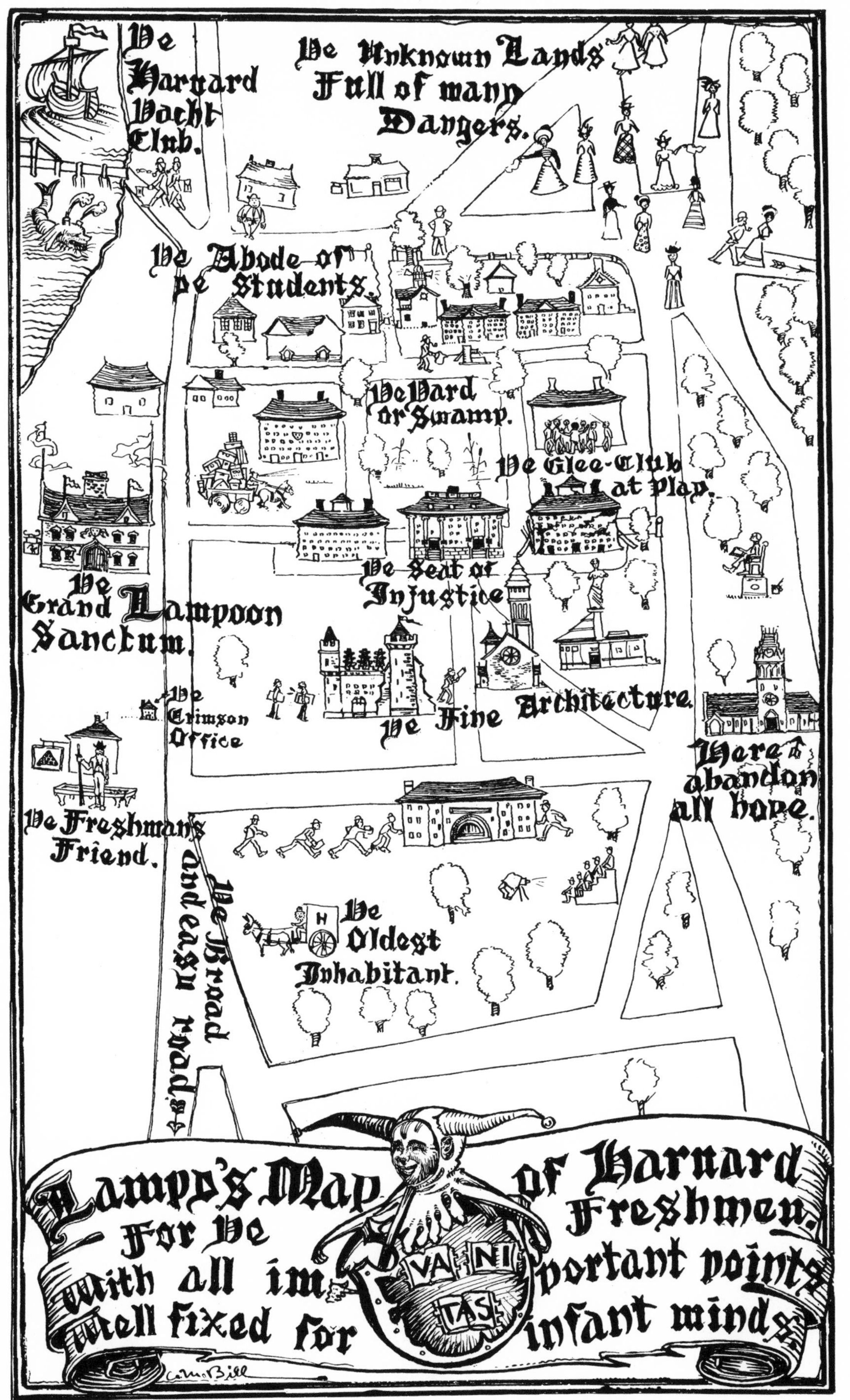

Carroll Bill/*Harvard Lampoon*

A SYLLABIC SYMPOSIUM

I

Inspire me, O Muse, with the indigo blues,
While I crib out of History's page,
And try to relate the most horrible fate
Of mankind since the Pliocene Age.
For those who are keen on this same Pliocene
Say many a man left his corpse
As a saccharine feast for the indigent beast,
The Dinosaur anthropomorps—
The Brachuocephalus-megalopopepsinous-dinosaur Anthropomorps.

II

But a new generation has given occasion,
To make their friend Anthro look pale,
And so I can tell of a tale that befell
To an innocent native of Yale.
Now a chemical gent, once, over in Kent,
Was toiling some law to refute
By mixing diethyl-percaesium-methyl
With pyrogal-chromate, dilute—
With sulphantimoniate pyrogal-chromate dilute.

III

But then with a smash, a scream and a crash,
The bottles blew up in a shake
The whole apparatus, and left him as flat as
The pancakes that mother can make.
And not only that, but he lay in a vat,
In an ocean, red-hot and incensed,
That sputtered and choked, and bubbled and smoked—
'Twas pyrogal-chromate, condensed—
'Twas sulphantimoniate-diethyl-methylene-percaesium-pyrogal-chromate, condensed.

IV

"Oh, get me," he cried, "ere it reach my inside,
An alkaline antidote—do!"
But what should it be—"Oh, hurry," says he,
"Get a sesquisulphuric or two!
Get a thiocarbaminide-tetramethyldiamidotriphenyl-methane-sesquisulphuric or two!"

V

Said the first assistant to the second assistant, "Where is this thiocarbam-etc., etc.?"
Said the second assistant to the first assistant, "I'll get the thiocarbam-etc., etc."
Yet e'en while they grunted and struggled and hunted,
He frittered and frizzled and fried,
In this polysyllabic, this Sanskrit-Arabic—
For a sesquisulphuric he died,
For a thiocarbaminide-tetramethyldiamidotriphenyl-methane-sesquisulphuric—he died!

Yale Record

ACT I

Scene—A Storm at Sea
Enter (R.C.) Desdemona in his dressing gown; Rigi, without.
DES.: What do you *(laughter)* think of *(cheers)* the Subway? *(Cries of "Hear, hear!" from the pit.)*
RIG.: All right, as a whole. *(Thunderous applause and laughter.)*
Quick curtain.

Robert Benchley/*Harvard Lampoon*

To be on a dais
With Thais—
How nais.

F. Scott Fitzgerald/*Princeton Tiger*

PROF: I'm sorry, Mr. Simp, but I found it necessary to flunk you. Do you know why?
SIMP: I haven't an idea.
PROF: That's exactly right.

Pittsburgh Panther

"Say, how did you get in the Glee Club?"
"Made first base on four bawls."

Stanford Chaparral

PAT—Say, Moike, phat's dhe diffyrunce bechune a man on dhe top av a hill an' one at dhe bottom av it?
MIKE—Will, phat?
PAT—Arrah, dhere's dhe hill av a diffyrunce.

Paul Bartlett/*Harvard Lampoon*

COMING OF AGE 1900-1919

HAVE YOUR CHANGE READY
HOW MANY?
INSTITUTE A SYSTEM OF TOLL-STILES AT THE VARIOUS GATES. . INCIDENTALLY THIS WOULD MAKE THE COLLEGE DORMITORIES WITHIN THE YARD MORE POPULAR
SPECIAL DISC GUNGA DIN
FRENCH IN THREE LESSONS
DR. B
SOME EPOCH-MAKING VICTOR DISCS MIGHT BE MADE BY THE TALENT IN THE FACULTY
UTILIZE THE ADVENT OF SPRING BY FITTING UP A FLOCK OF SWAN-BOATS FOR PLEASURE-RIDING IN THE YARD
THE DAYS WORK
FACULTY OWNERSHIP AND OPERATION OF THE CRIMSON WOULD BE ONE OF THE SUREST OF FINANCIAL ENTERPRISES.

A FEW (FOUR) SUGGESTIONS FOR MAKING UP THE UNIVERSITY DEFICIT

Robert Benchley/*Harvard Lampoon*

SPARKS FROM OLD ANVILS

Some Clever Sayings
of Themistocles

ας ενιβοδι ιρ σεεν κελλι;
ους λουνι ναυ;
ωβη θατ ιμπυλς.

Dying words of Nero to his
Mother, Agrippina
"Omnes laborant, sed pater!"

Twinkle, twinkle, little star,
How I wonder what you are.
Up above the world so high,
Like a diamond in the sky.
—Attributed to Copernicus

SOCRATES: Behold, I have a riddle to ask thee: What maketh more noise than a swine under a grate?
CRITO: I cannot possibly imagine, O Socrates!
SOCRATES: Behold, I shall tell thee. Twain.
CRITO: Is it necessary?
—From a hitherto unpublished dialogue of Plato

"Who was the first man in the Bible?"
"When it's ajar."
—Johann Wolfgang von Goethe
Harvard Lampoon

To the Editor of the LAMPOON:

I protest that the words which you put into my mouth in a recent issue of an undergraduate publication are utterly false. You misrepresent me as voicing the sentiment,"*ας ενιβοδι ιρ σεεν κελλι;*" I can prove that I never uttered such words, for, expecting trouble, I had Aristides accompany me to your sanctum. He is ready to swear that the words I actually uttered, as I thrust my Spearmint furtively into a hollow tooth, were,"*Θε φληφορ λαστς.*" I am disappointed that a publication with your high reputation should stoop to calumniate.

Sincerely yours,
R. CYRIL THEMISTOCLES
Harvard Lampoon

BUB: Why is a Saturday recitation like heaven?
HUBBUB: I'm askin'.
BUB: Not a damned soul there.
Yale Record

TO PROFESSOR PALMER

In the forty years during which Professor Palmer has been connected with the University, he has guided and inspirated thousands of students. —Crimson

Many months I've perspirated
Tutoring in Phil.,
While the tutors conspirated
To increase my bill;
For I've always aspirated
Through your words to know
Wise men who have expirated
Centuries ago.
Harvard Lampoon

At a consul's election, a quorum
Lacked a Senator, Rex Asinorum.
So they asked in a note
How he wanted to vote.
His laconic reply was "I'm Forum."
Williams Purple Cow

COMING OF AGE 1900-1919

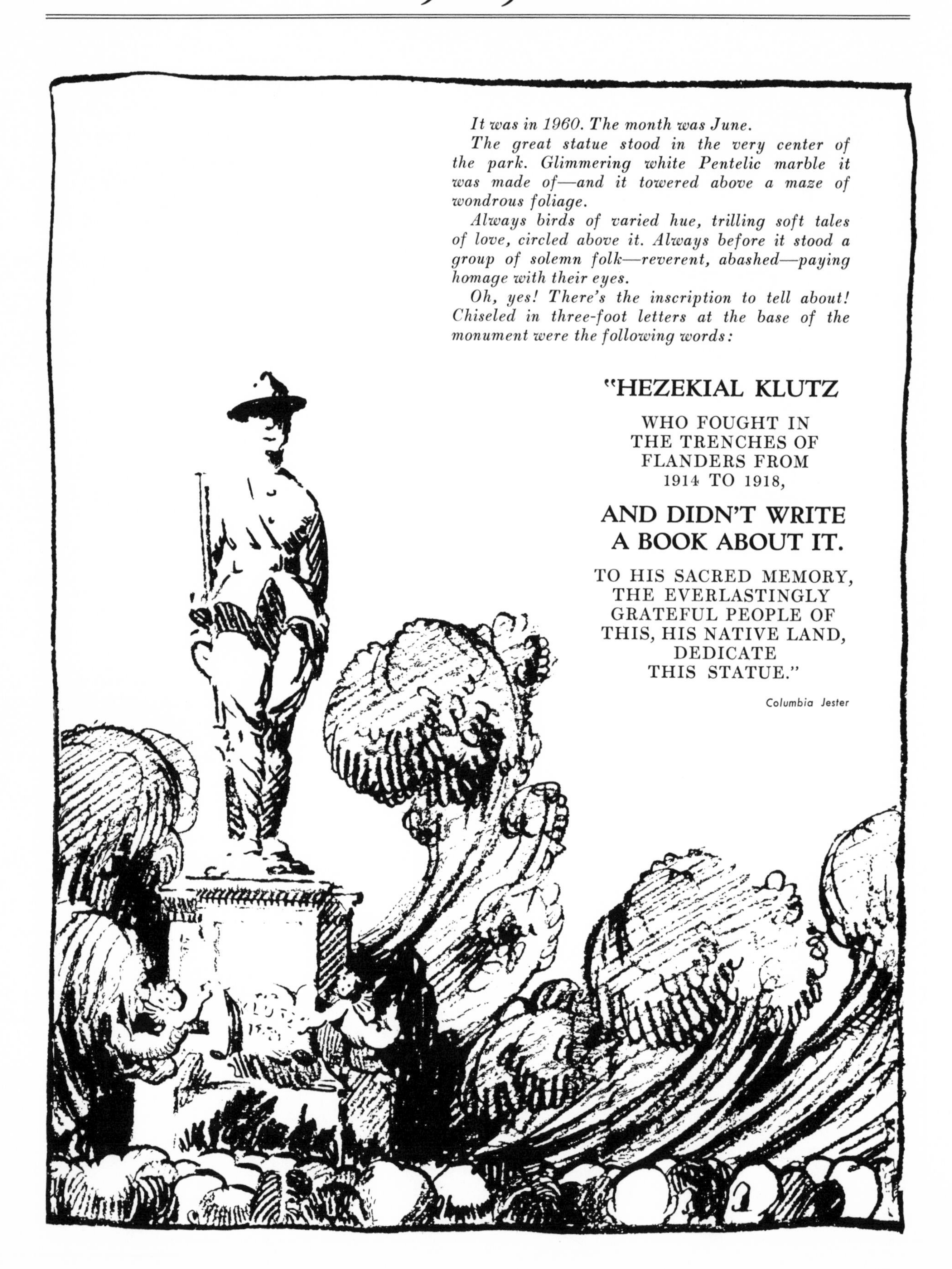

It was in 1960. The month was June.

The great statue stood in the very center of the park. Glimmering white Pentelic marble it was made of—and it towered above a maze of wondrous foliage.

Always birds of varied hue, trilling soft tales of love, circled above it. Always before it stood a group of solemn folk—reverent, abashed—paying homage with their eyes.

Oh, yes! There's the inscription to tell about! Chiseled in three-foot letters at the base of the monument were the following words:

"HEZEKIAL KLUTZ

WHO FOUGHT IN
THE TRENCHES OF
FLANDERS FROM
1914 TO 1918,

AND DIDN'T WRITE
A BOOK ABOUT IT.

TO HIS SACRED MEMORY,
THE EVERLASTINGLY
GRATEFUL PEOPLE OF
THIS, HIS NATIVE LAND,
DEDICATE
THIS STATUE."

Columbia Jester

WHEN UNCLE LOOIE BAGBY GETS DISCUSSIN' PANAMA

I.

THE boys in Pumpkin Center (that's the Perkins County seat)
Have formed a Town Debatin' Club, an' every night they meet
In Silas Greenleaf's Grocery Store, an' pass the time away,
Discussin' politics an' other topics of the day.
The Prohibition Question's been debated through an' through;
The Philippines has had its share of argumentin' too;
An' Congress wouldn't have to scrap or worry any more
If it could hear the Tariff talk in Silas Greenleaf's Store.

II.

There's old Doc Jones, an' Ezra Brown an' Hiram Wetherbee
(The same that ran for Sheriff in the fall of ninety-three),
They all have got opinions that they're pretty apt to air
About the Wimmen Suffrage an' the big St. Looie Fair.
But, say! for downright eloquence an' argumentin', too—
Jest drop in any evening 'bout the time the mail is due,
An' find a chair, an' settle back, an' take an' extra chaw—
When Uncle Looie Bagby gets discussin' Panama.

III.

He knows how many tons of dirt is dug up every day;
He knows how many men is there, an' how much is their pay.
He says if Congress hadn't been so all dod-gasted slow
That that old ditch would have been dug a year or so ago.
Sometimes he gets so heated he don't know just where he's at,
An' then I'm half inclined to think he's talking through his hat.
But jest the same we settles back an' takes an extra chaw—
When Uncle Looie Bagby gets discussin' Panama.

IV.

If Uncle Looie Bagby was in Panama, O my!
I reckon that HE wouldn't make them rocks an' gravel fly.
Of course, I must admit around the house he ain't no good,
But then, of course, it's quite another thing from sawing' wood
An' doin' such important things as helpin' Congress out.
He ought to be in Congress or the Senate I've no doubt;
But if you don't believe me, come around some night, an', Law!
Jest HEAR old Uncle Looie dig that ditch at Panama.

Princeton Tiger

LITTLE ACORNS

A Tragedy in Two Acts

ACT ONE

Time: March, 1606 A.D. Midnight.

Place: The tap-room of the Mermaid Tavern, London.

Enter a man, dressed in court costume. He throws his plum-colored cloak on a table and sits down. He pounds loudly, peevedly several times before a sleepy-looking waiter appears.

THE MAN: Here, boy, a tankard of good ale. . . . See that you fill it up, too. Brimming, and be quick about it.

WAITER: Yessir, savin' yer honour, sir, but it's after twelve, sir.

THE MAN: No matter. Bring me that ale.

WAITER: (without looking up) We has our orders, sir.

THE MAN: Orders don't apply to me. Do you know who I am?

WAITER: (rubbing his eyes) Bless me buttons, it's Master Will. Arksin' yer parding, sir, I 'adn't looked hup.

WILL: (as the waiter hurries about his order) These court balls aren't what they used to be, that they're not. You don't get the stuff to drink you used to get. What becomes of all the money you good Englishmen pay in taxes, I'd like to know. Fitting ships for that crank, Frankie Drake, more'n likely. From the table Lizzie sets, you'd think this was the Canary Islands! The country's going to the dogs, that she is! (The waiter brings his tankard, and he quaffs deep.) Aaaaah! (In a theatrical tone of voice)

"Before a tankard of good English ale
The drinks of other nations all must pale."

Here. I must put that down before I forget it. (He takes out a roll of MSS.)

WAITER: Ah, Master Will, ye're the poet! It surely must be fine to think of such things so quick.

WILL: It's a hard reputation to keep up. (He looks over his papers and shakes his head sadly.) And right now I'm in sore trouble.

WAITER: (quick in sympathy) Can't I help ye out with a couple o' shillin', sir? I'll never miss it.

WILL: It's not money I need, lad. Would God that it were! It's an idea I want. (The waiter sighs knowingly.) Here I am with this play of *Macbeth* on my hands that I've got to finish by next week, and I can't get started on the second act. Hold on, here's an idea. (He ruffles up his hair, scatters papers about, and starts to scribble. The waiter sits down and stares as if at a circus. Will mutters to himself.) Court of Macbeth's castle. Night. Banquo and Fleance. Torch. Here, boy, how's this? You be Fleance. I'm your master, Banquo. I'll say, "How goes the night, boy?" What'll you say?

WAITER: "Moon's up, yer worship. 'Tis nine o'clock of a fine clear night." How's that, sir?

WILL: (counts off on his fingers) One, two, one, two. Fair. But there's too much of it. Further, the moon isn't up, because I want it dark. Try again. Say what time the clock struck.

WAITER: But ye can't hear no clock out there.

WILL: Well and good; say so.

WAITER: "The moon is down; I have not heard the clock."

WILL: Most excellent. Then I'll say, "And she goes down at twelve."

WAITER: (objecting vehemently) I tak't 'tis later, sir.

WILL: (scribbling) Beautiful. Just finishes the line. Right to the syllable. "I tak't 'tis later, sir." Take care, boy, or you'll be writing better blank verse than I.

WAITER: 'Twas not blank verse. I meant it. Arksin' yer parding, the moon . . .

WILL: What care I what you meant? Let it pass. It is a good iambic line. Hold, take my tankard for another draught. There—that will do for my next line. . . . "Hold, take my sword." (He scribbles on.)

CURTAIN

ACT TWO

Time: February, 1917. Midnight.

Place: Living room in the home of Professor William Shakespeare Jenkins.

The professor sits at a table, grading papers; opposite is Mrs. Jenkins, darning the professorial socks.

PROF. J.: Numskulls! Porridge brains! (He makes savage red ink marks on a paper and throws it down.)

MRS. J.: I'm afraid your boys won't get very good marks this time, Billy dear, and if you flunk them all they won't like you any more. Don't be so cross.

PROF. J.: They ought to flunk, every one of them. They have the effrontery to elect a course under me, the greatest Shakespearean scholar of the age, and then they hand me papers like these! (He boils with righteous wrath while his spouse continues placidly to darn.)

MRS. J.: It's true you know an awful lot, Billy dear, but remember there was a time when you started out. Maybe one of these boys will be even greater and crosser than you.

PROF. J.: (unheeding) Here's a young fool tries to get by because he thinks I can't read his scrawl. Nor more can I! Bah! Just for that you'll flunk, sir.

MRS. J.: Let me try, Billy dear. I'm good on poor writing. Nobody but me can read yours, you know. (She takes the paper.) What's this first question about?

PROF. J.: (with the air of fighting it out for once and all) My dear girl, which of us knows more about Shakespeare?

MRS. J.: You, of course.

PROF. J.: Which of us knows more about teaching Shakespeare?

MRS. J.: Why, you, Billy dear, but . . .

PROF. J.: Which of us is conducting this particular class in Shakespeare?

MRS. J.: I know all that, but what is this first question?

PROF. J.: (yielding up his spirit) The question was, "Explain the following lines from *Macbeth*:

"Banquo: How goes the night, boy?

Fleance: The moon is down! I have not heard the clock.

Banquo: And she goes down at twelve.

Fleance: I tak't 'tis later, sir."

I had lectured on that passage for at least three days, my dear, and had fully interpreted the poet's meaning. The sinister aspect of "the moon is down." The fact that the guilty Macbeth had probably stopped the clock. The disputed antecedent of the word "she" in the third line; some scholars say it refers to Lady Macbeth, others with very good ground that it means the clock. I hold the opinion that "she" is some female character mentioned nowhere else in the play. Then there's Fleance's enigmatical speech. Nobody does know what that means. I think . . .

MRS. J.: Never mind what you think now, Billy dear; here's what this boy thinks: "If Banquo and Fleance lived today they would say,

"Banquo: How late is it, kid?

Fleance: Pretty darn late, I guess. Moon's gone down. I was asleep so I didn't hear the clock.

Banquo: I think it's later than that, sir."

PROF. J.: Why, the boy's a genius! Asleep! Think of that. Nobody ever thought of that before. "She" refers to the moon. Well, well, well. (He hops around in erudite excitement.) Hand me my Variorum Shakespeare, my dear. All as clear as day. I must telegraph dear Professor Hudson immediately. This will revolutionize Shakespearean study!!

(He rushes off. Mrs. Jenkins continues placidly to darn the professorial socks.)

CURTAIN

James Thurber/*Ohio State Sundial*

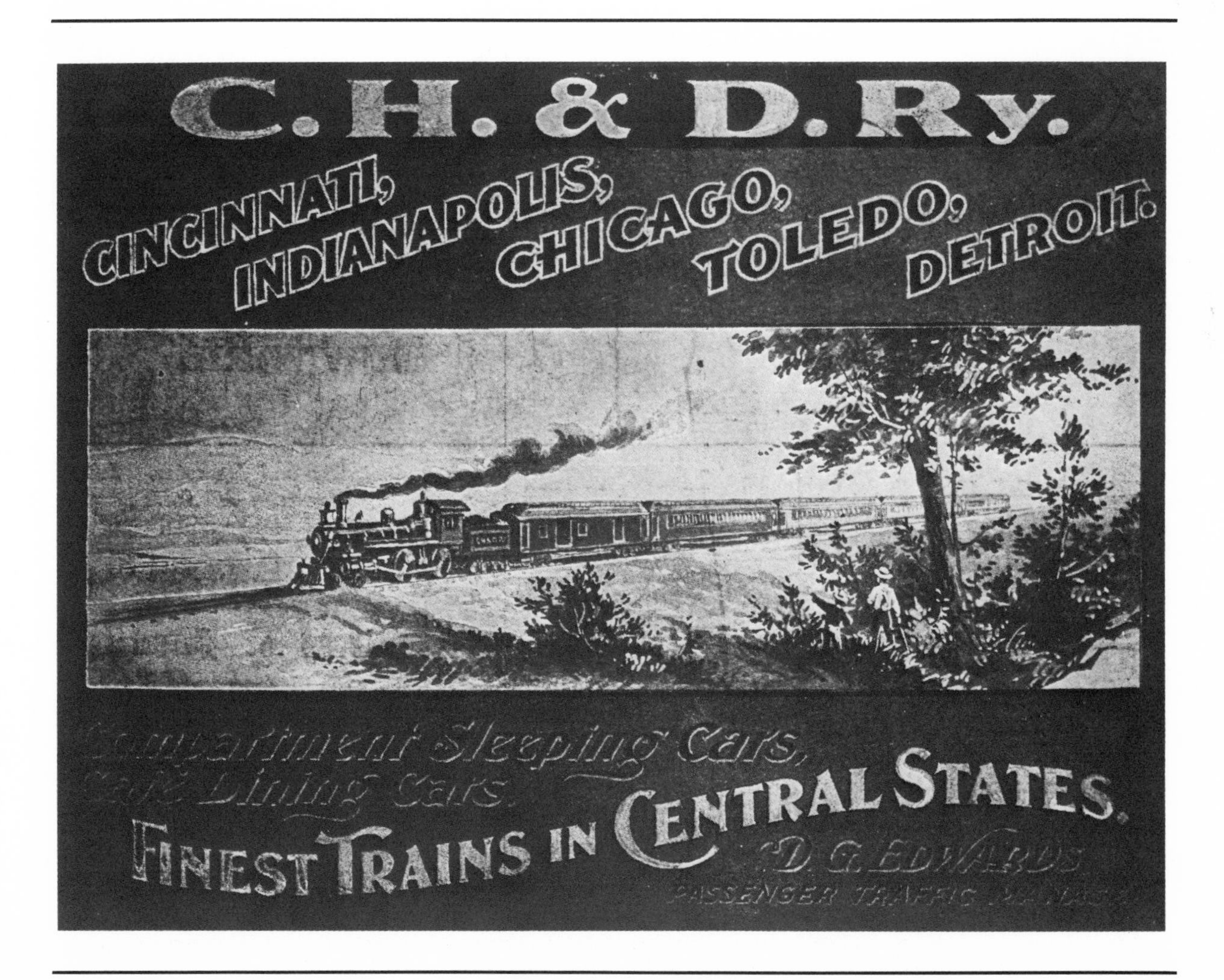

CAN THE ANIMAL THINK?

MRS. INANE FADDFUSSER THINKS SO!

This is Mrs. Faddfusser's prize cheese hound, Full O'Fleas, which is one of the links in a long chain of dogs. It was sired by the Yale Bull and damned by everyone.

THE keen enthusiast for the World of Pets will be delighted with the results of Mrs. Inane Faddfusser's recent experiments conducted at fabulous expense upon the members of her daring and unique household. Like the other women of her exalted station in the gold, marble, and satin plush society of New York, Mrs. Faddfusser has allowed in her family only dogs, cats, horses, birds, monkeys, and miscellaneous. The only kind of children tolerated are puppies, kittens, colts, . . . etc. These restrictions enable Mrs. Faddfusser to devote her entire husband's income to the investigation of brain power in what man, in his pride, has termed the *animal.*

Under the able (but, of course, expensive) management of M. Oilue Smirque various scientific tests have been applied to the dear pets to ascertain their mental capacity. Mrs. Faddfusser herself has passed satisfactorily many of these difficult examinations, some of which even her favorite monkey "Queen Wibbles" failed in, and she now feels qualified to make public her startling conclusions.

That the animals really do think is the natural hypothesis to be gleaned from a remarkable test made on "King Wubbles," the striped Hilarian lap-elephant, who was confined in a bird cage with the door left open. The animal actually did not quit the cage because the door was too small for him to get through. Such a brilliant streak of reasoning has been equaled only by "Prince Jiggles," the thoroughbred Hymalayan Jelly Fish, who brilliantly refuses food after each meal.

Mrs. Faddfusser's favorite pet, however, is "Princess Wobbles," a veteran point winner of old pleostocene stock, who, for over a year now, has remained unceasingly within three yards of her mistress. Mrs. Faddfusser has proudly refused to question the Princess' mentality by any tests whatsoever. She loves the animal dearly, and hopes to will it most of her husband's fortune.

Mrs. Faddfusser has very radical views on the care of pets and their important position in the social world. She offers below some invaluable hints for the better welfare of Petdom.

"For snakes, those perfectly darling and indispensable additions to the really fashionable drawing room, winter overcoats this year will be of flexible gas pipe. For dogs, a simple fragment of door mat with a light *sur-tout* of gold chain mail. The ponies and alligators are best excused from the dinner table when there is company."

Robert E. Sherwood/*Harvard Lampoon*

DO YOU BELIEVE IN FAIRIES?

By NELL DRINKLEY

There are lots of young girls whose parents have taught them to believe that love at first sight is worth two in a flat. This is an old-fashioned idea, my dear, and some day you will see how inevitable is the way of true love, but then it will be too late. Poor, dear, foolish little girl!

THE HARVARD LAMPOON

SEWING CIRCLE

The Sewing Circle is an exceedingly irregular department in the HARVARD LAMPOON. It is intended as the "woman's own forum," and in it housewives discuss the care of children and flowers, husbands and dogs, and offer suggestions for baby-tending, hair-removers, and dust-removers. Write only on two sides of the paper.

Will the sister who sent in the receipt for removing freckles from finger nails please tell me whether I may use the same method for getting rid of pimples on the eyelashes? I have soaked each eyelash for half an hour in a solution of cartrox and hot tea as suggested, but so far have noticed no effect.

I think that "Redundant" had better take up rowing as that always helps in such cases. — ESMERALDA P.

"Bewildered" asks what to do with radishes that are left over from breakfast. I myself was in a fix for a time until I found that by scooping out each one and filling it with crab-meat and powdered grape-fruit a tasty dainty might be made that would go well with oatmeal pie for tea.

Can anyone tell me how to make a harem skirt, bust 34, out of an old pair of tan sneakers and a last year's parasol? — DISTRAUGHT.

To "Pink Petticoat" — My child, too, often had convulsions while teething until I found a simple home remedy that calmed it very quickly. This is what I do. I get some cream from the nearest tobacco store and lay the child face down on a sofa. Then I heat it on the gas range until it simmers — try it time and again to prevent scalding — and feed it to it in tablespoonfuls. If it still cries add some lemon juice or a dash of oleomargarine. It will then usually drink it nicely. Be sure it is not too acid as that will make it restive and tends to bring on sore gums. After it has stopped drinking, pour it into a large fruit jar for another time. — CAREFUL MOTHER.

Can anyone tell me what baby means by winding its left leg around its ear and cooing chokedly? Is it bilious or is it just natural? — YOUNG WIFE.

DEAR EPPING, N. H.: — Was oh, so pleased to see your note in this column, and will love to give you any advice that I can. Girlie was three years old last month, and is full of mischief. Thank you ever and ever so much for your recipe for mock oyster stew. And oh — about that other thing you spoke of — never let it dry before you heat it, or it may burst. — SYMPATHETIC.

Will some of the sisters give a remedy for nitro glycerine stains on the teeth? My little Pearl ate some last Friday, and has been rather sullen ever since, and I think it must be mortification at the unsightly condition in which it left her teeth. — A BRIGHTON SISTER.

A CORN AND BEANS JABOT

FOR MRS. H.: — Begin with a rose center, wind thread 12 times around with tip of hook, and in the ring formed work 20 s c, 5ch, catch in 4th s c. Repeat until there are 5 loops of ch in each loop. Work 1 sc and 6 jt. This finishes the row. Make 7 sg, 4 gf sl tr around the petals, connecting the shells at each end, then make a row of 3 sc, picot 4 and 3 sc in each of the loops around the edge.

A NEW IDEA IN EMBROIDERY

One of our ingenious girl correspondents has made herself a dear set of lingerie shoe-strings, and has sent us the receipt for the readers of this column. They may be made while the eggs are boiling in the morning, for the ingredients are very easy to get, and we are sure that many tired house-wives will be glad to know of it.

Any druggist will be glad to give you any shoe-strings he may have in stock and these procured, the rest of the work is simple. First cover the shoe-strings with a frosting of glue. (You can obtain the glue at almost any place where they sell glue.) This done give them to baby (if any) to hold very still for twenty-six minutes until they are dry. Then rapidly chain-stitch the inner edge of each string. Our correspondent says that here you must be very careful about raveling, and to prevent this suggests running a gathering string of sheer pink dimity down the center and drawing it tight. The chain stitch may be done in Helen pink or Alice blue according to the way you like your eggs. All that now remains is the application of the lingerie, which can easily be done between courses at dinner by simply taking the lingerie and applying it to the shoe-strings.

DEAR SISTER; — Was it you who had the sick gold-fish and asked for help in these columns? You spoke of giving it a table-spoonful of potash after each attack. I should never do that until I had tried an application of ham poultice, followed by a brisk rubbing with a coarse dry towel. Try this on your sick gold-fish and let me know.

LITTLE LIGHT BEARER.

THE HARVARD LAMPOON

35th Year Cambridge, Mass.
Subscription Rate $2.75 per year

Friday, May 6, 1911

Foreign Offices

Abyssinia . . . . Hotel Toureen
Valdivostock . . . . . . 17 Kabsksz Place
France . . . . 8 Rue Matizm

Sun Rises Sun Set
In the East In the West

High Tide Low Tide

THE WEATHER

Forty-eight thousand nine hundred and three years ago to-day Wilfred H. Noah was born. Mr. Noah originated the phrases "Misfortunes never come singly," and "It never rains but it pours."

Officially:

FORECAST FOR CAMBRIDGE AND VICINITY: Fair to Middling; westerly winds in the west, easterly winds in the east.

FORECAST FOR NEW ENGLAND—Rain to-day and to-morrow, probably followed by clearing.

JOTTINGS

SpRinG?!!

Splendid!

Better not, Gordon!

Decidedly, Mr. Roosevelt.

And still Lombardy side-paddles.

Did Mrs. Eddy realize her coincidence, or is Dr. M. only in earnest?

Once more, Elevated! But beware the C. O. I. N. V.'s (Whichever!?)

If Major Jackson had been right, limp St. Patrick never so feebly! But the climb is up.

But the Mayflower doesn't *always* work that way, friend Thomas! Though hockey, we admit, has its Gladstones.

Beet-sugar, did you say, Mayor Smith? Nevertheless, those don't affect *his* tame orioles! Or was it gazelles? We forget.

With the price of beef rising, and Mr. Taft opening our pageant by a mere electric button—and yet Mexico plays the ace! After you, G. A. R. Veterans!

THE INTER-STATE COMMERCE COMMISSION

The report read last evening at the annual dinner of the Thimble-makers Union at the Hotel Lithuania brings to light several startling, if not prematurely fruitful facts which the voters of Boston might do well to cogitate upon. We have already remarked in these columns upon the seeming recusancy of the Committee on Ways and Beans on Beacon Hill, and with respect to the somewhat dehortative action of the Mayor in so prematurely shelving the Ma or Bottle Bill. Our readers will remember that in his inaugural address the Mayor expressly stated that for the sake of a few overcapitalized concerns such problematic performances as the "101 Ranch" and "The World in Boston" could not be without serious detriment to the fresh bloom of innocence of the thousands of theological students who loiter about the portals of our city, be allowed. And now Mr. Mayor, we ask you in all earnestness, what did you do with the franchise?

WORLD NEWS HOT FROM THE WIRE

CHARLESVILLE, PA. May 4:—While hunting for codfish in his back yard yesterday, F. R. Boggles discovered a collar-button he had thrown out the window at a cat nearly eighteen years before. The cat, according to Mr. Boggles, was in perfect condition.

TORPEDO, NEB. May 3:—Two horses belonging to Mr. Squirk, a former selectman of this town, died of delirium tremens while passing a lunch wagon near here to-day. By some mistake the stable boy had fed them with hops instead of oats and the sight of hot dogs fermented the horses. The horses were not insured.

To-day's Best Story

The following anecdote is told of Representative Henry F. Spiffkins, who afterwards became third assistant secretary to the Treasury. One day while on his famous Middle West Campaign he happened to be standing on the back platform of a trolley car conversing earnestly with the motorman when an evil looking policeman came up to him and asked him what he was about.

"I am trying to obtain some information," said the Congressman with a quiet twinkle in his eye.

"That don't go," cried the officer of the law angrily, "This ain't no barber shop."

"No need of that," answered Representative Spiffkins, simply, "I shave myself."

He was not troubled by the policeman again.

MAYOR THE BENEFACTOR OF YOUTH

NEW YORK, N. Y. April 29, '11. Mayor Gainer, while walking, as his custom is, along the east side to-day noticed some youngsters busily frisking about. "What are you doing?" he inquired. "Sellin' papehs," volunteered one of the youths. "Give me one," said Mr. Gainer giving the boy a penny. The youth was the center of an admiring throng all day.

BOY SAVES COMPANION

WASHAWASH, O. May 2, '11. While passing a swimming pool here to-day, John Squinch happened to notice a chum of his struggling in the water and making violent efforts to save himself. Waiting only to throw off his suspenders, young Squinch dove in. The water being only two feet deep in the deepest part of the pool, his first move was to secure his companion's feet and place them securely on the bottom. Then he led him ashore. The boy had been taken with a crab.

FOR OUR LITTLE READERS

TODAY'S PUZZLE

WHAT IS WRONG WITH THIS PICTURE?
Yesterday's answer—The man had no liver

COMING OF AGE
1900-1919

SOCIETY

Now that the sombre hues of Lent have been cast off, and the glorious pageantry of the budding mayflower blazes from the murmuring mother-earth on every fashionable hillside of the long North Shore, the smart-set leaders and society matrons are preparing for a last burst of sartorial glory before the dusty heat of summer drives the fevered aristocrats from the sweltering streets of busy Boston to the cool seclusion of Beverly and the invigorating though restful air of Bar Harbor. The pace becomes hotter and fiercer. There is no rest for the leader of fashion. Dog Shows, Horse Shows, Tincent Shows, teas, luncheons, and weddings continue with unabated furore to monopolize the spare minutes of the ambitious gadder.

It has been decidedly a week of weddings. On Monday the nuptials of Miss Notta Chaunce, eldest daughter of Mrs. Every Chaunce, and a prominent member of the Tincent Club and the 1907 Sewing Circle, and Mr. Laydeigh Killer, Harvard, '06, son of the Laydeigh Killers of Prude's Crossing, were celebrated at high noon in the Church of St. Brummel le Beau. The Rt. Rev. Tyem Tighte officiated. The maid of honor was Miss Wanta Mann, a noted horsewoman of the Social Drags, and a prominent member of the Tincent Club. The bride wore white chevaux-de-frise with hand-organdie trimmings, and carried clusters of dried prunes.

On Wednesday there was another brilliant affair, when Miss Taxie Cabot, the daughter of Mr. and Mrs. Hansom Cabot of Uncommonwealth Avenue, and a prominent member of the Tincent Club and the 1909 Sewing Circle, was married to Mr. Rushmore Pills of Pillsbury, New Jersey. Mr. Pills is well known in Boston through his cousins, the Stickeigh Pills of Chestnut Hill. He belongs to several of the most exclusive clubs of Pillsbury, New Jersey, and is a well-known sportsman in the Mosquito Hunt of Atlantic City. The couple will go to Europe on the SS. "Romantic" for a short honeymoon, returning *via* Reno in July. Miss Cabot wore a dainty gown of self-toned avoirdupois, with dashes of café-au-lait and demi-tassels of pistache. She also wore garden hose and force-pumps, the dernier cri of the Rue de la Paix, and carried a magnificent bunch of hot-house pineapples.

Quite the most ultra-ultra event of the week, however, was the annual production of the Tincent Club in Jordan Hall. The fashionable young ladies who took part in this season's pieces are now the receptive recipients of congratulatory congratulations on the success that attended their efforts. The chief parts were taken by prominent members of the Tincent Club.

Mr. and Mrs. Justin Clymer of Bay State Road gave a delightfully exclusive little dance at their country house, "The Pussy-willows," in Weedham, on Tuesday, in honor of their daughter, Miss Marie Wells Clymer. Many of the smartest debutantes and other prominent members of the Tincent Club were present, and altogether it was a very decolleté little affair. The whole interior of Mrs. Clymer's expensive residence was cleverly decorated in exact imitation of a scere on the Sahara Desert, and during the intermissions a concealed Bulgarian Band played selections from Slopski's "Dust unto Dust." A sand-storm, at an estimated cost of five thousand dollars, drove the guests to supper, which consisted of pickled zebra's tongues en cas, mock-camel soup, and Nubian ices. Supper was served in the palm-room, tastefully decorated to simulate an Algerian oasis. Mrs. Clymer is receiving congratulations on this charming idea.

A number of young people went out to the dinner dance given by Mrs. Baybeigh Bratz for her daughter, Miss Helena Bratz, of Cambridge. Mrs. Bratz comes of one of the most distinguished Colonial families, and Miss Bratz is a prominent member of the Tincent Club.

Mr. and Mrs. Patrick Mulligan gave an at home at their residence, 5B Vere de Vere Street, Chelsea, in honor of their debutante daughter, Miss Bridget Mulligan. After a delightful evening the guests went on to the K. of Q. Hop in Pullan Hall.

WHOSE CHILD IS THIS?

This picture was snapped by a *Lampoon* photographer, in the vicinity of Harvard Square, yesterday between 11 and 12 P. M. If the lucky parent will call at the *Lampoon* building any Thursday morning in May, between 7 and 8 A. M., accompanied by not less than three witnesses and a pack of calling cards, he will receive, as grand prize, one week's subscription to the Harvard Monthly and one pair Everwear Hosiery (special clubbing offer for this competition).

Robert Benchley, Frederick Lewis Allen, and others/*Harvard Lampoon*

COMING OF AGE 1900-1919

THE STREETS OF DURHAM

OR DIRTY WORK AT THE CROSS ROADS

(A Tragedy in Three Muddy Acts)

By TOMMY WOLFE

PERSONS OF THE PLAY

The Chorus ...... The Durham Police Force
History .... Himself
Father Time .... Ditto
Despair .. The Tar Heel Editor
Nemesis .... A Steam Shovel with an evil eye and devouring jaws
A Scheming Contractor .... Mr. John Q. Asphalt

Supported by an all star cast, including shopgirls, shoplifters, mill people, ill people, butchers, bakers and candlestick makers. Trinity students dressed neatly but not gaudily in light pink shirts with green collars, together with the rest of the native population.

ACT I

SCENE I

The curtain rises on a dreary prospect. Coming faintly through the driving rain one hears the mournful whistle of the Bull Durham factory. Nemesis, in the form of a steam shovel, stands by quietly with a cold sneer on his evil face. A few belated ducks swim languidly around in some of the more shallow puddles; the others are too deep. Enter two members of the Durham police force, dressed in their native regalia, and heavily armed with rubber boots. One is a sergeant, the other a plain cop. On their respective bosoms are pinned the insignia of their order, viz., namely and to-wit:

A field of green embossed and cut diagonally by a streak of yellow, the whole surmounted by two beer bottles, rampant. The orchestra plays softly the opening strains of Danny Deever.

"What are the whistles tooting for?" said Sgt. McElrade.

"Another day of Durham Bull," the new policeman said.

"What makes you look so green, so green?" said Sgt. McElrade.

"I just fetched in from Appletree," the new policeman said. "For the frost was on the pumpkin and the cawn was in the bin, I hadn't had a bit of rest in Gawd alone knows when. So I joined the Durham force on Wednesday mornin'."

"What's that so pink against the sky?" said Sgt. McElrade.

" 'Tis the student shirts of Trinity," the new policeman said.

"Methinks I see a tinge of green," said Sgt. McElrade.

" 'Tis the collars to the shirts you've seen," the new policeman said.
"For their student body cometh in their winsome boyish way,
They're done with registration and they're marching en masse
To the Malbourne and the Orpheum and goodly cabaret
Belike you'll need your foive before the mornin'."

Enter a group of Trinity students with a gleeful shout, singing the good old business college songs.

SCENE II

College stuff: Chorus on your left, Trinity gathered around Maypole erected in center stage.

TRINITY STUDENTS: Let us gather 'round the maypole, comrades, in our happy boyish way,
Today let us be merry, tomorrow come what may.
If I should fall asleep, just wake me, wake me, brothers dear,
Tomorrow'll be the maddest, gladdest day of all the year.
For I'm to be queen of the May, brothers, I'm to be queen of the May.

(The whole chorus hits a high note as the curtain relaxes and falls.)

ACT II

SCENE I

Same as before. Enter three Durham belles whom we shall call Mary, Kate, and Minnie, mainly because those are their names.

MINNIE (in consternation): O Gawd, girls, look at the mud!

KATE: It's really quite obtuse of the authorities to permit these intolerable conditions.

MARY: I should worry; mine are silk. (They cross the street, their cheeks suffused with the delicate shy flush of maidenhood, a chorus of admiring "oh's" and "ah's" from Trinity students collected on the corner.)

TRINITY STUDENT (enthusiastically): Boni stuffi. (Latin for "good stuff".)

SCENE II

Enter Tar Heel editor, dazed. His mind is wandering. Casts wild despairing glances toward the streets.

TAR HEEL EDITOR (laughing hysterically): "O Fireman, save my pop-eyed child," the frantic mother cried, but the frog climbed a sycamore tree and sighed, as he sharpened his sting with a file. (From a ballad of mountain dew.)

"O mother, hear that rattling noise?" a little girl once said.

"Cheer up, my dear, 'tis your father's voice, the poor nut's brains are dead." (An old Durham folk song.)

TAR HEEL EDITOR (regaining sanity for a moment): O God, I would I were a duck.

ACT III

Same as before. Enter John Q. Asphalt, a scheming contractor, and his co-conspirator, Nemesis, the steam shovel. Asphalt is a man with a fat hog-like face, a derby hat and prematurely grey eyes. No self-respecting playwright ever describes Nemesis.

NEMESIS: When shall we two meet again? In thunder, lightning, or in rain?

ASPHALT: Preferably in rain. The trouble with thunder and lightning is that their bark is usually louder than their bite. Now rain is a slow but sure assistant. Why, if it keeps on raining, I won't finish this job until the spring of 1979.

NEMESIS: We'll pave this street with asphaltine and take it up again I ween, for when they find the sewers missed, they'll want 'em in real quick I wist.

Yes, if my wops will only stick fast
We'll tear them up from Hell to Breakfast.
And after that it's easy, then—
From Breakfast back to Hell again.
And if our methods cute don't fright 'em.
We'll keep 'em up ad infinitum.
NEMESIS (admiringly): You're a man after my own heart. (Arm in arm the two conspirators sneak around the corner and drink to the day with a bottle of Bevo, pilfered from Gen. Julian S. Carr's cellar.)

SCENE III

Enter chorus of natives singing the native song of lamentation.
Chorus:
We never get to see the neighbors,
Since they ripped up all our streets, bejabbers.
And it's us that's telling yo' we're sorry,
That we let them fix our streets, begorry.
We sure did pull a big fat bone
When we let 'em do it, ohchone, ohchone!

(In the distance can be heard the hoarse, grating chuckle of Nemesis, followed by the high falsetto cackle of Asphalt.) The natives shiver and look at each other muttering: "I reckon we had better be getting along home, there's dirty work ahead."

SCENE IV

Forty-seven years have elapsed. During this time the audience gets tired of waiting and goes out. The curtain rises on the same street as in Act I. It is still raining. Nemesis, the steam shovel, has moved two blocks down the street. History and Father Time make their first appearance; they come in together and converse.
FATHER TIME: I'm gittin' tired of waitin'.
HISTORY: It took me twenty-seven years to write a history of the war.
To count the graves, the tombs and biers,
Also the near beers—but I'll swear
In thirty-seven different lingos
There, Durham streets have all the jingoes
Beat that ever jingoed. Now my song
Is something like this, "Oh, Lord, how long!"
FATHER TIME (fiercely): I'm an old man an' I deserve some consideration. It's all the fault of that young scoundrel there (he shakes his fist at Nemesis whose back is turned).
HISTORY: Let's fix him.
TIME: Done. (He pulls his trusty Smith & Wesson from his pocket. His gun coughs and spits fire. Nemesis falls, mortally wounded, shot through his waistcoat and with his suspenders cut to ribbons. With a joyous shout the chorus of natives [including students and police force] rush out on stage uttering noises of delirious delight.)
FIRST NATIVE (hoarsely): At last! At last! We are saved. Drink! Drink! Strong drink! (The popping of corks may be heard and we gaze upon a wild debauch of intoxication as the natives reel from the effects of eleven bottles each of Pepsi-Cola. They continue their wild orgy of joy, putting pennies recklessly in chewing gum slots and laughing insanely as they stagger around. Finally two or three of the more sane ones come forward and sing the native song of Thanksgiving.)
CHORUS: From the muddy lands with which our feet were shackled,
To this freedom, with hope's brightest lamp imbued,
Is the farthest cry that ever roared or cackled,
Or one might say, farthest cry that ever crewed.
Come let us hence
To some point thence
To celebrate the death of dull Misgiving,
To crown our joy with feats of great Thanksgiving;
Yea, since the corkscrew's lost its pull
Let's open up a can of Bull.

(The natives scream with delight. They are still screaming as)

THE CURTAIN FALLS

Thomas Wolfe/North Carolina Tar Baby

An Intelligent peasant named
Brgrstpkskverst
Said in Russian, "This country is cursed!
They're too rich over here
But *my* conscience is clear,
Last November I voted for Hearst."

Morris M. Osborne/Harvard Lampoon

PRINCETON
NURSERY RHYME

Compulsory Chapel

We love weekday chapel,
They keep it so warm,
And if we don't go there
'Twill do us no harm.

Princeton Tiger

1909: "Isaacstein has married an Irish waitress."
1910: "He always was fond of music but I didn't know he went in for Jews' harps."

Dartmouth Jack O' Lantern

COMING OF AGE 1900-1919

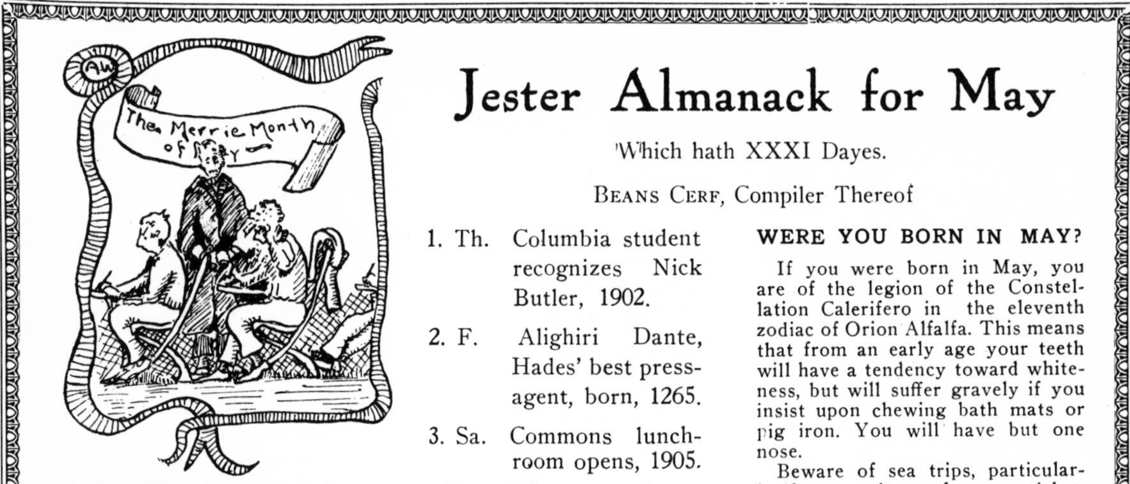

Jester Almanack for May

'Which hath XXXI Dayes.

BEANS CERF, Compiler Thereof

1. Th. Columbia student recognizes Nick Butler, 1902.
2. F. Alighiri Dante, Hades' best press-agent, born, 1265.
3. Sa. Commons lunch-room opens, 1905.
4. Su. First joke about Commons coffee. 1905.
5. M. Menorah and Newman club give joint dance. 1961.
6. Tu. Newly elected student board ceases to greet electorate by their first names. 1919.
7. W. Chorus men's union goes on strike. Box office records at every theatre broken. 1919.
8. Th. Frat bands taken out of camphor. 1919.
9. F. William Penn and his son, Waterman Penn, shoot crap with the Indians, and win all the wampum in Philadelphia, 1683.
10. Sa. William Penn prohibits gambling. 1683.
11. Su. President 'Wilson takes a walk without Mrs. Wilson 1919.
12. M. Spec gets a big Columbia story on the same day as downtown papers. 1879.
13. Tu. Levering Tyson shows Jester board the money it ought to get as its share of the S. A. F. 1919.
14. W. New edition of the Subway Sun out. *Frost.*
15. Th. Spec. managing board meets. Harold Cone loses twenty dollars. 1919.
16. F. Mark Twain meets Brander Mathews. 1891.
17. Sa. Talcott Williams trims his mustache. 1904.
18. Su. Nero begins burning Rome. 64 B. C. Columbia studes begin burning midnight oil. 1919 A. D.
19. M. Exams. begin. 1919.
20. Tu. Mr. Hylan announces that he is the best Mayor New York ever had. 1919.
21. W. Giant rooters begin thnking of next year. 1919.
22. Th. Columbia professors hold annual theatre party. Hurtig and Seamon's mobbed. 1919.
23. F. Bill Hearst subscribes to the Tribune. 1947.
24. Sa. Student finds book he wants in the Library. 1890.
24. Su. Amendment prohibiting smoking. dancing, cussing, and breathing passed in the U. S. 1922.
26. M. Prof. Steeves acquires"in the nature of things" and "on the face of things." 1899.
27. Tu. J. M. Barrie born, 1873 Nurse remarks how "quaint and "whimsical" he is.
28. W. Journalist succeeds in entering Journalism elevator. 1914.
29. Th. American citizen seen leaving Bronx subway train. 1917.
30. F. Memorial Day. School of Business student takes a bath. 1918.
31. Sa. Napoleon invents new kind of French pastry and names it after himself. 1805.

WERE YOU BORN IN MAY?

If you were born in May, you are of the legion of the Constellation Calerifero in the eleventh zodiac of Orion Alfalfa. This means that from an early age your teeth will have a tendency toward whiteness, but will suffer gravely if you insist upon chewing bath mats or pig iron. You will have but one nose.

Beware of sea trips, particularly if you can't pay for your ticket. Come to think of it, you better beware of land trips too. In short, beware of trips. Your flower is Pillsbury's and your gem is the Pork Chop. Avoid little men with large ears, and large men with no ears at all.

Being a son of the Constellation Calerifero, you are fearless. handsome, brilliant, and anything else you'd like to be. We aim to please. At some time in your life you will probably eat a bowl of tripe. Try to conquer the difficulties that will beset your path to success. Remember that John Wanamaker only had $20,000,000 when he began.

Don't marry a red-headed woman. This is good advice no matter what month you were born in.

ANECDOTE

No one is fonder of an innocent drollery than General Pershing, the noted leader of the A. F. F. It is related that he was riding in a Ford motor car one day this spring with a Colonel, and the machine was misbehaving scandalously, his proverbial good nature was not ruffled.

"They ought to add the motor in this thing to the casualty list," he said suddenly.

"Why is that?" asked the Colonel, struck by the strangeness of the idea.

"It's missing in action!" 'exclaimed the General. And even the Ford joined in the hearty burst of laughter that followed this sally.

Bennett Cerf/Columbia Jester

THE *CRIMSON* CANDIDATE
HIS KINDERGARTEN OF VERSES

I

FAREWELL TO LIFE

The *Crimson* made a call for men
Who had, like me, a ready pen,
And as I came I stopped to sing—
Good-bye, good-bye to everything.

To books and fussing, town and class,
To dinners and the brimming glass,
To ease and comfort, youth's wild fling—
Good-bye, good-bye to everything.

Oh, fare you well forevermore,
All joys I've tasted heretofore,
The theatres where angels sing—
Good-bye, good-bye to everything.

Through all the day and all the night
I work and work with all my might,
And from the stool my legs I swing—
Good-bye, good-bye to everything.

II

SNAPPY THOUGHT

The *Crimson*'s so loaded with ads and such things
Its readers should all be as happy as kings.

III

MY CLASSMATE

You, too, my classmate, read my rhymes
For love of unforgotten times,
And mourn your friend, a sacrifice,
Who on the *Crimson* altar lies.

IV

WHOLE DUTY OF CANDIDATES

On yellow paper we must write
Our tales both colorless and trite,
And we must speak when spoken to
And swear that what we wrote was true.

V

BED—A VISION

I cannot go to bed at all,
At dawn or when the shadows fall,
But if the *Crimson* Board I make,
Then I need ne'er from slumber wake.

VI

A CONFESSION

I like the *Lampoon* very much,
I like its verse and jokes and such,
I revel in its "By the Way"—
But I must keep this dark, they say.

Earl Derr Biggers/Harvard Lampoon

RADCLIFFE WINS AGAIN
or

The Prize Play

at the

Bijou Dream

Scene: Room with piano, silk cushion, and rubber plant—latter to represent high life and tragedy. . . . Enter Mary, carefully looking away from audience—several minutes' wait.

VOICE OF PROMPTER: Ah, well!
MARY: Ah, well!
VOICE OF PROMPTER: Ah, well! 'Tis enough.
MARY: (loudly) Yes!!
VOICE OF PROMPTER: (loud whisper) Say, "James," g'wan brace up.
MARY: James!
(Enter James with dish of ice cream.)
MARY: Ah, you've brought my writing (sees ice cream) . . . I mean sherbet.
JAMES: Madam, Lord Hawkhurst waits without.
MARY: Without what? (Startled silence.) I mean show him in.
(Enter Hawkhurst in dress-suit with light pink vest and four-in-hand tie.)
HAWKHURST: Mary, will you marry me?
MARY: Ah, me lord, I had rather stay in my little Italian villa . . .
VOICE OF PROMPTER: No, no, not that. Say "Cur!"
MARY: Cur!!
HAWKHURST: Ah, Mary, will you follow me off? . . .
MARY: (loudly to herself) The stage?
HAWKHURST: To the land of the Might-have-been?
MARY: No!! Never! cur! (Trips over rubber plant.)
VOICE OF PROMPTER: I am going back to the farm.
MARY: So am I.
(Exit.)
(Three minutes' silence to watch rubber plant and—Curtain.)

John P. Marquand/Harvard Lampoon

Princeton Tiger

The Daily Princetonian

VOL XXXIV. No. 12 PRINCETON, N. J., SATURDAY, MARCH 13, 1909. PRICE FIVE CENTS

MAP SHOWING COURSE OF H. I. M. UN HUNG'S MESSAGE

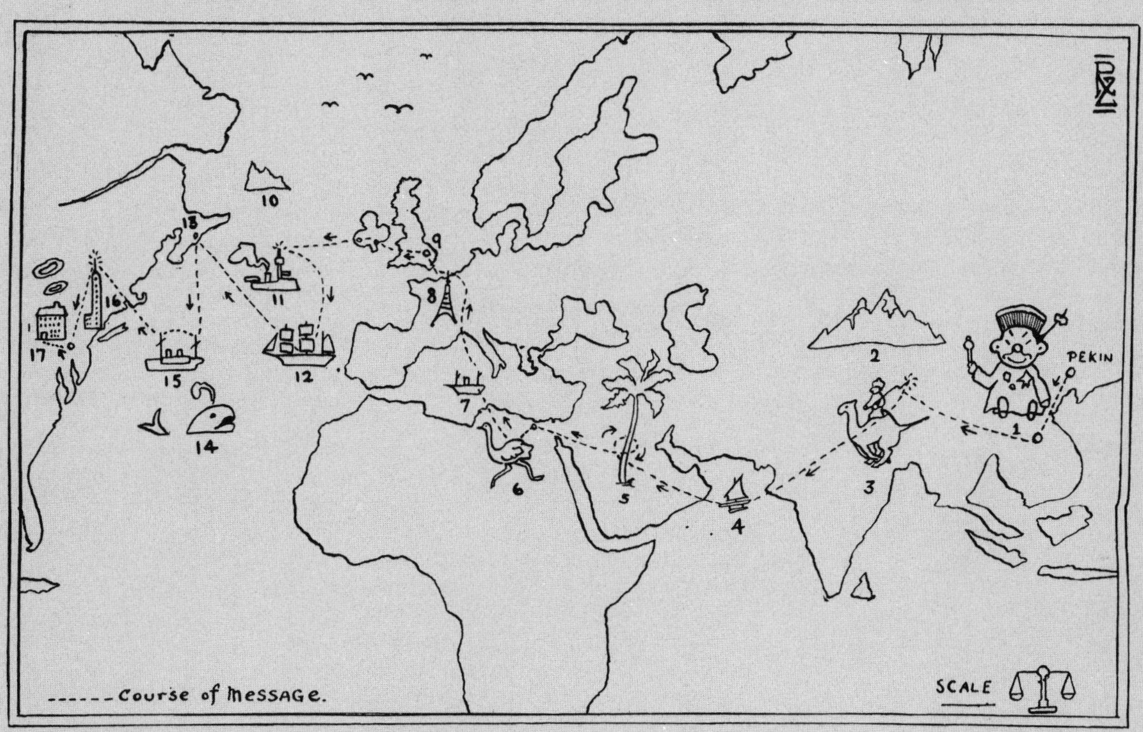

EXPLANATION: 1—His Imperial Highness Himself; 2—Mountains; 3—Camel; 4—Catamaran; 5—Date Tree, showing short circuit; 6—Ostrich; 7—S. S. Sassafras; 8—Eiffel Tower; 9—London; 10—Iceberg; 11—H. M. S. Dreadnot; 12—G. S. Sea Bass; 13—Halifacts; 14—Whale; 15—S S. Colic; 16—Singer Building; 17—Princetonian Office.

WIRELESS TELEGRAPHY.

History and Review of the Season.

Wireless telegraphy was not discovered until some time ago. The reason is that it is invisible. This makes it even more difficult to see than would be otherwise the case.

Its presence was first suspected by the German scientist Squertz in 1888. It was viewed with even more suspicion in '89, and finally with open alarm in '92.

Experiments were made by Marconi and others, but these were not regarded seriously till augmented by the inconceivable accomplishment in our issue today.

At present the problem is to invent an air-ship that cannot be made to roll or pitch by wireless waves.

PRINCETONIAN—Copies of this issue will be on sale forever.

EXTRA! EXTRA? YES, EXTRA

Something Never Before Attempted in the History of Advertising!!!—Via Wireless: Pekin to Princeton—Infant Emperor Sends Winged Words of Chinese Congratulation

**"Greetings to my Chinese friends.
Signed—Un Hung"**

This was the message that Un Hung, the baby Emperor of China, sent to the now famous *Princetonian*. Authorities are unanimously agreed that it is the simplest message ever received at this office, but owing to the fact that there are no Chinamen here at present it is not as all-inclusive as might be hoped.

HOW THE THING WAS DONE.

This startling achievement was only accomplished by the cordial cooperation of the *Princetonian*, the Amalgamated Wireless Societies of Siberia and the Chinese Marine Intelligence, better known as the Wun Lung Gon.

COURSE OF THE MESSAGE.

On the whole the message had a delightful voyage. Once, however, in Hindustan no relay could be found, but a friendly and intelligent monkey supplied the missing link.

RECEIVING THE MESSAGE.

It is not strange that the youthful despot should use his native tongue. The message, however, was unusually pregnant for that sort of thing. It was "Goo, Goo, Goo"; three "goos" in all; each distinctly audible to the three members of the reception committee, for each one heard one "goo" and that makes three (3x1=3).

THE CAPTIVE WIRELESS MESSAGE.

The wireless from the Chinese Emperor is now on view at this office. It is the only one in captivity and no one interested in Science, Zoology or Publicity should fail to catch a glimpse of

the little fellow. The Chinese wireless message will be on exhibition between the hours of ten and four daily and will be fed a cold storage battery egg every afternoon at three. ~~Admission 50 cents.~~

THE WEATHER.

(*From U. S. Government Bureau, Washington, D. C.*)

Muddy today and yesterday. Stout boots advised for adults, gum-shoes for the little ones.

Princeton Tiger

COMING OF AGE
1900-1919

Willard Dickerman Straight and André Smith/Cornell Widow

THE DYSPEPTIC CANNIBAL

A cannibal was seated on a green Pacific isle,
With the temperature at ninety-nine degrees;
His dress was rather scanty, in a truly savage style,
Just a pair of Boston garters round his knees.

But he didn't seem quite happy, for now and then a groan
Escaped—which tore his savage breast in two;
And he chanted in a melancholy, meditative tone
The ditty that I now repeat to you.

"I've eaten hostile tribesmen without a single question,
I've feasted on the yellow, black, and brown;
But I never have encountered such a fit of indigestion
As accompanied the minister from town.

"I have tried the Uambago, boiled and roasted, baked and fried,
I have chewed the woolly Oolah stuffed with yam;
But for all the after-symptoms from the dishes I have tried
I wouldn't give a Bamballooadam.

"But I caught this missionary calmly strolling on the main;
Cooked and served him dressed exactly *comme il faut*
But a feeling deep within me makes it disagreeably plain
That the missionary surely is *de trop*.

"I have eaten hostile tribesmen with the greatest of urbanity;
I've feasted on the yellow, black, and brown.
But to eat a missionary was the acme of insanity.
You cannot keep a good man down."

Yale Record

THERMOS
THE BOTTLE

"Have a Drink on Us"

We can give it to you Hot or Cold Anytime—Anywhere

Pints - - - - $3.00 up
Quarts - - - - $5.00 up

We also make Thermos flasks, decanters, tea and coffee pots, humidors, and jars for solid foods

American Thermos Bottle Co. of New York
Broadway and 27th Street, New York City

College Shoes

Distinctive Styles for Men and Women

Great Variety

Wide Range of Prices

Alexander

Sixth Ave. and Nineteenth St.

For Early Summer
KEISER BAT WINGS

In self stripes, figures or plain colors

Silks specially woven
Slip easily under fold collars

Keiser-Barathea, bright all silk, in over sixty plain colors, three qualities

Grand Prize, St. Louis World's Fair, for Quality, Workmanship and Style

Bear this Label

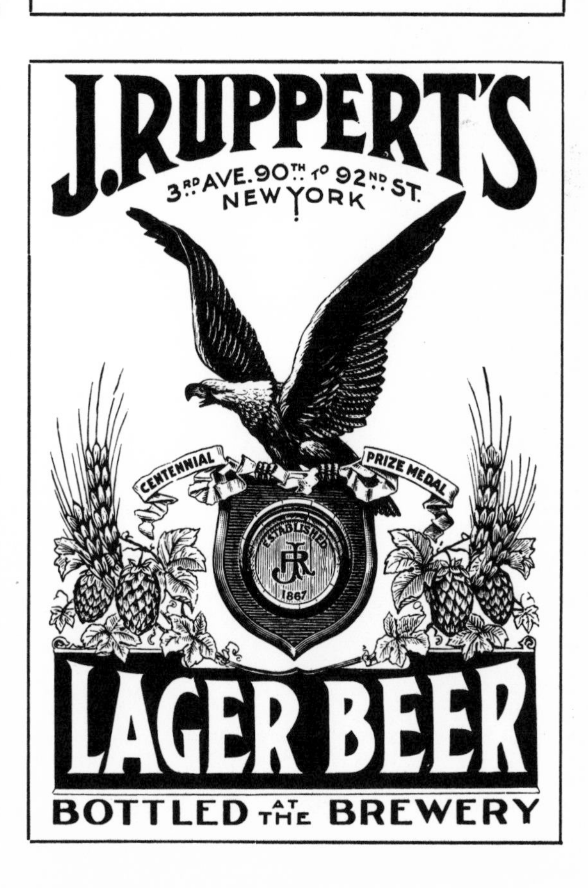

PROSPEROUS & COLLEGIATE

1920-1929

"The funniest thing about a woman is her sense of humor."

Bowdoin Bear-Skin

the June issue

from start to finish is a world-beating magazine

"Finishing Neck and Neck" an incomparable John Held, Jr., cover.

four winners in the June humorous and fiction classic:

Frank R. Adams
Thyra Samter Winslow
Charles Collins
Robert Benchley

An artistic steeplechase — no handicaps by:

Franklin Booth
Arthur William Brown
R. F. Schabelitz
Ralph Barton

The very best from the leading college comics—and the second installment of "GLITTER" by Katharine Brush.

COLLEGE HUMOR *is always eager to secure the work of Collegiate Humorists. Send us your best material during the summer vacation.*

COLLEGE HUMOR *now has vacation openings for college men who will work on a salary and bonus arrangement, for a ten weeks period. Go-getters with previous sales experience wanted.*

Your best efforts when accepted, will popularize your Comic with millions in

College Humor

"The Best Comedy in America"
Chicago

"Now look here, young man, it's much too cold up here for that big electric fan; you just turn it right off."

Johns Hopkins Black & Blue Jay

If all should fall for the same kind of stuff.
Fielding K. Smith/*Utah Humbug*

The White Stove

(A DRAMA OF NORDIC BLONDS AFTER HENRIK IBSEN)

CAST

Oswald Gijkberg.
Mamma Gijkberg, his wife.
Hjalmar Gijkberg, his son.
Selma Gijkberg, his wife.
Svaärdsen, a lunatic.

(Note: Gijkberg is pronounced Svaärdsen. Svaärdsen is pronounced *vice versa.)*

ANY ACT.

(. . . The Gijkbergs are sitting around the white tile stove (no Nordic home should be without one), eating cheese. There are mirrors on the walls and chairs on the floor. The Gijkbergs are on the chairs. The cheese is on a plate. . . .)

Oswald: Life is not worth living.

Mamma Gijkberg: No.

(A shot is heard from around the corner.)

Hjalmar :What's that?

Selma: That's old Rejvking shooting himself.

Hjalmar: What, again?

Oswald: Yes; he's a poor shot.

Mamma Gijkberg: That's too bad. He should practice more.

(The mirrors fall from the walls. They break.)

Hjalmar: There go the mirrors. That means bad luck.

Mamma Gijkberg: God!

Selma: My God!

Oswald: Good God!

(Enter Svaärdsen. He is a lunatic and is stone deaf.)

Hjalmar: Here is Svaärdsen. He is crazy.

Mamma Gijkberg: Yes, poor Svaärdsen! He's crazy.

Oswald: They all are.

Selma: I never knew that.

Svaärdsen: How's that?

Hjalmar: You're a lunatic.

Svaärdsen (not understanding him): So's your old man.

Hjalmar: Is that right, old man?

Oswald: Yes—and no.

Mamma Gijkberg: What can we do about it?

Hjalmar: Let's kill ourselves. (He eats the last piece of cheese. This is symbolic.)

Svaärdsen: Here's a pistol.

Oswald: Thanks. I'm first. (He shoots himself, but the pistol does not go off.) *Svik hjaäd!* (This is a Nordic oath literally meaning "My gosh!" However, usage has taken the objectionable profanity from its meaning until now it is the equivalent of our "dear, dear.") The pistol is no good. *Svik Hjaäd!*

Hjalmar: What can we do?

Mamma Gijkberg: God knows.

Svaärdsen: The stove! The white stove!

(He jumps in the stove. All the others follow his example save Mamma Gijkberg. She is too fat to get in.)

Mamma Gijkberg: I always was unlucky. (She sits for five hours staring at the stove. Then she walks around the room and discovers the empty plate.) Good God! They've finished the cheese. (She starves to death.)

(*Curtain.*)

T. S. B., Jr. and R. C. Osborne/*Yale Record*

First Bumma—*I beg of you, my dear Stanislaus, prithee leave and deposit thyself in a body of running water. Doubtless you comprehend the connotation of creek?*

Second Bumma Bumma Bumma—*Of course, my dear Absalom, of course. One who organizes and administrates an emporium of fluid and edible sustenance.*

(Translated)

1st—"*Aw, go jump in a creek. You know what a creek is, don't you?*

2nd—*Sure. One of those guys what runs a restaurant.*"

Wiley Padan/ *Utah Humbug*

IN ENGLISH A

PROF: Decline 'to go.'

SON OF '26: I won't go.

Stanford Chaparral

MONTHLY DIALECT STORY

"Boy, what kinda seegar is dat you is smoking?"

"Nigger, dat's a quarter seegar."

"Quarter nothing. You never pay no two bits for a seegar."

"I didn't say nothing about dat. De boss he smokes three quarters and I smoke a quarter." *George Washington University Ghost*

OLD SKINFLINT: Here, boy, what's this you were shouting? "Great swindle—60 victims!" I can see nothing about it in the paper.

NEWSBOY: Great swindle—61 victims! *Harvard Lampoon*

DEW YEW?

He had met her at his first formal. They had left the floor for a few moments and stepped into the garden. Summary:

SHE: (softly, sweetly, and suggestively) Some evening.

HE: (in a little more ordinary tone of voice) Yeah; some evening!

SHE: (s_1, s_2, and s_3) (also accidentally dropping her handkerchief) Some moon.

HE: (bending) Yeah; some moon!

As he recovered the lost article he noticed that the grass was damp; and rising with an inspiration (and replacing his monocle), he poured forth:

HE: Some dew!

SHE: (s_2, but emphatically) Maybe, but some don't. Let's go back and dance!

(Exit) (Exit) *Middlebury Blue Baboon*

One: I'm going to kiss O. U. goodbye.
Two: You certainly started out well with your date last night.

Frank Shaw/*Oklahoma Whirlwind*

WHY NOT?

The Almanac, the Almanac—
It tells the strength of ipecac,
Contains the dope on foreign trade,
The sum of eggs our hens have laid,
Statistics on the the deaf and dumb,
The size of Webster's cerebrum;
But why not use a coupla slugs
To tell just when one necks and mugs?

The Almanac, the Almanac—
It lists the records of the track,
The altitude of Cobleskill,
The mountain peaks of Ellenville,
The export rate of mules and swine,
The mileage of the Erie line;
But why not tell the public this:
The proper way to give a kiss?

The Almanac, the Almanac—
It tells about ammoniac,
The time to plant your garden seeds,
The dates of all heroic deeds,
Requirements for copyrights,
The voltage of electric lights;
But why not spill a line to beaux
To tell them how they should propose?

Theodore M. Bernstein/*Columbia Jester*

Rushin' love Utah Humbug

Gulp: "You say that's your sister? I thought she was abroad."
Ulp: "No, she's a damn'nice girl." Brown Jug

HOTSY TOTSY

Is oo mama's umsey-wumsey?
Does oo love her lipsey-ipsies?
Creepy-eepy, closey-osey.
Hugsey-wugsey, tightsy-wightsy.
Honey, bunny, little sweetie.
Darling-arling, sugar-ugar.
Willsie always lovesie-ovesie.
Pettsey-ettsey, holdsey-oldsey.

When I hearie-earie suchie
Talksie-alksie in my earsie.
Then you bet I knowsie-owsie
Thatsie-atsie Spring is heresie.

Joe Catnip/*Columbia Jester*

"Did you notice," asked one lady of another, "that Mrs. 'Awkins 'ad a black eye?"

"Did I not?" was the answer. "And 'er 'usband not out of prison for another week. I don't call it respectable, I don't."

Arizona Kitty-Kat

Judge—Do you plead guilty?

Defendant—Yes.

Judge—Please address the court correctly. Yes what?

Defendant—Yes, you damned old monkey. *Wisconsin Octopus*

Princeton Tiger

In The Shadow of Their Goal Posts

HOW DAVE PORTER KEPT SOMETHING AWFUL FROM HAPPENING BY DOING SOMETHING GREAT

IT WAS ONE of those crisp autumn days, just nicely browned and not even scorched on the edges,—the Day of Days, the day of the game between Oak Hall and Frank Merriwell Military Academy. As Dave Porter took his seat in the Oak Hall "rooters' section", between his mother and his "girl", Miss Lavinia Tootle, the school eleven swept onto the field.

"Hurray for the team, fellows!" cried Dave Porter, leaping from the seat he had just taken. And into the crisp autumn air rang the well-known slogan of Oak Hall:

Football, baseball, basketball, track athletics, soccer, checker-playing, tennis, golf, fishing and various other forms of sport—HOO-RAY!
Who are we, who are we, who are we? GUESS!
No, guess again! No, guess again! Oak Hall? Yes!

Then, "Toot, toot!" went the referee's whistle. The Great Game was on, and the spectators resumed their conversation.

"Due to what causes are you not playing, Davie?" coyly chirped Lavinia to Dave Porter.

"Well, you see, it was this way," explained Dave, flushing. "As you may recall in 'Dave Porter In The Air', I was pursuing Lew Flapp in an aeroplane when he pushed me out and I sprained my wrist. I then fell into the ocean and caught tonsillitis, as related in 'Dave Porter Under Water'. Also, I have been suffering from hay fever, as you may remember from 'Dave Porter Among the Flora and Fauna'. It is only as a result of a number of personal letters to Mr. Ford and Mr. Ivins that I came back to Oak Hall, as related in this volume, which is complete in itself but forms part of the Dave Porter series. So I am not on the team."

"Indeed!" said Miss Lavinia, archly, and Dave flushed again and then refilled.

In the meantime all was not going well with Oak Hall. Their rivals had already run up about one hundred points, and Mr. Stronge, the coach, began to suspect something. "Whatever can be the matter, boys?" he called from the sidelines to the team. But nobody had any suggestions.

Continued on page 72

Oswald Orecruncher Jr., who possesses his own jaguar-skin coat and sports roadster chariot arrives on the Neolithic campus!

William B. Banks/*Johns Hopkins Black & Blue Jay*

Continued from page 70

"Block that kick!" yelled the stands as the play progressed.

"We beg pardon?" queried the team.

"Get that man!" howled the stands.

"Which one?" asked the team, putting their hands to their ears, and even more mystified than ever.

But Dave Porter's eyes were growing narrower and narrower, for he began to see what was wrong. He had caught sight of Lew Flapp in the Oak Hall band, playing his trombone with a sinister smirk. "Listen!" he said to himself.

"One, two, three, four!" went the Oak Hall quarterback, calling signals.

"Oomph, oomph, oomph, oomph!" would go Lew Flapp's trombone, drowning them out as fast as they were called.

Then Dave Porter remembered. He remembered that he had seen Lew Flapp, although a member of Oak Hall, wager a large sum of money that Merriwell would win. (Lew Flapp was a sneak.)

"Stop!" cried Dave Porter, leaping out of his seat to the astonishment of his mother. "There is dirty work afoot!" Rushing pell-mell into the midst of the school musicians, to the amazement of the spectators, he thrust his arm down Lew Flapp's trombone and pulled it inside out, so the only way Lew could play it was to get inside of it. This effectively quashed the first of Lew Flapp's mean tricks.

And yet this was not all. Dave Porter's keen eyes had seen the goal posts move ever so slightly. Stalking across the field, followed by the coach and most of the team, he tilted the visitors goal posts up and disclosed a pair of castors upon their bases. "The field is at least twenty yards too short," he said, sternly, as he picked up the posts and carried them back to their proper place.

"Dave Porter made a forward pass"

"Good for you, Dave!" said Mr. Strong, with a kindly smile, which was echoed by the stands. "If you want to, you can play!" So Dave Porter went down to the locker-rooms and got dressed.

As his mother was pinning him into his jersey, she said softly to him: "Remember, Dave, you are your father's son." This cheered Dave up considerably.

Now back on to the field went Dave, and the well-known cry of Oak Hall rang out to greet him. The ball was in the hands of the rival eleven. Their first play was a forward pass. The ball sailed within a quarter-inch of Dave's head, and landed beside him with a sickening thud. Dave leapt down into the excavation thus created, brought the pigskin to the surface, unlaced it, and emptied out a large cannon-ball. "Flapp again!" he said between his teeth.

And now Dave was carrying the ball for Oak Hall. Down the field came charging as one man the scarlet-clad forms of the rival eleven. All of them were headed straight for our hero. What should he do? Only a moment did he pause. Then, with a sudden flash of inspiration, he turned and ran. As he had already run through three series and nine editions, he soon outdistanced his pursuers. Then, as they fell panting and exhausted behind him, he turned again, and leaping over their prostrate forms, he loped easily back down the field for a touchdown. You ought to of seen the stands!

His steady toe piloted the pigskin unerringly through the air for the goal after touchdown, when, to the astonishment of everyone, it was seen to halt in mid-air between the posts and then leap back at him. Dave bit his teeth, climbed up the goal posts and tore loose a large piece of chicken-wire which Lew Flapp has fastened there. "Some day that sneak will go too far!" he muttered.

As the rest of the Oak Hall team had been able to take a much-needed rest during this spectacular activity of Dave Porter's they were now easily able to score many more points. Higher and higher the score kept mounting. Finally Dave could stand it no longer. He paused in the middle of the field and raised his hand. "Fellows," he said earnestly, "we do not want to make enemies." Then, turning firmly and cubing his already square jaw, he ran determinedly down the field and planted the ball between the goal posts of the rival team. This made the score only 207 to 106, in favor of Oak Hall. A wild burst of kindly applause arose from both stands at this noble act. Then the whistle blew, and the Great Game was over.

The frenzied mob lifted him onto their shoulders and carried him round and round the field until he became dizzy. But Dave spied four eyes far away in the grandstand, and, staggering over the shoulders of the mob, he came to his mother and Lavinia, and took one in each hand. Then he turned modestly to face the admiring multitude.

As the gray November dusk was clouding the field, three stalwart forms were seen to detach themselves from the throng and approach our hero.

"We are the three Rover boys!" said the first.

"We are Merriwell grads and we saw you play!" said the second.

"Hit it up! Hit it up! Hit it up!"

"Will you come to Columbia?" said the third.

"Yes!" said Dave Porter.

"The workout" – that's where you find what men or clothes are made of College men say our clothes always "make good" in style and wear

"The Oak Hall assistant managers, Hart, Schaffner and Marx, cheered madly as Dave Porter made his smashing tackle."

At this moment Dave espied a familiar figure sneaking out of the gates half-a-mile away. "Lew Flapp!" he ejaculated with his mouth wide open. "He must have resigned from the band. I wonder to what dirty work he will next give attention?"

But he was not to find this out until the next book, "Dave Porter In His Search For Santa Claus," and, knowing this, he readily forgave him.

"First fellow in the locker-rooms gets a ginger-snap!" cried Dave. And off he tore, with his mother at his heels. And here let us say goodbye.

Perry Ivins, Corey Ford, and T. C. Mueller/*Columbia Jester*

Dartmouth Jack O'Lantern

"Alice, do you think you'll be warm enough going out in that dress?"
"Warm enough? Why, Mother, if I took off another stitch I'd be naked!"

Princeton Tiger

A SONG WITHOUT WORDS

"........ ....," announced the butler.

As I bowed she rose and greeted me with a smile. "....," she invited, making room for me on the sofa beside her.

"....," I replied.

Her eyes laughed saucily up at me.

I moved closer.

"....," she threatened, putting a pillow between us as a safeguard against such movements.

I turned my back. Silence. I waited.

"....," she coaxed.

No reply.

"....," pouting now.

"....," I whispered as the pillow fell to the floor.

"....," struggling.

The door opened. Wild confusion.

"....," said she, clumsily greeting her mother.

"....," I added, looking up from the fire that I had been punching vigorously.

"....," was her laughing reply.

There was an embarrassing pause. Molly poured out the tea.

Her mother glared. I wished I had not come.

"....," said I, looking at the heavy clouds outside.

"....," her mother answered frigidly.

I took my hat and gloves.

"....," said her mother, ignoring my proffered hand.

Molly blushed.

The door closed behind me.

"....," said I, softly.

Stanford Chaparral

TO A ROSE

What is this thing that shakes its shaggy head at me?

It is a rose.

Thank God for roses

Is my diagnosis.

Captain Jimmy Haverson/Toronto Goblin

"I've had a shower every day this week."

"I suppose you're getting married?"

"Gosh, no; doctor's orders."

Annapolis Log

Three college men went to heaven and knocked at the pearly gates. Out came St. Peter.

"Who are you?" he said to the first.

"I'm Brown of Harvard."

"Enter, Brown of Harvard." He turned to the second. "Who are you?"

"I'm Stover of Yale."

"Enter, Stover of Yale . . . And who are you?"

"I'm Smith of Ohio State."

"Where's your fee card?"

Ohio State Sundial

SUSCEPTIBLE AUDIENCE

PROFESSOR: I am going to speak on liars to-day. How many of you have read the twenty-fifth chapter of the text?

Nearly every student raised his hand.

PROFESSOR: Good! You are the very group to whom I wish to speak. There is no twenty-fifth chapter.

Yale Record

WARM CANINE

I'm a little prairie flower

Growing wilder hour by hour.

No one ever cultivated me.

Ha, ha. I am wild.

Maine Mainiac

When the skunk gets halitosis,
When the possum falls asleep,
When the chipmunks blow their noses,
When the bear lets out a cheep,
When the trout eat up the salmon,
When the robins leave the state,
When the muskrats die of famine—
That's when I'll graduate.

Oregon State Orange Owl

"Eve's Dropping"

Monk Antrim/*Stanford Chaparral*

"It's impossible to tell those twins apart, isn't it?"
"It's hard for them too. They even borrow money from each other without knowing it."

Brown Jug

When the persistent joke teller insists on relating his dumbest joke for the fiftieth time in spite of all sorts of protestations, assume your most charming manner and arising with a graceful flourish degenerate into this:

"Have you ever heard the joke about the potato clock?"

A volley of "No" and "Tell it" bursts forth.

"Well, every morning, I get a potato clock."

Rice Owl

BLUE BELLS

Hear the news,
Mournful news,
We must lose our golden booze.

No longer may we hear the note
From the shaker's nickeled throat,
Or the tinkle, tinkle, tinkle of the glasses on the tray.
The tintinabulation of the glasses on the tray,
See their crystalline array.

And my soul is filled with blues
Musing sadly o'er the news
Of the losing of the booze.
Booze, booze, booze, booze, booze,
Musing o'er the losing
Of the booze.

Johns Hopkins Black & Blue Jay

PÈRE GUILLAUME–CHEMIST

"You are lit, Father William," the young man said,
"Though perhaps in the morn you'll regret it,
But the thing I should really be pleased to find out
Is—where did you manage to get it?"

"You would like to find out," the old codger replied,
"Just how I am able to do it?
The process itself is as simple as sin—
I set up a still, and I brew it!

"In the days of my youth," Father William went on,
"I studied at Chemistry's forces—
But the profs and myself could never agree,
And I flunked every one of my courses.

"Yet the facts which I learned, and retained in my dome,
Before I was asked to leave college,
Enable me now to evade the dry laws,
Because of superior knowledge.

"So every young man," the old sinner raved on,
"Should take as much Chem as he's able—
Then with tea-kettle, stove, and some old garden hose,
He can drink himself under the table."

C. F. MacMullen/California Pelican

The shades of night had glided down
Long since on the spires of Hadley town.

On the chapel steps, so the story ran,
Stood a Holyoke maid and a Dartmouth man.

In a voice that was husky and low, said he,
"Won't you walk around the lake with me?"

Quoth the Holyoke maid in a mournful tone,
"But I can't go without a chaperone."

The Dartmouth scholar raised his head,
"I'm sure you won't need one with me," he said.

"Then," quoth the maid, so sweet and low,
"Then," quoth she, "I don't want to go."

Mount Holyoke Ravin'

The Blue Pencil

HOW A SPEC NITE-ED WOULD CONDENSE THE GETTYSBURG ADDRESS FOR A CROWDED FRIDAY EDITION

Lincoln's Gettysburg Pa., Address.

~~Fourscore and seven~~ 87 years ago our fathers brought forth ~~on this continent,~~ a new nation, conceived in liberty and ~~dedicated to the proposition~~ stating that all men are created equal.

Now we are ~~engaged in a great civil~~ at war, testing whether that nation ~~or any nation so conceived or so dedicated,~~ can long endure. We are met on a ~~great~~ battlefield of the war. We ~~have~~ come to dedicate a ~~portion~~ part of that field, as a ~~final~~ resting place ~~of those who here gave their lives that that nation might live.~~ of the men who died here. ~~It is altogether fitting and proper that we should do this.~~ (Edit Bull)

But ~~in a larger sense~~/we cannot dedicate, ~~we cannot~~ consecrate, ~~we cannot~~ hallow this ground. The ~~brave~~ men, ~~living and dead~~, who struggled here ~~have~~ dedicated it ~~far~~ above our ~~poor~~ power to add or detract. The world will ~~little~~ not note, ~~nor long remember~~ what we say here, but it can never forget ~~what they did here~~ their work. ~~It is for us~~ The living, ~~rather, to~~ should be dedicated ~~here~~ to the ~~unfinished~~ work which they who fought here have ~~thus far so nobly~~ advanced. ~~It is rather for us to~~ We should be ~~here~~ dedicated to the ~~great~~ task remaining ~~before us~~ - that from these ~~honored~~ dead we ~~take increased devotion for~~ become more devoted to that cause for which they ~~gave their last full measure of devotion. That~~ died. We here ~~highly~~ resolve that these dead ~~shall not have died in vain~~ honor ~~that~~ this nation, ~~under God, shall have~~/a new birth of freedom, and ~~that~~ the government ~~of the people, by the people, and for the people,~~ shall not perish. ~~from the earth.~~

Columbia Jester

"O, clerk, there's something the matter with the keyhole in the door to my room."
"That so? I'll look into that tonight."
Theodor S. Geisel (Dr. Seuss)/*Dartmouth Jack O'Lantern*

BLANK VERSE

John asked Clara
To take
A walk with him
And pick flowers.
But Clara's brother
Came along
And so
They picked flowers.

North Carolina Boll Weevil

THE DICKENS YOU DON'T!

"Did you see Oliver Twist, Aunty?"

"Hush, child, you know I never attend those modern dances."

Pittsburgh Panther

HAWKSHAW HIMSELF

The famous detective arrived at the scene of the crime.

"Heavens," he cried, "this is more serious than I thought. The window has been broken on both sides."

Minnesota Ski-U-Mah

GREEK

A stranger was being shown through the house of the Boston chapter.

"And is this the lodge room?" he asked.

"Well," was the reply, "it is rather lodge, but the living room is much lodger."

Hamilton Royal Gaboon

JOKE ABOUT A CROW

HE: Why is a crow?

SHE: Caws.

Ohio State Sundial

THE GEMOT BLUES

"Father, may I go to the Prom?"

"No, my darling Abie;

Mother and I go out tonight—

You'll have to mind the baby."

Columbia Jester

"Gladys must be a wild girl."

"How's that?"

"I heard her father say he could hardly keep her in clothes."

Pennsylvania Punch Bowl

"Hi, keed, can you spell 'weather'?"

" 'W-E-O-A-T-H-E-R,' How zat?"

"Terrible. That's the worst spell of weather we've had in a long while."

Brown Jug

"Why should Jack Dempsey be World's Champion?"
"Well, who's got a better right?"

Dartmouth Jack O'Lantern

A NEW ELEMENT—"WOMAN"

Symbol—Wo.

A member of the Human family.

Occurrence: Can be found wherever man exists. Seldom occurs in the free or native state. Quality depends on the state in which it is found. With the exception of Massachusetts state, the combined state is preferred.

Physical Properties: All colors and sizes. Always appears in a disguised condition. Surface of fact seldom unprotected by coating of paint or film of powder (composition immaterial). Boils at nothing, and may freeze at any moment. However, it melts when properly treated. Very bitter if not used correctly.

Chemical Properties: Extremely active. Possesses a great affinity for gold, silver, platinum, and precious stones of all kinds. Violent reaction when left alone by men. Ability to absorb all sorts of expensive food at any time. Undissolved by liquids but activity is greatly increased when saturated with spirit solutions. Sometimes yields to pressure. Turns green when placed next to a better appearing sample. Ages very rapidly. Fresh variety has great magnetic attraction.

Note: Highly explosive and likely to be dangerous in inexperienced hands.

MIT Voo Doo

The demure young bride, a trifle pale, her lips set in a tremulous smile, slowly stepped down the long church aisle, clinging to the arm of her father.

As she reached the low platform before the altar, her slippered foot brushed a potted flower, upsetting it. She looked at the spilled dirt gravely, and then raised her child-like eyes to the sedate face of the old minister.

"That's a hell of a place to put a lily," she said.

Ohio State Sundial

FABLE: Once there was a campus politician who was clean, upright and noble.

Columbia Jester

"Oh, Mabel—I love you the worst way!"

"Don't become discouraged, Jimmie; you're improving!"

Pittsburgh Panther

HE: Have you tried the new elevator dance?

SHE: No, what are the steps like?

HE: There aren't any.

Maine Mainiac

"My dog took first prize at the cat show."

"How was that?"

"He took the cat."

Harvard Lampoon

There was a young girl named O'Neill,
Went up in the great ferris wheel,
When half way round
She looked at the ground,
And it cost her an eighty-cent meal.

Bowdoin Bear-Skin

If all the Democrats in Vermont were placed end to end . . . how damn foolish they both would look. *Middlebury Blue Baboon*

A certain romantic young Mr.
Had a girl and he often Kr.
But he asked her to wed
And she solemnly said:
"I can never be more than a Sr."

Cornell Widow

Ikey and Pat were wounded in an engagement in the Argonne. A priest making his rounds found them. After giving the Irishman the last rites he went over to Ikey and said, "Do you believe in the Father, Son and Holy Ghost?"

Ikey groaned and rolled over.

"Oi, Oi! Here I am dying and you ask me riddles."

Georgia Tech Yellow Jacket

"Hey Jack, let's have another look at that map."
Curtis A. Peters (Peter Arno)/*Yale Record*

STUDE (to pretty little co-ed): So you are from Long Island?
CO-ED: Yes, indeed—a Great Necker.
Hamilton Royal Gaboon

A modern bachelor is a man who has no children to speak of.
Dartmouth Jack O'Lantern

Minneapolis and St. Paul are still at it. Something must be done about those two towns. This one comes from St. Paul.

A Minneapolis man drifted into the sister city, looked superciliously at a fruiter's display, picked up a big watermelon and asked with a sneer:

"Is this the largest apple you have in St. Paul?"

"Hey!" bellowed the proprietor, "put that grape down!"

Oregon State Orange Owl

Flapper—"Is the fish fresh?" Waiter—"I don't know. It hasn't said anything yet"

Allan Rudyard Crawford/*Toronto Goblin*

HE: How many Commandments are there?
SHE: Ten.
HE: Suppose you were to break one of them?
SHE (hopefully): There'd be nine.

Brigham Young Y's Guy

I kissed her in the moonlight,
My head was in a whirl;
My mouth and eyes were full of hair—
My arms were full of girl.

Princeton Tiger

I kissed her in the garden,
And my brain was rather gladdish;
My coat lapel was powder white—
My lips and cheek were reddish.

California Pelican

I kissed her in the parlor,
I felt myself grow faint;
I breathed a lot of cheap perfume—
I tasted too much paint.

Colgate Banter

I kissed her in the vestibule,
I yearned for more and more;
I went to kiss her once again—
But kissed the closing door.

Notre Dame Juggler

I kissed her in the lamplight,
And wondered if she knew my past;
She said, "I've heard a lot about you"—
Then I knew it couldn't last.

Grinnell Malteaser

I kissed her in the darkness,
And then I didn't care;
I made another wicked stab—
But all I kissed was air.

NYU Medley

I kissed her in the ante-room;
The last kiss, I declare,
For tho we didn't know it then,
Her demon aunt was there.

Brown Jug

Curtis A. Peters (Peter Arno)/*Yale Record*

GAMES FOR THE WEE ONES

Since little girls cannot be trained too early for the trials of life. *Blue Baboon* has evolved the following charming bit of recreation, which has a purpose:

Each player is given a shovel or a pick with sharpened edges. The little boy from across the street is placed in the center of the circle formed by the players. His hands and feet are tied and a gold piece is placed in his pocket. The players then try to take the coin from him using only their picks or shovels. Time is called at the end of five minutes, and if the little boy is still alive, he gets the prize. He deserves it.

To develop a love for the great out-of-doors, *Blue Baboon* suggests this little game:

The mother who is giving the party carefully fills her oil stove with gasoline, and, closing all the windows, shuts up the children in the kitchen, first giving each one a handful of matches. After telling the little tots that each is to see how quickly she can light the stove, the mother goes calling on some friends in another part of the town. When she returns, she will find the children very much spread out all over the out-of-doors.

Kindly Visitor: *"I'd like to see convict 515, please, if he's in."*
Theodor S. Geisel (Dr. Seuss)/*Dartmouth Jack O'Lantern*

Mothers who wish their daughters to make their own clothes when they grow older will find this little bit of fun an excellent seed for later fruition:

If the party is at the home of Mrs. X, for example, all the mothers whose children are present will bring to the house their best gowns, frocks, and dresses. These will be placed in a pile on the floor, and each child will be given a large pair of scissors. While the mothers solve cross-word puzzles in the next room, the children will be remodeling the dresses, and at the end of the afternoon, the little girl who has the most number of unique creations will be declared the winner. The husbands will be the losers.

When a man's feet are all out of his shoes, it's poverty, but when a woman's are, it's style.
Gray/*Oklahoma Whirlwind*

QUESTION BOX

For this issue only we are conducting this department for the benefit of those little tots who still play with dolls, but who, perhaps, are troubled by those questions which arise in the lives of even the youngest.

Dere Editor:

I am five years old, but I ain't never walked home yet. I just finished "Jorgen" and it's all Blah! This permanent lipstick stuff is the bunk too. I want to know what's the latest bob.

Yrs till prohibition means something,
Yvette Maloney.

Dear Yvette:

In the toy department at Wanamakers you will find the duckiest little mechanical dogs imaginable. And I'm glad to hear that you say your prayers in the morning as well as at night.

Dear Editor:

I want a man. He must be tall, good-looking, and must have scads of money. I am really only forty-five, altho my friends tell me I don't look more than thirty. Where can I find him?

Anxiously,
Susan G.

What Is She Saying?

THERE IS NOT A $500 Prize

For The Best Answer

But go right ahead and have a good time guessing - it's so simple - do you get it? - of course - that's right

She wants **The Brown Jug**

Take The Hint

Please send **The Brown Jug** for the year 1922-23.

To ____________________

At ____________________

Enclosed find $1.75

S. J. Perelman/*Brown Jug*

Dear Susan G.:

Your present inhibitions are due, no doubt, to excessive palpitations of the cordex. See Freud, "On Dreams," p. 361.

Dear Editor:

This morning when Mother wouldn't give me Castoria I shot her, and then when Father got sore I pushed him out of the window. We live on the fifteenth floor. I am eight years old. What's a five-letter word for an undiscovered island in the South Seas?

Cordially yours,
Mabel DeMedeci.

Dear Mabel:

You sure have gave us the one big laugh of the week. What a wow that was about your old man! Have you heard the one about the traveling salesman in Hackensack, N.J.? Send us a stamped, self-addressed envelope.

Miss H. M./*Middlebury Blue Baboon*

"What do you charge for rooms?"
"Six dollars up."
"But, Madam, I am a student."
"Then it's six dollars down."

Carnegie Tech Puppet

There once, in the city of Limerick,
In the Irish county of Limerick,
Was born a Limerick
Who slung a mean limerick,
And invented the verse-form, the limerick.

Harvard Lampoon

"Bill, you don't know how I miss that cuspidor."
"You always did miss it. That's why I threw it away."

S. J. Perelman/*Brown Jug*

Weary Alumnus (mechanically): "Oh, all right, I'll subscribe."

Bruce Russell/*California Pelican*

THE CAMPUS REACTS TO JACK AND JILL

1. As Explained by the Campus Bozo

"My Gawd! What a pair of dizzy boids! The poor bloke and his bimbo went up the ____ ____ hill to get a ____ ____ drink of water and came bellywhoppin' down the other side. What dumbbells! My Gawd!"

2. As Investigated by Dean Hawkes

"Ah! Good-morning, Mr. Jack . . . what is this I hear . . . about a little affair . . . with a Miss Jill . . . up the side of a hill . . . pail of water . . . fell down . . . when can your father see me? . . . good-day. . . ."

3. As Summarized by Professor Weaver

"Now, these two creatchahs, I take it, traveled up theah side of theah hill in order to imbibe of some puah watah. Jack, it seems to me, lost his sense of what might be termed equilibrium and, in accordance with theah laws of Natchah, pro-gressed downward, being immidgitly followed by Jill."

4. As reported in *Spectator*

JACK AND FEMALE COMPANION
MEET WITH SERIOUS MISHAP

Jack '27 and Miss Jill, Barnard '28, were the victims of a disastrous mountain climbing expedition on Wednesday afternoon. They are students of Geology and were on a field expedition to the Palisades. They tripped over a piece of Manhattan schist, rolled down the East bank of the Hudson and landed in the water.

Both Jack and Miss Jill are in St. Luke's Hospital, suffering from broken crowns.

5. As It Appeared in *Morningside*

Jack! Shade of immortal Apollo!
Jill! Spittin' image of Diana!
Up the hill!
Up! Up! Up! Up! Up! Up! Up! Up! Up! Up!
Arrived!
Down the hill!
Down! Down! Down! Down! Down! Down! Down! Down!
Blooie!

6. As It Appeared in Triolet Form in *Jester*

Young Jack and Jill went up the hill
To fetch a pail of water.
Of course it's true! Don't be a sill;
Young Jack and Jill went up the hill—
They tried to love but took a spill:
You should have seen the slaughter!
Young Jack and Jill went up the hill
To fetch a pail of water.

Alan M. Max/*Columbia Jester*

CONDUCTOR: Shamokin! Shamokin!

IRISH PASSENGER: No, playin' cards.

Penn State Froth

He—Don't you detest the person who interrupts your conversa—

She—And takes the words right out of your mouth?

Denver Parrakeet

"I can't serve as a juror, judge: just one look at that prisoner made me know he is guilty."

"Silence in the Court! That's the prosecuting attorney."

Denison Flamingo

If we're married on Christmas Eve, will we be "Yule-tied?"

Milton Caniff/*Ohio State Sundial*

Since the "Talkies" came . . . Hollywood is *stronger* than ever for OLD GOLDS

"A year or so ago, Hollywood didn't think much about its vocal chords or its voices. We were in the *silent* drama then. But the coming of the 'Talkies' has changed things. Lovely stars, leading men, 'heavies' and ingenues are guarding their throats with zealous care . . . and smoking OLD GOLDS. It didn't need the 'Talkies' to win me to OLD GOLDS. I've been smoking them since they came to Hollywood, two years ago. But it's great to know they are kind to the voice, when the voice has assumed a new importance!"

(SIGNED)

WALLACE BEERY *transport pilot No. 3298,* now appearing in "Tong War" tells how the movie stars are guarding their throats with OLD GOLDS.

Why not a cough in a carload?

OLD GOLD cigarettes are blended from HEART-LEAF tobacco, the finest Nature grows . . . Selected for silkiness and ripeness from the heart of the tobacco plant . . . Aged and mellowed extra long in a temperature of mid-July sunshine to insure that honey-like smoothness.

On your Radio, OLD GOLD-PAUL WHITEMAN HOUR . . . Paul Whiteman, King of Jazz, with his complete orchestra, broadcasts the OLD GOLD hour every Tuesday, from 9 to 10 P. M., Eastern Standard Time, over the entire network of the Columbia Broadcasting System.

eat a chocolate, light an Old Gold, *and enjoy both!*

FLY OVER HOMEWOOD

$5.00

CALL PIKESVILLE 577
FOR AN APPOINTMENT

Every student should get a bird's-eye view of Johns Hopkins University and the surrounding country, including Lake Roland and Pimlico Race Track.

Two of these ads, if presented jointly before January 1st, will entitle the bearers to a sight-seeing ride over Homewood at the reduced rate of $4.00 each. *No single rides can be given at this price.*

Park Heights Flying School, Inc.

PARK HEIGHTS AVENUE AND OLD COURT ROAD
PIKESVILLE, MARYLAND

OPEN ALL
YEAR ROUND

LIEUT. OTTO MELAMET
CHIEF INSTRUCTOR

Brown Jug

FIFTH AVENUE **B. ALTMAN & CO.** NEW YORK CITY

CLOTHES CONFIDENCE

Properly clad, one loses consciousness of clothes. It is the man not quite sure of his appearance who lacks confidence on the links. Altman Sports Clothing will eliminate an appreciable mental hazard . . .

MEN'S FURNISHINGS—FIRST FLOOR MEN'S CLOTHING—SIXTH FLOOR

SOPHISTICATED? GAWD!

1930-1939

HOW TO GET RID OF A ROOMMATE

ONE OF the major problems around school is that of getting rid of a crummy roommate. Unless the roommate is female, the following four methods should be considered for dispensing of said C.R.

1. *The Practical Approach.*

In the first place, you should greet your crummy roommate affably enough, but warn him that your hours are slightly inconvenient. This won't bother the C.R.; he will just say, "Oh sure, that's all right." But don't let that bother you either.

The first night he sleeps with you, come staggering in at two in the morning. Trip over a chair, and curse audibly, then turn on the light and make a great show of examining your foot and swearing out loud. Get undressed, throwing your shoes around the room; it is a good idea to hit him in the face with one, if you can manage it. Follow this up by waking him and giving him a long, tedious account of your night's activities, telling him the funny things you did when drunk, etc. Punctuate the recital with horse laughs and hearty slaps on the back and stomach, also face, chest, neck, nose, etc.

Set your alarm clock (and make it a lusty one) for five in the morning. When it wakes you up, don't turn it off; let it ring itself out. Get dressed, taking a new suit out of the closet and throwing his stuff around as much as possible, your excuse being the darkness of the room. Splash around plentifully while getting washed, drying your face on his scarf. Strop your razor heartily, and chant, *fortissimo*, "Stormy Weather" while shaving to the accompaniment. If he has awakened by this time, resume your anecdotes of the previous night, making sure to repeat yourself as much as possible. Borrow five dollars from him and warn him that you won't be around 'til late tonight. Walk out leaving the water running (across the floor) and slam the door. Pop your head in again and say, "Well, keep your nose clean!"

2. *The Macabre Approach.*

Correct diagnosis of the C.R.'s disposition is important. If you judge him to be a rather nervous, high-strung sort, this approach should work. At any rate, either you or he will move out.

When your roommate comes in the first night, you will see to it that the light has been removed from its socket; place something fuzzy or hairy over the switch, possibly an otter. As the C.R. walks toward the center of the room in darkness, his face will be brushed by a piece of liver which is hanging from the ceiling. Liver in such a situation has a remarkable effect.

See to it that something yielding is in his bed when he sits on it; pillows will do, although something that squirts is preferable. When he lies down another piece of liver should flop in his face. You should pause for a while; then as a final touch burn some cellophane in the back of the closet and squeak weakly.

The next morning, bring the subject of conversation around to wharf rats. This done, mention casually the large, ugly, man-eating wharf rat which was harpooned by a B&G fusileer two years ago. The odor, you will remark, is really not so bad, if the stomach is in good shape. Caution him to eat lightly and to refrain from walking about the room in his bare feet, else he might lose a toe. The only way to escape it, you say, is to move from the dorm. If this doesn't dislodge him the first

West Point Pointer

time, keep it up with added variations for a couple of nights. If you've judged your victim correctly, you can't lose.

3. *The Menacing Approach.*

If this fails, your tactics had best assume a more aggressive tone. For instance, as soon as possible after you have been introduced to him, tell him you are intercollegiate boxing champion, and say, "Old boy, I'm going to make a man of you." Order him to put up his dukes, and slap him around the room for ten or fifteen minutes. Tell him that's enough for the first day, and you'll increase the time gradually to an hour within a week or so. This requires a fair physique.

A clever variation is to tell him your hobby is knife-throwing; ask him to volunteer to stand up as the dummy, and you'll ring him around with knives. If he refuses, keep slinging knives around the room anyway. Knife the cigarette out of his mouth, the hat off his head; pin his theme to the desk with a knife while he's writing it. Send a knife quivering into the wall in front of him as he walks out of the room. If you can nick him now and then, and draw a little blood, it helps somewhat.

This requires some practice, and there is of course the inconvenience of killing him by mistake. At any rate, say it was by mistake.

4. *The Fantastic Approach.*

While melodramatic, this approach has a great appeal for a C.R. of the more imaginative type. If nothing else, he will probably turn to religion, and you know how *they* are!

When you first meet your roommate, act with an air of restraint and mystery. Invite him out to lunch and as you munch herbs and leaves, chat about the esoteric similarity of Shintoism and the Yoga cults. Then see to it that he doesn't return to the room for at least an hour.

And in that hour? Why, you are putting on a turban, a layer of Stein's "Sallow Hindu Prophet" greasepaint, donning a sheet and inverting a goldfish bowl, being sure to first remove the goldfish, for the C.R. might be too deeply affected to find live goldfish in his future.

When your roommate returns to the room and penetrates a thick haze of incense, he will see you sitting cross-legged, looking up at the ceiling and intoning aimlessly. Something from "Winterset" will do.

After about three minutes, stop. Stare at him in hypnotic fashion, and inform him that you are about to initiate him into the mysteries of Is and Yurko, twin gods of the stormwind. Tell him that the incense is hasheesh fumes. You then chant gibberish for five minutes; drawing a dagger, you then hand it to him, saying that he is the sacrificial lamb and must perform hara-kiri, but that the god will make him whole again after he has stabbed himself. He is likely to edge toward the door nervously, muttering something about going out for a pack of cigarettes. You leap in front of the door and inform him that if he doesn't perform the act himself, you will have to do it for him yourself within the next two weeks. Bow low, repeat the words "Ishu hasheesh Yurko" three times, and stalk out.

Though this method is rarely employed, it never fails to draw a little note pinned to the door that evening: "Sorry—had to move. Rent too high."

Herman Wouk/Columbia Jester

"Do you mean to say this sofa is stuffed with Pekinese dogs?"

Ad F. Reinhardt/Columbia Jester

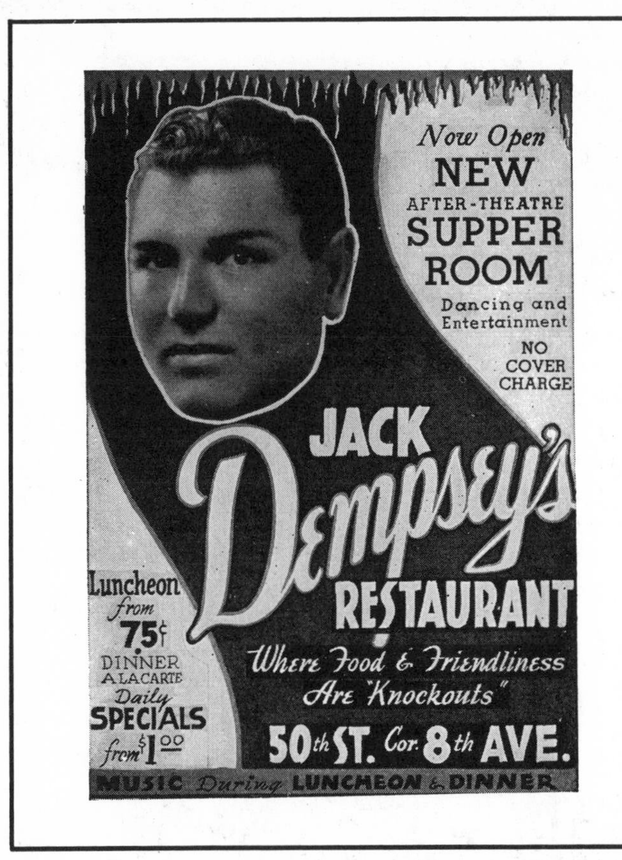

"How do you find yourself these cold mornings?"
"Oh, I throw back my covers, and there I am."

Lehigh Burr

Little Jane walked into the corner drug store and said her mama wanted some tissue paper. The clerk wrapped up three rolls and handed them to her.

"Charge them, please," she lisped.

"Certainly," replied the clerk, "but who are they for?"

"All of uth," sighed the little girl as she walked out.

Sewanee Mountain Goat

CHEMISTRY PROF: What is the outstanding contribution that chemistry has given the world?

FROSH: Blondes.

Washington State Cougar's Paw

"Yessum, Pa told him to join a fraternity. He said he couldn't afford to keep him in clothes." Robert C. Ruark, Jr./North Carolina Buccaneer

FOLLOWING is a condensation of Shakespeare's *Titus Andronicus*. Even the most ardent Shakespeare experts are willing to blame this one on Francis Bacon.

ACT I

Scene: The city of Rome.

Titus. I want blood. Who amongst our Gothic prisoners is the noblest? I have lost twenty-one of my twenty-five sons in the Gothic wars, and the souls of the dead call for revenge.

Tamora, Queen of the Goths. An .840 average, and he still wants revenge.

Alarbus, son of Tamora, is brought forward.

Lucius, Quintus, Martius, and Mutius (Titus' remaining sons). Here is the noblest, sire.

Titus. Good. Slice him up and feed him to the fire.

Exit Lucius, Quintus, Martius, and Mutius with Alarbus.

Tamora. You rat.

Re-enter Lucius, Quintus, Martius, and Mutius.

Titus. How's Alarbus?

Lucius. Roasted.

Titus. Well done.

Lucius. Yes. Well done.

Enter Lavinia, Titus' only daughter.

Lavinia. My father, I presume.

Titus. Pleased to meet you.

Enter Marcus, Andronicus, the Tribune, brother of Titus.

Marcus. H'yar. Get your late *Tribune.*

Titus. What, my brother dead?

Marcus. Well, well. Titty!

Enter Saturninus and Bassianus, sons of the late emperor. They are razzing each other.

Sat. Bassianus!

Bass. Yeah?

Sat. Brrrack! (*All of you B'klyn readers recognize this as the Bronx cheer.*)

Bass. Look here, Saturninus.

Sat. Yeah?

Bass. I made you look! I made you look!

Marcus. Who shall become emperor, O Titus? Saturninus is in favor of Saturninus, and Bassianus chooses Bassianus. Have you any preference?

Titus. No. I'll pick Saturninus.

Sat. Thanks. And I'll pick Tamora.

(*Grabs queen of the Goths.*)

Bass. And I'll pick Lavinia.

Titus. Why you filthy rat!

Mutius. Don't get excited, Pop.

Titus. What, you too?

(*Stabs Mutius to death.*)

All. Tsk, tsk. Naughty, naughty Titus.

Exeunt omnes.

ACT II

A hunt in the woods near Rome. Enter Tamora and her lover, Aaron, the Moor.

Aaron. Highness, don't you love to curl up with a good book?

Tamora. No. I'd rather curl up with a nice page. (*Remark through courtesy of Ervin Druckerman.*)

Aaron. Tamora!

Tamora. No. Today!

Aaron. Highness, after the death of Alarbus. Don't you hate Titus' guts?

Tamora. His guts? I hate his whole Andronicus.

Enter Lavinia and Bassianus.

Bass. Our empress alone with her Moorish servant!

Lavinia. I predict a dark issue of this.

Tamora. Go on and snitch!

Bass. I will.

Enter Demetrius and Chiron, Tamora's surviving sons.

Dem. Hello folks.

Stabs Bassianus.

Chiron. Hello folks.

Stabs Bassianus.

Tamora. Why, you dirty louses.

Dem. Look! A woman.

They rape her, and pull her tongue out, and chop off her hands so she can't snitch.

ACT III

Rome.

Enter Titus, his son Lucius, his brother Marcus, and Friend.

Titus. There's something rotten in Rome. The Senate blames Martius and Quintus for the murder of Bassianus!

Friend. It isn't so bad. Beheading is a very pleasant death.

Enter the Moor, Aaron.

Aaron. If one of you guys will chop off an arm and send it back with me the emperor says he'll send back your sons.

Titus. Good. Why didn't he tell me before?

Lucius. Let me!

Marcus. No. Let me!

Titus. O.K., you two boys choose it out, and go get an axe.

Exeunt Marcus and Lucius.

Titus. O.K., Aaron. While they're gone, bite off my arm.

Aaron does so.

Re-enter Lucius and Marcus.

Marcus. Why, you awful cheat.

Lucius. We'll never play with you again.

Aaron. Pity the poor guy. His petting days are over.
Exit Aaron.
Enter Lavinia. She looks dopey.
Lucius. Whatsa matter, sis?
Marcus. Look at her arms!
Titus. That's what she gets for biting her nails.
Re-enter Aaron.
Aaron. The emperor was only fooling. Here's your arm back, Titus. May I drop these heads in the corner there?
Exit Aaron.
Titus. A great darkness falls over me. I'll never see a son anymore.
Marcus. Come. Let us advise the world of our grief.
Exeunt Titus and Marcus carrying heads and Lavina with Titus' arm between her teeth.
Lucius. I'll take my grounds to the Goths and brew a rebellion against the emperor.

ACT IV Scene 1
In the palace.

Tamora. What news of Rome?
Saturninus. They say that young Lucius Andronicus prepares to storm the gates of Rome with a huge Gothic horde.
Tamora. I knew I should have had that rat bumped.
Sat. Well, what can we do now?
Tamora. I'll fix me up some rat-poison.

ACT IV Scene 2
The home of Titus Andronicus.

Titus. Woe! Grief! Misery! Despair! Sorrow! Anguish! Distress! Pain! Wormwood! Boy, I must be feeling lousy.
Enter Tamora.
Tamora (coy). 'Lo, Titty.
Titus. You! Out, slimy witch!
Tamora. Who, me?
Titus. Yes, you. Are you not wily Tamora?
Tamora. Who, that stinkpot? No. I only smell like her. My name is Revenge. I hate Tamora. I shall help you to even the score for what she has done to you. I am your friend.
Enter Chiron and Demetrius.
Titus. Vile creatures! Away! Away!
Chiron. Away down south in Sicily.
Titus. Aren't you Chiron and Demetrius? Don't you go around committing rape and murder?
Dem. No. But it's a good idea.
Tamora. These are my assistants here, like myself, to do your bidding.
Chiron. Yes. What can we do for you?
Titus. If you see anybody who looks like you, you can stab him for me.
Tamora (*aside*). The fool is a lunatic. I'll have him call the leaders of the Goths to his house, and then, by cunning, make them enemies of Lucius and him.
Titus. Well, what would you of me?
Tamora. Call Lucius and the Goths to your home, that we may plot to overthrow the wicked empress.
Chiron. Yes, we'll put her on her back.
Dem. That's our specialty.
Titus. So I gathered. Good. I'll send my brother Marcus.
Tamora. Until then, I and my assistants must leave you.
Titus. Not so. Leave me with Rape and Murder. I'll have need of them.
Tamora. O.K., Andy. Adios.
Tamora leaves Chiron and Demetrius with Titus.
Titus. They think I've lost my head. Well, I haven't, but they will. (*Calls.*) Publius, Caius, Valentine! Lavinia!
Enter Publius and others. Lavinia with knife between her teeth.
Titus. Tie these guys up.
Chiron. What a cheap trick!
Titus cuts his head off.
Dem. Isn't it!
Titus cuts his off too.
Titus. You ain't seen nothing yet.

ACT V
The following day at the house of Titus.

Enter Emperor Saturninus, Tamora, and friends; Lucius, Marcus, and Goths; Titus, dressed as a cook, and Lavinia veiled. All take seats at table.
Titus. Romans and friends. In honor of this occasion, I have baked a cake. (*Places it before Tamora, who eats hungrily.*)
Titus. And now guess what I'm going to do.
All. What?
Titus stabs Lavinia.
Titus. Surprised?
Tamora. Sort of. This is a gooa pie here.
Titus. It ought to be. It's full of chopped Chiron and Demetrius.
Stabs Tamora.
Saturninus. Oh, a game, huh?
Stabs Titus.
Lucius. Let me play too.
Continued on page 99

SOPHISTICATED? GAWD! 1930-1939

BOY MAKES GIRL

Hemingway

"I love you, dammit. I love you, Alice."

"Oh, you're drunk, dammit. I'm going to Spain, dammit."

"Don't go, dammit. I love you, dammit."

W. C. Fields

Come, my little passion flower, and let me inundate you with emotion.

Dostoyeffsky

"I love you, Raskalnalov," whispered Sonia. Raskalnalov paled. He hadn't expected this. What did she mean by it? What was her motive? He searched his mind for the possible trap she might be leading him into. Cold chills were shivering up his spine and his knees were trembling. Finally, slowly weighing each word, he, too, whispered, "And I love you, Sonia Soniavitch."

Gertrude Stein

And seeing that it is not that which it is not but rather is that which is not what it is and seeing pigeons purple pigeons in the red grass it is you.

Walter Winchell

Your B'way correspondent reports that Gwendolyn Twinkler-Moultke, of the Follies, and S. S. Bustard, the artichoke king, are sizzling and should be middle-aisling it soon.

Thomas Wolfe

O night. O day. O earth. O sky. (O nuts. Skip three pages.) . . . "I love you, Julia."

Karl Marx

"You make me class conscious, Natasha, and for that I love you."

Time

Tuesday, Nov. 9: Pittsburgh's tipsy Rufus J. Figgear, 72, and Milwaukee's scrawny Abigail Doughbeer were today married by Rev. Ugh. Said Mrs. Figgear (nee Doughbeer), "There's no fool like an oiled fool."

Pittsburgh Panther

In keeping with the trend in contemporary journalism, *Point* has adopted the practice of labeling its stories, articles, etc., according to the editors' opinion of their authenticity. Propaganda will be marked as such. Truth will out, and so on. So, hereafter, *Point* readers should follow the printed key in determining the source and identity of each item.

P. . . . . Propaganda
D.P. . . . . Dirty Propaganda
W.M. . . . . Well Maybe
P.P. . . . . *Point* Propaganda
P.R. . . . . Partly Rumor
A.R. . . . . All Rumor
L. . . . . Lies
F. . . . . Fact
F. Fiction
H. Hooey
W.C. . . . . Who Cares?

West Point Pointer

Tarnished waist plate, tarnished waist plate, scratches on waist plate, spots on waist plate, tarnished waist plate, tarnished waist plate . . . .

Paul S. Deems/West Point Pointer

Music Lover

Some time ago we heard a story about the first violinist in the Philharmonic Symphony Orchestra when Stravinsky was conducting it. We've told it so often now and thought of it so many times that we've decided to get if off our chest once and for all.

It seems that during the rendition of Beethoven's Fifth, Stravinsky noticed the first violinist straining and frowning, making faces, and acting generally as if he were in pain, although his playing was, as usual, perfect. Naturally Stravinsky was much concerned, thinking the first violinist had had a sudden attack of whatever first violinists are susceptible to. As time went on beads of perspiration burst out on the poor fellow's forehead, his face became paler and paler, his actions more agonized. During the intermission, Stravinsky asked his first violinist in great consternation if he were ill.

"No," replied the violinist, "I'm all right."

"Then what's the matter? Surely something must be wrong."

The first violinist insisted that he was in excellent health.

"Perhaps you don't like my conducting," said Stravinsky, who was beginning to become annoyed.

"No, no! Your conducting is fine."

"Well, then, what's the matter? Don't you like my appearance? Is there something wrong with me?"

"No, you're fine. You're very good."

"Is there something wrong with your violin? It sounds all right."

"No, my violin is fine. Nothing the matter with my violin."

By this time Stravinsky was definitely annoyed with his first violinist. Here was a man who went into paroxysms of agony while playing, who kept insisting that there was nothing wrong with him or anyone else. Stravinsky got a sudden inspiration.

"Ah!" he said. "I know. You don't like Beethoven."

"No, Beethoven's a fine composer."

Stravinsky exploded. One might have detected a little trace of froth around his lips. This violinist was impossible.

"Then what is the matter?"

The violinist looked crestfallen. He looked up and down several times, looked around him, and wet his lips. Finally he sighed and said, "I hate music."

Columbia Jester

"On this play, remember, Lehigh center gets rammed to hell."

Penn State Froth

▼

Continued from page 97

Stabs Saturninus.

Aaron the Moor is dragged in.

Lucius. You!

Aaron. Yes, me.

They all stab Aaron.

Aaron (the hard-bitten guy). Ouch. That hurt.

Lucius. Yes. But not enough.

THE CURTAIN DESCENDETH

Henry Lefer and Ervin Druckerman/ CCNY Mercury

AS WHO LIKES IT

Dramatis Personae

LUCIUS, *prince of Sparta*
SEBASTIAN, *buddy to Lucius*
ANTONIO, *duke of Kent*
MARCELLUS, *brother to Bernardo*
BERNARDO, *brother to Marcellus*
BLOT, DULL, TORPID, LIVID — *varlets of little interest*
LADY MARGARET, *wife to Lucius*
FANNY, *a pleasant wench*
MISTRESS THICKLY, *hostess at the Red Eye Inn*
Attendants, Hautboys, Soldiers, Murderers, Officers, Sailors, Priests, Ghosts, Ham Actors, and Hallucinations.

ACT I

Scene I. England, Sparta.

Thunder. Alarums. Excursions. Enter Hautboys *with torches. Exeunt severally with torches and bodies.*

Enter Lucius.

Lucius. If love be food or food be
Love then am I in a state most bord'ring
On the undernourished. For as the
Falcon[1] coursing down the wind does
Look about and see the object of his
Choice, swoops down and misses it by
A smart two feet, so I, though by
The pangs of love am prick'd, do yet
Have naught to do but be by hautboys
Followed—

Enter Hautboy *with torch.*

Hautboy. Did you call me?

Lucius. No.

Exit Hautboy *with torch.*

But would I could the comely Margaret
Call, or better yet the lass called Fanny
That I did recent see. She was a paragon
Of something I know not what[2]
But fly all that; affairs of state
Do me divert.

Enter Clown.

Clown. Good morrow, sir.

Lucius. Oh my God.

Clown. Nay, not your God, good sir, for
Were He yours He would be nobody else's
Which is certain to be a lie since you
Know what that means and being the means
Would make you the extremes, which would
Be far from hot.

Lucius. Here's gold for you.[3]

Clown. For me?

Lucius. For you.

Clown. Oh, you shouldn't.

Lucius. Shouldn't what?

Clown. For who's the man to tell what
Is should and what is shouldn't? For
If I should say to you you shouldn't
And you should say to me I should
Then I should be shouldn'ting you
And you should be shoulding me, and
That would be

(*Sings*)

With a hey diddle and a hey hey-oh
Sing nonny nonny nonny and a hey hey hey
With a diddle diddle diddle and a hey etc.

Lucius. Thou hast a quick wit; here's gold
For thy pains.[4]

Clown. (Aside) Thank you.

Lucius. You're welcome.

Clown. (Aside) Let's get out of here.

Lucius. All right, but you don't have
To shout. (*Exeunt.*

Scene II. A garden. *Enter* Antonio.

Antonio. Ah, here it is that I my Fanny
Last did see. 'Twas here she said that she
Would soon be back, but now some fifteen
Moons are come and gone[5] and she is not
Returned.

Hamlet.[6] O, what a rogue and peasant

[1]Falcon. Coleridge explains this as being a hunting bird called a falcon, that would sometimes course down the wind, but Kit. contends that it refers to the type of one of the U. S. Army observation planes, known as the Curtis Falcon.

[2]This rather vague statement has been explained by Coleridge by the fact that Lucius was probably tired and had just fallen into the footlights, thereby ruining his train of thought. Kittredge contends that this line was written by Bacon, and should therefore be dismissed without further notice.

[3]"Here's gold for you": *Nobody* has been able to explain the Elizabethan habit of giving these clowns money, since it certainly did not get rid of them, and if anything made them hang around longer. cf. MSND III ii 108, Ham IV iii 137, AWTEW I, II, III iv 120-173, Macb V ii 20-300.

[4]"*Thy pains*": This indicates that it hurt the clown just as much to carry on like this as it did Lucius to listen to it, but the gold end of it still remains a mystery. Kittredge suggests that perhaps in those days giving a person gold was like kicking him in the face, in which case this is explainable, but that, as he admits, is purely a rough guess.

[5]Coleridge suggests that this was really only one moon, having reappeared, or completed its cycle fifteen times. Other references to many moons, however, (Folio and Quarto, iii 2 V 265) seem to indicate the possibility that the people of the time believed that there was a new moon for each month.

[6]The appearance of Hamlet in this scene is rather mystifying. Lowes points out that many of the Elizabethan writers thought nothing of borrowing (the word "plagiarize" was not yet in use) plots from each other, but the author of this play certainly went the whole hog, if that is what he was trying to do. And to make matters worse, it makes no sense at all.

Slave am I! Is it not monstrous that this
Player here, but in a fiction, in a dream
Of passion, could force his soul so to
His own conceit that from her working
All his visage wann'd, Tears in his eyes,
Distraction in's aspect, a broken voice
And his whole functions suiting with
Forms to his conceit? and all for nothing!
For — for —
Antonio. For Hecuba.
Hamlet. That's right, for Hecuba.
(Exit, muttering.
Antonio. And now at last I am alone
And I may my envisage heal[7] which
As the surly Ethiop does stand out in a
Bank of snow doth make me mocked by
Idle boors who have time for but to
Stand and sneer. Out with it!
Out! out! damned spot![8]
And now I have the plot. I to my
Fanny right will go, but better to
Pursue my suit I shall my puss disguise
In manner that no man shall tell from
Where or why I came. *(Exit.*

ACT II

Scene I. England, Sparta.
Enter Antonio, *disguised as a girl of twelve.*
Antonio. And now is my disguise complete,
And I have but to wait until my Fan
Comes gaily past when I her will salute
And she mistaking me for what I'm not
Will easier listen to my love. Hark!
Who comes?
Enter Fanny, *disguised as a sailor.*
Fanny. (Sings) Oh, Mademoiselle from Armentieres, parlez-vous—
Antonio. Hail, friend.
Fanny. Hello little girl.
What are *you* doing tonight?
Antonio. I'm going home.
Fanny. Is there a fire?
Antonio. No, but my mother bade me—
Fanny. Thy mother—pah! A fig for
Thy mother. If thou comest with me thou
Shalt see things and people the like of
Which thou hast never seen before.
Antonio. I dassn't. *(Aside)* What is
To be done? I would fain with this stranger to drink or so imbibe, but yet that
In this guise can I not, or if I should
So would I lose my purpose with my Fanny.
Fanny. All right, little girl, no harm.
Enter Clown.
Clown. Hello, Antonio, Hello, Fanny.
Antonio. I am not Antonio. Here's gold
For secrecy.
Fanny. Call me not Fanny. Here's gold to
Keep thee quiet.
Clown. Well, that was easy.
(Exit.
Antonio. Well, now I must to my mother
Run, or else she will be sore angered.
Fanny. Adieu, small girl, and if you
Should a man called Antonio see
Direct him to come hence. I would have
Words with him. *(Aside)* Methinks that
Is the only way that I my Antony
Can see. He is so bashful otherwise
That I in this rig up must get. Ah, well.
Antonio. I shall. *(Aside)* and what
Can this varlet of me want? I do not
Cater to the fleet.[9]
(Exeunt severally.
Scene II. Sparta, England.
Alarums. Enter Hautboys *with torches, Attendants, and* Mistress Thickly.
Mistress T. What ho, my merry yokels,
Is this not a day that would make the
Dullest dope a poet and then again the
Poet to a dope[10]? I feel it in my
Bones that there will this day be
One of those mass marriages the
Like of which has not been seen
Since last the Bard of Avon was around
With all his players.[11]
Enter Clown, *singing.*
Clown. (Singing) With a hey nonny—
Enter luckily Lucius, *disguised as a bass viol.*
Lucius. Tum du de dum dum.
Enter Antonio, *still dis-*

Continued on page 113

[7]*"Envisage heal"*; This is a rather rare use of the word "envisage." C. submits that it means "face," and supposing that either he has fallen down or Hamlet has struck him with his sword. K. prefers "mend" for "heal," and, by substituting "beltstrap" for "envisage" concludes that A's pants were falling down.
[8]Cf. *Macbeth* V ii 37.

[9]This line is missing in the Folio; in another of the early editions it is spoken by Hamlet, who has suddenly reappeared. C. emends it to read "garter for the feet," which is better.

[10]Dope. Here the meaning is somewhat obscure. C., without reading the context, suggested "narcotic" as a synonym. K. suggests the emendation of "pope," which only complicates things a little more.

[11]Possibly a contemporary comment on Shakespeare and his players, although it is not clear whether or not the marriages were in the script of S.

WAITER, THERE'S A FLY IN MY SOUP

. . . TO END ALL SUCH JOKES

"Waiter, there's a fly in my soup."
"Yeah, we ran outa turtles."

▼

"Waiter, there's a fly in my soup."
"All right! I'll bring you a fork."

▼

"Waiter, there's a fly in my soup."
"Shh—he may be a *Silver and Gold* reporter."

▼

"Waiter, there's a fly in my soup."
"That's strange. What kind of soup is it?"

▼

"Waiter, there's a fly in my soup."
"I won't tell anyone if you won't."

▼

"Waiter, there's a fly in my soup."
"That will be ten cents extra, please."

▼

"Waiter, there's a fly in my soup."
"Okay, here's a fly swatter."

▼

"Waiter, there's a fly in my soup."
"Indeed? I guess we just forgot to put it on the menu."

▼

"Waiter, there's a fly in my soup."
"That's no fly. That's the manager."

▼

"Waiter, there's a fly in my soup."
"I'm not the waiter. I'm the manager."

"Waiter, there's a fly in my soup."
"That must be the one the Brooklyn Dodgers are looking for."

▼

"Waiter, there's a fly in my soup."
"Yes, I know. That's better than half a fly."

▼

"Waiter, there's a fly in my soup."
"Where did you think they went in March?"

▼

"Waiter, there's a fly in my soup."
"Ah, cornered at last."

▼

"Waiter, there's a fly in my soup."
"Wait 'til you see the coffee."

▼

"Waiter, there's a fly in my soup."
"Shh—all the customers will be wanting one."

▼

"Waiter, there's a fly in my soup."
"What do you expect with the blue plate? A humming-bird?"

▼

"Waiter, there's a fly in my soup."
"That's not a fly, that's Raisin Delight."

▼

"Waiter, there's a fly in my soup."
"That's all right—it's Friday."

▼

"Waiter, there's a fly in my soup."
"Well, do you blame him?"

"Well anyway, I got their goddam cheese!"
Stanford Chaparral

"Waiter, there's a fly in my soup."
"Yes, sir. This is the Beta house."

▼

"Waiter, there's a fly in my soup."
"You see, our cook is a former tailor."

▼

"Waiter, there's a fly in my soup."
"Yes, sir, look at those muscles."

▼

"Waiter, there's a fly in the bottom of my tea cup. What does this mean?"
"How should I know? I'm no fortune teller."

▼

"Waiter, there's a locomotive in my soup."
"Yes, sir—this is a training table."

▼

"Waiter, there's a fly in my soup."
"It's all right, he won't drink much."

▼

"Waiter, there's a fly in my soup."
"Fly, hell! That's the *Dodo* editor."
Colorado Dodo

CLUB LIFE AT HARVARD
"He's a bit shy at first, but he's a good fellow when you get to know him."

Nathaniel Benchley/*Harvard Lampoon*

THE ART AND HEART OF JOURNALISM

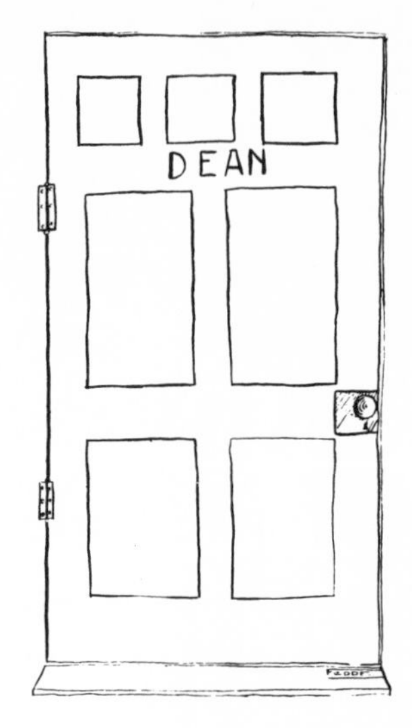

"Your deal, Sir"
Williams Purple Cow

DEMOCRACY could not last two minutes without newspapers. It might last three minutes, but not two minutes. This statement may sound dogmatic, but in such vital matters as this it is better to be dogmatic than kittenish.

Since America is a great one for democracy, it is essential that every schoolboy be familiar with the elementary aspects of journalism.

At the start, we must distinguish between journalism and newspaper writing. A man who, for a salary of $25 a week, takes inconsequential facts and slaps them into a story so that they appear to be world-shaking, is a newspaper man. A journalist does exactly the same thing, but because he spreads the inconsequentialities on a little thicker he gets more money. To be a journalist you must know how to fill four columns where an ordinary newspaper man could only fill one; you must know how to read hidden meanings into meaningless facts, to "interpret" by the yard irrelevant events about which most people don't give a hoot; and how to repeat the same thing six or seven times over, making it sound altogether different each time. A journalist ofter makes as much as $35 a week. If he makes more than this he is either a propagandist or a publicist, in which case he doesn't bother with facts, but merely interprets events.

All the parts of newspaper writing can be demonstrated by tracing a news happening from the time it occurs until it appears in the paper. Let us suppose Mayor La Guardia passed the Health Commissioner on the street last week and, not having seen him for a few days, called out to him:

"Hello, Rice, you old son-of-a-gun! What have you been doing with yourself these days? Has your wife gotten over her cold yet?"

All the City Hall reporters are within hearing, so they dash down what they hear, dash over to a telephone and call up their city editors. The city editors each take a puff on their cigarettes, connect the reporters with "re-write" men, and after several passings about the story appears in type. The only story that will approximate the facts will be that sent out by the press associations. The Associated Press story will read:

> Mayor Fiorello H. La Guardia of New York City yesterday passed Health Commissioner John L. Rice on a street adjoining the City Hall and greeted him as though he had not seen him for several days.
>
> Meeting him on Centre Street, La Guardia said:
>
> "Hello, Rice, you old son-of-a-gun."
>
> He added, "What have you been doing with yourself these days?"
>
> Smiling, La Guardia concluded:
>
> "Has your wife gotten over her cold yet?"
>
> Rice did not reply.

This story was written by a newspaper man. It is insolent, terse and straight. If only the first paragraph is printed, the news is out.

The New York Times, the journalists' newspaper, will run the story on Page 1, column 8, with a two-column headline, the story jumping over to Page 14, where it lays over 2½ columns, not counting cuts (photographs). The story will begin:

SPLIT IN FUSION NEARS AS MAYOR LOSES HOLD; RICE WILL BOLT SOON

HIS OVERWORK BLAMED

La Guardia Shows Signs of Strain, His Temper Heightening Now

SNUBS HEALTH OFFICIAL

He Passes Commissioner on Street and Suggests Inattention to Job; No Reply Given

CALLS HIM A 'SON-OF-A-GUN'

Remark Thought to Refer to Epidemic of Colds Now Besieging City; Tammany Is Jubilant

Weather: Fair, rain.

DAILY  RECORD

Don't you dare print any of this stuff. **BOSTON'S LITTLE TRIBUTE TO CULTURE** If you think this ought to be 2nd class mail, OK. We think it is first class.

Vol. 241. No. 103 28 Pages Boston, Tuesday, May 8, 1934 PRICE 25 CENTS

NAB EINSTEIN, YALE PRESIDENT, HITLER, HARVARD STUDENT IN LOVE NEST RAID ON EAST LYNN APT.

Story on Page 3

Womanhood is a state more to be worshipped than scorned. It is a true gift from the gods. We put women on a pedestal and are glad to leave them there as long as possible. Here is a woman who was on a pedestal for nineteen days, three hours and five minutes. Nineteen days, three hours and five minutes of playing-around-time for hubby. That's what she gets for her pedestal-sitting.

Inventor? Cedric Cantalover, explaining the moves of a new game, a cross between checkers and dominoes that is said to be taking the West by storm.

Mayday on the Hill is the caption for this photo. It is far and away the best action picture we have. The two policemen are arguing about whether or not the man on the street who is lying nursing a head-wound is called John Gselcin or John Gselkin. There is no difference in pronunciation and both men gave the same address. The woman gave some other name and is being trundled off, as you see, to the wagon. She is going to go to jail. There she will be in jail and a fit subject for the jailer. She is sort of a fat old hussy anyway and we are content to see her go. That leaves only the man in the background, waving, to be mentioned. He gave his name as John Gzelcin and complicated the name situation further. He said he lived next door to the other two guys. He is a communist and therefore probably goes to Harvard, which even has a red banner. We think all Harvard men are communists. This means you.

Harvard Lampoon

DAILY RECORD PLATFORM

1—War with Japan by Christmas.
2—Quell communism at Harvard.
3—Probe love nests in Greater Boston.
4—Play up New England murders; not ones in other sections.
5—Probe and quiz all hub affairs which need quashing.
6—Eradicate sex education in schools; it is hell on circulation.

Who Knows It

There is a lot to be said about Harvard students and other rich men's sons who think that just because they have a lot of liesure time they can spend it pestering the life out of the working classes who are the backbone of this country of ours which was discovered in 1492 by Christopher Columbus. That is a long tradition of working classes. Four hundred and forty-two years.

But very few people seem to know that in this country there are no class distinctions which say to the young working man:

"You are a working man. Now go and work."

The four hundred and forty-two years of tradition in this country say, instead:

"You are the backbone of the country. Now go and work."

We think you will agree with us that this is a much better state of affairs.

But just the same, Harvard students shouldn't pester the working classes. Let's put a stop to this sort of thing.

More Art Exhibits

At a recent art exhibit there was a picture of a nude. Now we have all heard about culture and we thoroughly endorse its tenets. But when it gets to putting up for public exhibit a picture of a nude it is too much. American men have put woman on a pedestal and when some dirty foreign art man puts her on the wall, instead, and in the nude, which is a private state with most American women, it is just too much. The model that posed for the picture probably never intended the pictures that were made of her in that private state to be hung up for public inspection. We must try to put a stop to it. A law against posing in the nude might do the trick.

Make the artists stop putting up such lewd pictures and leave it to us.

Yes and No

A man said "The Daily Record is a disgrace to Boston". Some say yes to this. Others say no. Perhaps neither side is right.

Good Old New England

There is much too much of a tendency in Boston lately to recognize other parts of the country.

If we New Englanders are to get anywhere in this world we must stand together and blow our horn for the old home region.

The New England Chamber of Commerce has done a lot but there is a lot more to be done.

It might be a good idea to cut off all railroads and communications with other parts of the country.

It might be a good idea for the newspapers to confine their news stories to New England. We have always done our bit along this line, won't the others join us?

It might be a good idea to move the whole works to the interior of Alaska where there is no chance for outside interference and we can have our murders and our culture in peace.

It might be a good idea to have a good idea.

Why Men Love Women

A professor in an interview published in this paper says women are loved by men because of a methyl radical.

That is perfectly absurd. Men love women because women are the most lovely things in the world. We have always endorsed the policy of most Americans to put women on a Pedestal.

Letters From Our Readers

PATRICK J. MURPHY

I wish to express my earnest approval of the nomination of Patrick J. Murphy, of South Boston, as Assemblyman by the Democratic Party. Although he is at present engaged in the coal and trucking business, Murphy is not without political experience. His earlier occupation, that of filling-station operator, kept him in close touch with the People. Murphy loves the People.

He is also a family man and a defender of American womanhood.

We need more men like Murphy.

PATRICK J. MURPHY.

KILL 'EM ALL

Do most Americans realize that over there on the other side of the Pacific is a nation of sixty million men, women, and children, all belonging to the Mongolian race?

These Japs are planning a little joke on us. After grabbing Manchuria, they will seize Hawaii and the Philippines. They they will send a fleet of planes over to drop bombs on California.

The best thing to do would be for us to send our navy over right now and shoot every single man, woman, and child in Japan.

Then the joke would be on them.

I for one would like nothing better than to stick a bayonet into one of those little yellow fellows.

WHITE MAN.

AGAINST IT

I speak as an Irishman. My father came to Boston because he did not like the English government. But the American government is worse, I don't care who hears me.

We starve while the capitalists grow fat.

They say the government is giving the poor man a New Deal. But I say, down with the government! Whatever it is, I'm against it.

J. J. O'B.

CATERWAULING

Last night I was unable to sleep because of the continual yowling, screeching, and caterwauling of a group of love-lorn cats outside my window.

Something has got to be done about it.

The best way is for somebody to collect all the tomcats in Cambridge and let a veterinary take definite measures to deprive these unpleasant animals of the seat of desire and mollify their dispositions.

If this it not done, either the cats or the humans will have to pack up and leave Cambridge.

CAMBRIDGE CITIZEN.

HOCKEY

Aggies won Aggies win won won Aggies is a Aggies is a Aggies won win Aggies I mean Aggies win Aggies.

I mean I think Aggies won win is won is won is two Aggies is Aggies. Aw Hell!

G. STEIN.

Paris.

RADIO

Gee, I think Gertrude Niessen is swell. He's a lot better than Morton Downey, don't you think? And gee, I wish they would can some of this high-brow classical stuff. I bought my radio for five rocks and I can't waste my time listening to Lady Esther or Victor Herbert, or any of that high-hat junk.

PROF. FENELON WEATHERBY BIGELOW.

Cambridge.

HARVARD HUNGER

In my capacity as dancer in a Minsky revue, it is customary for me to do a good deal of my performance in somewhat scanty (abbreviated) costume. Hitherto this has not bothered me. Embarrassment, to me, was unknown.

But last night there was a bunch of Harvard boys at the show, and, honestly, you ought to have seen the poor things. They looked simply ravenous. It was then that I felt embarrassed, for the first time.

Give me tired business men, and keep me away from those Harvard boys!

FAN DANCER.

Toonerville Folks

INQUIRING REPORTER

What do you, as a Daily Record reader, think of the Daily Record?

Rodney Fluttermush, bricklayer, on Washington Street:

I never think. I find it hinders one in one's business. I lay bricks, you know. Chickens lay eggs and I lay bricks, ha-ha. All I have to do is to put one brick on top of another, with a slight dash of plaster in between. I haven't thought since my wife Amanda had triplets, in 1924.

Rodney Fluttermush

Rupert Musheltut, philosopher, in a Washington Street gutter:

It is my opinion that the above-mentioned Daily Record, in depth of comprehension and broadness of scope, is the most noble embodiment of all that is to be desired in journalism. The Record's philosophic point of view is extremely meritorious; in sagacious and far-sighted vision it is practically peerless; and in many other ways it is pretty good. Of course I can neither read nor write myself but I have a dandy time looking at the pictures.

Rupert Musheltut

Miss Abbie Mutterflush, hog-caller, on Beacon Street:

That is a question that I as a daily reader of the Bangor Commercial have been wanting to answer for years. Thank you very much for asking me. You had a perfect right to.

Abbie Mutterflush

Herbert Hoover, retired, on Atlantic Avenue:

I think Roosevelt is doing as well as could be expected. The C. W. A. is actually making streets grow in the grass out in Arizona. I think Roosevelt is doing as well as could be expected. I am also of the ipion that i' Franklin D. Roosevelt keeps on the way he's started he is going to make the best governor New York ever had.

Miss Fanny Shuttermush, idiot, on Dorchester Avenue:

You do say the funniest things. I have read the Daily Record ever since I was knee-high to a knee-action wheel, and I want to tell everybody how the crossword puzzles have broadened my mind. In fact, after twenty consecutive years of your cross-word puzzles, I am practically the most broadminded person I know.

Fanny Shuttermush

Edgar Luttersiush, moron, on Canton Avenue:

I think Roosevelt is a good man. I think Mussolini is a good man. I think Hitler is a good man. But what about Nila Cram Cook? And what about the Daily Record? After all, what's sauce for the goose is sauce for the gander. That's what I'm always saying to myself. I am a Republican.

Fedora Sputterthrush, man, in Picadilly Circus:

I am a religious man. I go to the Cathedral every Sunday to clean up after the pigeons. One can't have spent his life in the shadow of a cathedral without becoming impregnated with a deep, religious faith. I believe in God and the Daily Record.

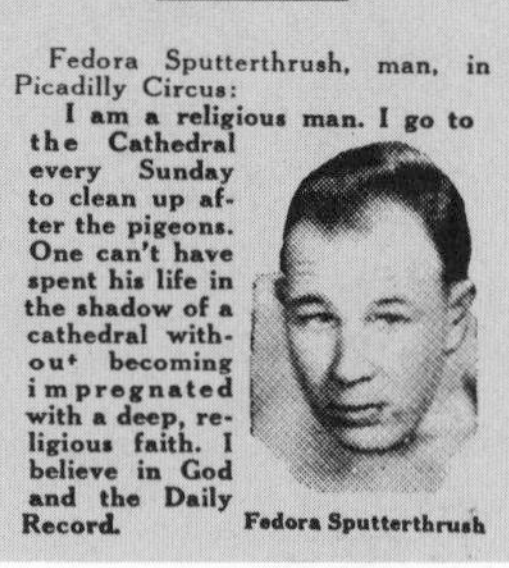

Fedora Sputterthrush

An early split in Fusion ranks, which may ease the way for a Tammany victory at the next election, was predicted by city political leaders last night after they viewed with growing concern the development of an intra-administration conflict over policy between Mayor La Guardia and Health Commissioner John L. Rice.

That tense relations between the two officials have existed to a greater or lesser degree for many months has been apparent to persons close to the Mayor. But an incident occurred yesterday morning which clearly demonstrated that the Mayor is not inclined to conceal any longer his dissatisfaction with Dr. Rice's administrative methods. Mr. La Guardia passed Dr. Rice on a street near City Hall and, using language stronger than has been heard in official quarters since the regime of Richard Croker [formerly the leader of Tammany Hall], accosted him and intimated that he was considerably displeased with the Health Commissioner's lax conduct of his office.

Dr. Rice's failure to reply to what was said to be an affront was viewed by persons close to him as an indication that he is biding his time, in preparation for the day when he will, it is considered likely, seize control of the Fusion party, move for Mayor La Guardia's dismissal, and effect a coalition with the so-called "old guard" Socialists and Republicans in the hope of staving off the expected onslaught by Tammany Hall next Fall.

The distinction between newspaper writing and journalism should now be clear. The *Times* story will run on for several columns much like the above, with conflicting but anonymous statements from "high authorities" invented by the journalist himself, giving tone to the journalist's finespun theories. The full text of the words which actually passed between the Mayor and Dr. Rice will appear near the end of the story, on Page 14, column seven, bottom of the page, right next to a story about a party Mrs. John L. Rice will give at the Biltmore tomorrow for the benefit of underfed street cleaning department employees, and to which Mrs. La Guardia and other prominent officials' wives have been invited.

Other papers will go to the *Times* better, running exclusive interviews with Dr. Rice's brother-in-law, a feature article on Mrs. Rice's cold, a historical story on the history of the term "son-of-a-gun" in New York politics, a signed article by James J. Dooling to Tammany on What This Means to Me, and possibly a *Herald-Tribune* or *Sun* story about a petition signed by 50 leading clergymen protesting violently, as men of God but primarily as citizens, against the use of abusive language by city officials who are guardians of the people's trust. The whole thing will be forgotten by the next morning.

All this is known in the newspaper office as "coverage," and in the outside world as "freedom of the press."

Other, more detailed aspects of newspaper work are:

1. HEADLINE WRITING—Very tricky indeed. The most irksome thing about writing headlines is that they must fit, letter for letter, in the narrow space of a column. This forces you to write:

REPUBLICANS FLAY LEGISLATIVE BODY AS BATTLE APPEARS

which sounds as if the Republicans beat up somebody just before a war; actually you mean that the Republican Party criticized the Committee on Legislation of the National Economy League, just before George Gordon Battle stepped to the front of the House of Representatives, where the charges were being made. But type, as all of you have been told before, is not made of rubber.

2. SYNONYM HUNTING—The chief indoor sport in the newspaper world. There is an unyielding law of the trade against repeating the same word (with the exception of prepositions, "the" and "a" and other unavoidable word-helpers) in the same paragraph; some papers extend the ban to an entire article. This compels the writer to hunt for synonyms for every conceivable noun, adjective and verb he uses. If he uses the word "conference" in his first paragraph, he must refer to it afterward as a meeting, a convention, a conclave, a session, a parley, a powwow, an assembly, an assemblage, a council, a congress, congregation, caucus, palaver, and so on into the French. The reader often wonders if he is reading about the same meeting. The synonym hunt applies also to people's names: if an outfielder is named Hank Melange, and comes from East Hackensack, the newspaper writer will call him Hank Melange just once; after that you hear about the left-handed fury from East Hackensack, Hackensack Hank, Blanc Melange, the Jersey Blowout, Mrs. Melange's little son Hank, Mr. Melange's proud chip off the old block—et cetera. Again, when a man gives a speech, he doesn't simply *say* the words he uses, but also asserts, declares, avers, maintains, states, holds, contends, insists, points out, shows, and demonstrates them. Synonym hunters often find it easier to shoot up department stores during the rush hour.

3. PUBLICITY RELEASES—Commonly called handouts. These announcements often run into many pages, all properly marked for publication, and tell all about the 25 guests who heard Mr. Timothy Squire's son recite "The Old Oaken Bucket" last weekend at the home of Mrs. Squire's sister, Nellie. Unless the person issuing the release is a friend of the editor's or an advertiser, the release is used to keep the furnace going when the night staff moves into the slot.

4. COLUMNISTS—The people who get the best pay on a newspaper by disregarding all the trade rules and writing what they can get away with. Strangely enough, columnists often begin as journalists.

5. EDITING—A lost art, now reduced to the business of correcting mistakes in spelling, omitting "the" and "a" as often as possible,

cutting damaging facts, and marking for type. Editors used to use blue pencils, but discarded them because the psychological state induced by reading copy was low enough. Editors are commonly stout, are light smokers, and climb trees only when pressed.

6. PROOF ERROR—The last resort of a scoundrel. A communicable disease akin to German measles.

7. STICK—A paragraph. The word is derived from a Scandinavian term meaning "glug."

These are the less frightening aspects of journalism. A thorough acquaintance with them will no doubt prove beneficial to Rover Boys and all others upon whom the older generation is looking for faith and security in these parlous times. But anyone seriously considering becoming a newspaper man or even a journalist is advised to get acquainted with the publisher's daughter first. This is known as "getting in by the back door," and saves a great deal of trouble. If a publisher hasn't a daughter, look for one who has. If no publisher has a daughter, and no one's daughter has a publisher, then you might try the stage. There are plenty of daughters there, and you can always find a place to sleep in the second balcony when you're out of a job.

J. Stanley Morgenthal/*Columbia Jester*

LITTLE ORPHAN ANNIE, THE SLUT

By Harold G. Fluttermash

DUMB DORA

By Jimmy Fluttermash

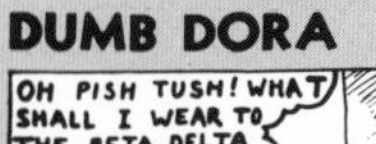

TARZAN, THE OLD MAESTRO

By Edgar Rice Fluttermash

Here is the old maestro snapping asunder some chains. They are large chains and hard to snap asunder. But he does it.

Here is the old maestro choking some Roman soldiers. Why any Roman soldiers ever appear in this strip is a mystery to me. They are large soldiers and hard to choke. But he does it.

Here is the old maestro choking a snake. Always a snake. Snakes, snakes, snakes . . . hush! that way lies madness. It is a large snake and hard to choke. But he does it.

The old maestro makes another cow a widow. He shoots the bull. Listen: "Now, apes, in just two easy lessons I can give you a musculature like mine. Maureen O'Sullivan thrown in for 25c extra."

Harvard Lampoon

You too can take advantage of all the world has to offer. Just forget about your grasshopper mind for about five minutes and lend an ear to our lesson. No need even to clip a coupon. It's all here. Take it away.

How to Carry on Brilliant Conversation.

Everybody wants to impress everybody else with his brilliant conversation. Unfortunately not everyone knows how this has caused more trouble than Communism and the Rhythm Method. However, brilliancy in conversation can be learned in one short lesson and gets you farther than the Culbertson system and telling that sweet young thing that you're mad about her.

Three topics are essential. You've got to be able to talk about (1) books you've never read, (2) plays you've never seen, and (3) neuroses you've never had.

The most kosher critics of the country use several ways of describing a book. It is an important contribution to the history and criticism of the period it portrays; it is an important record of artistic achievement; it is a notable realistic romance; it is an absorbing and mature piece of writing; and it's a penetrating social document. Any one of these will be a panic if tossed off between the meat course and the celery.

The style of the book is either recherche, which is a thirty-five-cent word and practically pays for the meal, or else it is tough and extroverted, in the James Cain tradition. If it's a lend book, it's faintly reminiscent of Proust. If you haven't any idea what the hell the book's about, just say that it resembles Hemingway and let it go at that.

The hero is either a country boy who meets a city girl or a city girl who meets a country boy. Ever since the war it has been a literary tradition (that's also an impressive phrase) to have the girls seduce the boy. This is undoubtably just another labor-saving device which will soften the fibre of modern manhood.

If you look shyly at the caramel custard and mumble something about the rape that takes place in chapter seven, this will give you a chance to remark that rape has always fascinated the erotic consciousness of the world's writers, including Shakespeare. It also demonstrates your tremendous erudition and leads to some very pleasant cracks.

You must always remember that a play is significant, dull, socially conscious, bawdy, or something that George Abbott dragged in. If it's a revival, it's never as good as Barrymore or Sarah Bernhardt did it thirty years ago. It must also be remembered that Maurice Evans is the only actor on the American stage that can play Shakespearean parts. All players under forty are obvious Hollywood material. It will thrill the girl sitting next to you who is making so much noise with the spaghetti if you mention a couple of producers by their first names and repeat what Alfred Lunt never said to you about what Noel Coward says when he wakes up in the morning.

Somewhere between the coffee and the third act of *Mourning Becomes Electra,* you can bring in the story of how your Uncle Jim was bitten by a horse and then became a Manic Depressive. This is a good opening, because it leads to talk about all sorts of mental disturbances. Let the other guy tell the first story and then raise the ante. You will always know someone who was a little bit more psychotic than anyone else, and if somebody does come up with a dilly, you can always subdue them by mentioning that you think that Freud isn't all he's supposed to be. This can be kept up until one of you loses his voice. The subject is very easily changed to defining life and saying that it resembles a plum-pudding, a hay stack, a snowy day in January, Jack Benny's wise-cracks, and your underwear after the laundry is through with it. This makes you sound cynical and a bit of a Bronx Alexander Woollcott.

As the women rise to give you a chance to crack the dirty joke you've been saving all evening, you can climax your brilliant repartee with a remark such as: "Anyway, Bach is an ass," or "Frankly I don't think we have anything to worry about over Communism," or "Lemon juice, however, is very good for bunions."

How To Write A Sophisticated Movie.

The picture should start with

Crawford getting a rubdown. She is dressed very charmingly in a towel and an engaging smile. Gable and Grant, who always play in this kind of stuff, always make their entrance by sliding down a bannister or breaking up the water-polo by jumping into the pool with all their clothes on. This demonstrates in some mystic way that they have been bosom pals since their first cream-puff way back in Spencerville Prep. It proves, too, the interesting fact that all young people these days are very gay and have clothes and time to waste.

By this time, Crawford is dressed and she grabs the two young men by the arm. They walk vigorously to the bar, making a few smooth cracks to demonstrate their overwhelming sophistication. Such as: Have you any oranges in the kitchen and will you please marry me? Having passed all your psychology courses, you can realize that Joan is in love with both of them. This is technically known as a triangle and will prove to the Hollywood mogul that you've got a good idea. A few of Noel Coward's cleaner epigrams, lifted and marcelled, convince the audience that this is the Vanity Fair squad to the cuff-link. The three principals banter with a high-ho and a pip-pip Jenkins all through the picture. The sadder they are, the more flippantly do they laugh-clown it. This is known as tragedy and is exceedingly moving.

How they do it, you really don't know, but sooner or later the three of them eventually land in Bridgeport, Connecticut, with four cents and a Baltimore trolley token, adding the devil-may-care touch to it all. This also provides a chance for them to put in a hitch-hike scene, or something else just as ducky.

Nobody knows who's in love with whom until the last reel, giving everybody who doesn't like the picture a chance to make a couple of bets on the side. When one of the leads leaves the lovely girl at the altar, the other boy steps in and it turns out that, of course, this is what should have happened in the first place, because she's been in love with him all along. A theme song such as "Isn't Love Blind?" might help.

There is also the rich dowager (cynical, but with a heart of gold) who swears like the chairman of a holding company, can drink anyone under the table, and lets everyone know that the facts of life were well known when she was at her prime. She hints about several gay romances with spur bearers of her day and tells everybody to marry everybody else.

The intrigue is represented by a rich, perfect blonde, who knows a collar-ad when she sees one. She manages to detain Grant for several hours and Crawford naturally assumes that he has been kidding her along. This blonde is a bitch who has realized that the course of true love depends on which person can think up the most inane and childish way of passing the time.

The fade-out, a milestone in social consciousness, consists of Joan and the oh-yeah guy kissing in front of a porthole while the Guy With The Pathetic Look waves frantically from the pier.

Follow these rules, and you're made.

Ralph de Toledano/*Columbia Jester*

Try Skill at Gigolette

Fill in the sections in which you see the damned little dots with a pen or a pencil or anything else you want. When you black them in you will have some kind of a crazy design the clue to which is given below the Gigolette. The Latin is correct which is more than can be

HARTE

MEDIO TUTISSIMUS IBIS!

said for a lot of the stuff that goes in this department. To the first 25 sending in solutions to Lampy we will give original drawings from the issues of Lampy printed since January 1st, 1934. Name the drawing you want, and maybe you'll get it.

Daily Crossword Puzzle

Seventy-five pairs of seats to the Roundout Theatre will be awarded to the first 150 people who send in the correct solutions. This means that none of the people can sit together. Figure it out for yourself.

That, to us, is a shame.

VERTICAL

1—Many an unscholarly student has not been so fortunate as the three little pigs in evading this old schemer.
2—Where mineral waters chase ulcers instead of rye.
3—Handle with care! or you're apt to get a tat in exchange.
4—Mencken says that women in this condition are ugly. But how, then, can truth thus always be beauty?
6—Exclamation of sudden revelation.
7—Easy to take out, expensive to bring out, eager to be out; glamorous in Philly, gaudy in New York, godawful in Boston.
12—Post-grad test-tuber, first year administrator.
14—This guy made a good gin, so they're still yelling about him down at Yale.
15—Poor, proud beef-steak! to find you like this under a poached egg.
19—A yellowish color, akin to that "dark-brown taste."
21—A famous American beauty.
22—Slang for mazuma.
23—A rival institution.

HORIZONTAL

1—Home grounds of Blue-laws, Blue-bloods, and Baked-beans.
5—Call this a gat, if you prefer.
8—This moves in all the best circles.
9—In this half of the day the Harvard man is accustomed to debauch, sleep, and perhaps study. (abbr.)
10—This kind of man makes a hit with the cave-girls. (Just ask them)
11—Preposition of place.
12—A stocky, short-legged horse, who, by the way, likes corn like his name.
13—Sal Hepatica or these salts, it's just a toss-up.
14—How's that? (In dear old London town)
17—There. (French)
18—This lady vetoed the Harvard coeds' ambition to display themselves in a naughty dramatic club play. (It's her first name)
Here's the head of the course. Ask him.
20—Does History I make you nervous or jumpy, girl.
24—Often in church, but never a bride, this little
25—Complete the quotation: "FI, FIE,——, FUM."
26—Lampy got this organization's numbers last fall.
27—Ingredient peculiar to Russian pineapples.
28—One type conceals a yolk,
In another sits the stroke.
29—Nothing without this verb.
30—The glee club is minus many a first-tenor because this happens to his voice.

Solution on Page 27

Harvard Lampoon

"Gee, Miss Odolovanovitz, I wish you would let me call you just 'Sophie.'"
Whitney Darrow, Jr./Princeton Tiger

Facts and Figures of 1936

Hearst and Mae West
Totalled the best
Salaries throughout the nation.
It's apropos
They should rank so—
Both deal in exaggeration.

Pittsburgh Panther

A Dark Outlook

An old darky had been riding a mule for some time when he came upon a native man and asked him the distance to Birmingham.

"Twelve miles," was the reply.

"Giddap, Napoleon," cried the darky and started off again. After a while, he met an old mammy, and, upon asking her the distance to Birmingham, he received the same reply, "Twelve miles, brother Rastus."

"Giddap, Napoleon," he shouted, and the mule marched on.

After another hour, the old man met a little child. "Chil'," he said, "how far is I from Birmingham?"

"Twelve miles, Uncle." The old darky wiped his brow.

"Giddap, Napoleon, we's holdin' our own."

Brown Jug

NO FUN IN BED

Lines from the Infirmary

Traitor! Traitor! Ogden Nash
Writes his poetry for cash!
A soul that sings its songs for
money's
Like a bee that eats its honey;
Stupid soul, and stupid bee,
Stupid everyone but me.
Ogden, lucky Ogden Nash
Sells his poetry for cash.

Robert Lax/Columbia Jester

▼

DUMB HUNTER: How do you detect an elephant?
GUIDE: You smell a faint odor of peanuts on his breath.

Princeton Tiger

▼

An old linotype went askew
With its naked machinery in view.
It made love to the press
In this state of undress
Saying gently, "etaionshrdlu."

Cornell Widow

"Wait a minute, honey, until that person turns the page."
Readie/Temple Owl

SPEECH WITH COGNAC

SOME IDEAS are all right. Some are not.

Making a whisky sour with cognac and no ice is an all right idea (even if it does taste perfectly lousy and waste good cognac) because you can do something with it. All right, wise guy, just because you're obvious is no reason for me to be.

On the other hand, I now am in possession of three perfectly foul little theories which are no good to anyone, particularly myself. They are, I hasten to add, completely fascinating and quite effective in keeping me from the more enjoyable pursuits of my abnormal existance, as laughing immoderately at a small and scabrous Irishman I happen to know, pasting bookplates in books, and not drinking beer.

I have three, but you shall know only two: the first I shall conceal, since I have a sentimental attachment for it, and since the title of the theory is much more interesting than the theory itself.

Being an inspired evangelist, in argument I invariably undertake with sublime confidence to instruct any group of more than three people not cretins or women in the more difficult concepts of political science, philosophy, economics, monetary exchange (sometimes known as the Black Mass), theosophy, and the pre-natal education of female children.

This is done by way of defense: when you casually mention that you hope to hell William Randolph Hearst does not sleep too well and is sometimes bothered by belching after meals, people glare at you and say, "Oh, you're a Communist! What would you do if

a. The Japs came over and raped your sister?

b. Your sister was nationalized?"

I used to say that I hated the bejesus out of my sister and would be tickled to death if a. *and* b. happened.

My sister got annoyed.

Anyhow, I found out that they never wait for the answer to that or the next three questions and by the time you get around to answering a question, it is invariably the one about "Well, aren't conditions in Russia the same as in Germany and Italy? Isn't there a controlled press, no free speech, curtailment of civil liberties? Isn't Russia just as nationalistic?"

The answer to that proved to be my "Wild Berry Theory of Nationalism," which is much too good for the likes of you. Three whisky sours, made not with cognac and with ice, will convince me that you are an eminently good guy, and worthy to know this gem. Mail will reach me at the *Jester* office for the next three weeks. After that, the relief bureau will be only too glad to put you in touch with me.

The second is the "Swimming Pool Theory of Communism": it goes like this, and is automatically set off by the question, "Why are you a Communist? You have lots of food to eat, a new suit with side vents, and pimples all over your chin? Nu?"

Answer: one is placed in the world, as one is placed in a swimming pool. One must make adjustments to the world, one must equate oneself with surroundings, one must assume some position of understanding to the things around. One must relate himself to the swimming pool, or sink. Sink equals die. Now, the equation to the world may be done in a number of ways, by religion, smoking opium (fill in your own) or (watch out, here it comes) by Communism. In the swimming pool you may use water wings, swim sidestroke, or use the crawl with a six-beat kick. I have found that I am most pleased in a swimming pool with the crawl with a four-beat kick, which I hope to raise to a six in short order.

The third theory doesn't seem to fit in anywhere, but I hope to steer conversation that way shortly, to use "The Post-Toasties Theory of the Social Contract." I shall do it subtly, by saying, "What do you think of the Social Contract?"

The social contract is when everybody gets together and says we will surrender some of our rights if everybody else does so that we shall not kill everybody off immediately. (If this lucid explanation is not enough, go read the books yourself.) The difficulty is that it works by majority rule and you wonder who started the first meeting to decide about majority rule and whether majority rule was decided by majority rule.

Now, if you will run out and get a box of Post-Toasties you will see a very pretty picture on the front showing a girl holding a box of Post-Toasties which has a picture on the front showing a girl holding a box of Post-Toasties which has a picture on the front and so on with a deep brreath.

This is also handy for explaining infinity.

Now get the hell out of here and leave me alone.

Robert Paul Smith/*Columbia Jester*

PREFACE FOR PROFESSORS

BY PROFESSOR HERBERT L. JACOBSON

(Fill in the blanks and save yourself hours of trouble thinking one up. Guaranteed for any textbook you can write.)

The need has long been felt for a modern text which would at once satisfy the requirements of the second year high school and the first year of college studies in . . . . while providing a non-technical introduction for the intelligent layman.

In this work the author has avoided alike the conservative stand of Professor . . . . and the radicalism of Mr. . . . . because he believes that only through an unbiased exposition of the relevant facts, rather than through a controversial development of untried theories, can the ultimate truth be ascertained. However, the question of . . . ., as yet unresolved in the public mind, has been omitted advisedly as better suited to the public forum than to a factual examination.

This text is, however, truly *modern*. Material on . . . ., so prominent in older, physically cumbersome and mentally unwieldy works on this subject, has not been included, so that the beginner may not be discouraged at the outset by the sheer ponderosity of the treatment. Chapter . . . ., on . . . ., is, so far as is known to the author, the first discussions of these new developments to be published in a book of like scope.

Attention is directed to the treatment of . . . . in chapter . . . ., which, by the prefixion of a brief review of its historical development, makes the erstwhile difficult subject easy to comprehend. Particularly useful to the student will prove the set of questions on the context appended to each chapter. These are designed to discourage rote learning and to encourage the gradual development of facility in synthesis. Similarly the full chapter outlines to be found in the Appendix should not be used to shirk work, but rather to stimulate original thinking along guided lines.

The author's wife interpreted and typed his notes. Miss . . . ., the Headmistress of Miss . . . . . .'s School for Young Ladies, read the proof and offered many helpful criticisms and suggestions. The charming librarian of the college, Miss . . . ., graciously worked overtime to supply most of the books listed in the extensive bibliography.

In conclusion, the author wishes to affirm that the sins of omission and commission are his alone, and to beg the indulgence of the serious-minded reader for those few humorous anecdotes he has included as illustrative material. . . . .
College, 18 . . . . ., 19 . . . . .

Herbert L. Jacobson/Columbia Jester

Summer

Sumer is icumen in
(Lhude whistle traffique coppe)
Sparrewe peepeth, poodle leapeth
Aardvark sleepeth in the zoo;
Sumer is icumen in
Murie sing cuccu.
Busse upon the Dryve ironne
Sauntre saylors in the sunne,
Traffique maketh toote and screeche,
Longen folk for Brighton Beache,
Sumer bringeth awful dinne,
Shut-up dmne cuccu!

Robert Lax/Columbia Jester

▼

HE: Baby, I can read you like a book.
SHE: OK, but lay off the Braille method.

Princeton Tiger

"Amos and Andy Who?"
San Diego State Cacti

Continued from page 101

guised as a small girl.

Antonio. How now, friends.
All. How now.
Enter Fanny, still disguised as a sailor.
Fanny. What ho.
All. What ho.
Enter Sebastian, *disguised as himself.*
Sebastian. And what, pray tell, is all
This fil de ral and fal da ral about?
All. We should know?[12]

[12]As it stands, this is the last extant line of the play, the rest being happily lost. The way things are going, however, it is easy to deduce that Lady Margaret will marry Antonio, Sebastian will marry Fanny, the clown will marry Mistress Thickly, and the rest will just take off their disguises and go home, if they are wise, about in the middle of the epilogue that Lucius will be giving.

Nathaniel Benchley/Harvard Lampoon

We must mention the gigolo in the leper colony who was doing quite well until his business started falling off.

North Carolina Buccaneer

▼

And then there was the man on relief who was so accustomed after years of unemployment to having everything done for him that he went out and married a widow with three children.

NYU Medley

▼

A traveling salesman was caught in a storm. There was no shelter in sight but a farmhouse some distance down the road. He knocked at the door. The old farmer came to the door. He looked at the wet salesman.

"I'm sorry. My daughter's not home," he said, and slammed the door.

CCNY Mercury

▼

Wabbits have a funny face,
Their private life is a disgrace.
Oo'd be surprised if oo but knew
The awful fings that wabbits do—
And often, too.

Yale Record

▼

Then there was the guy who had a dirty joke tatooed on his forehead—and was his face read!

Arizona Kitty-Kat

"Sir, I've lost my amoeba."

John J. Sullivan/*Yale Record*

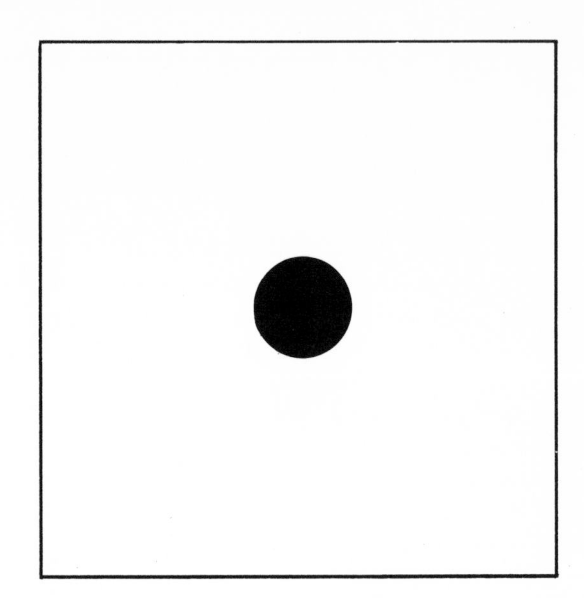

NOW to explain why the cartoon shown on this page and drawn by a member of the *Gargoyle* staff is the best in the issue:

All the primary aspects of good cartooning considered, the cartoon displayed here is the most perfect of the whole shebang. It has everything a good designer could pray for.

Balance

We have already proved its balance since it has been on a *Garg* desk for three years and shown absolutely no signs of falling to the floor.

Unity

The principal of unity is one of singleness of thought. Without a doubt an observer will not be hindered by confliction of unity in this cartoon. The spot in our cartoon is a perfect example of unity. Note the marvelous arrangement.

Emphasis

In emphasis the important element in the cartoon is situated so that it will make its great appeal to the sight of the observer. Certainly you will agree that the dot is immediately seen and is given doggone emphasis.

Rhythm

This is the re-occurring stress of a line or color or something so that a rhythm is formed. Look at the cartoon. Now blink your eyes and notice the re-occurring spot. Pretty, isn't it?

Proportion

Notice how carefully centered the spot is. On all sides of the spot is an equal amount of whiteness. The proportion is perfect. *Mon Dieu*! fine stuff!

Harmony

This is a blending of the elements in the composition. Note how well the dot blends into itself. Note how the white blends. Everything blends all over.

Grace

This is typified by an economy of force and a display of just plain grace. There certainly was an economy of effort used when this cartoon was made. The spot is a perfect circle. If nothing else this is a composition of grace . . . pure and *simple*.

And that is how good cartoons are made. . . .

Richard Humphries/*Michigan Gargoyle*

Bad start - be explicit
Say "eighty-seven"

"fathers"?

Fourscore and seven years ago, our fathers brought forth upon this continent a new nation, conceived in liberty, and dedicated to the proposition that all men are created equal.

Now we are engaged in a great civil war, testing whether that nation, or any nation so conceived and so dedicated, can long endure. We are met on a great battlefield of that war. We have come to dedicate a portion of that field as a final resting place for those who here gave their lives that that nation might live. It is altogether fitting and proper that we should do this.

But in a larger sense we cannot dedicate, we cannot consecrate, we cannot hallow this ground. The brave men, living and dead, who struggled here, have consecrated it far above our poor power to add or detract. The world will little note nor long remember what we say here; but it can never forget what they did here. It is for us, the living, rather, to be dedicated here to the unfinished work which they who fought here have thus far so nobly advanced. It is rather for us to be here dedicated to the great task remaining before us: that from these honored dead we take increased devotion to that cause for which they gave the last full measure of devotion; that we here highly resolve that these dead shall not have died in vain; that this nation under God, shall have a new birth of freedom; and that government of the people, by the people, and for the people, shall not perish from the earth.

repetition of sound

bad word

"gigantic" or tremendous would be better

Too many "we's"

you said this once

tr - Rule 194, p. 6

Too many monosyllabic words

very trite sentence

??? meaning?

Use another word

spelling!

Wrong word - you mean "subtract"

awkward

Rule 194, p. 6

make up your mind

bad

almost unintelligible

too many small words - strike it out

(trite word use "colossal"

Rule 74, p. 90

sp.

sp

change around

Not bad. Too much repetition. There are six "thats" in the last sentence alone. You use verb "dedicate" six times. More variety in the choice; your words are too simple. Try again - you are improving.

C-

Professor Glunk

Doodles Weaver/*Stanford Chaparral*

When in Lafayette

There is an old soldier who lives down in the circle of Easton. Once in a great while a shrill blast from his trumpet cracks through the air. He does this not only to show that he is still alert, but also in proof of an old tradition. The tradition that he has kept going for Lafayette is to blow the trumpet every time a virtuous young girl goes past his post. The last time the old soldier blew his horn, which was many many years ago, the girl about whom the note was blown turned and with a twinkle in her eye said: "You think you know everything, don't you?"

Lafayette Lyre

Out of the Depths

Here's one I just resurrected out of the ash barrel, where it has resided for several years. If you still remember it then you shouldn't be in college, because everyone is dead that first heard this one.

It seems that there was a cigar store on a corner that had two of these automatic lighters. You know the kind, where you pull a little chain and a flame spurts up. One of these was at the back of the store and the other near the door. Every morning a little insignificant-looking fellow would walk into the store just at nine o'clock, go to the back, light a big black cigar, and then walk out. He never bought anything.

After this had kept up for several weeks the proprietor grew tired of it, and determined to put a stop to the practice. Accordingly, the next morning, when the little man entered and lit his stogie, the owner fixed him with a baleful glance and said, "Say, look here. There is a lighter at the front of the store. Why don't you use that?"

The small fellow cast a surprised look in his direction, and said calmly, "You don't know who I am!" Then he walked out.

The proprietor was somewhat startled, but tried again the next day, only to receive the same answer. Then on the third morning he called for a showdown. The little man appeared promptly at nine and walked to the back of the store, where he lit his cigar.

"Wait a minute," bellowed the boss. "I told you twice before that there was a lighter at the front of the store. Why don't you use it?"

Again came the calm reply, "You don't know who I am."

"All right, just who are you?"

"Why, I'm the fellow that lights my cigar with the lighter at the back of your store."

And it wasn't until then that the owner really realized who the little man was.

Brown Jug

Most People Don't Realize

1. That collegiate flivvers have been "out" for at least three years.
2. That slickers and pennants are almost never seen on college campuses.
3. That balloon trousers haven't been worn since the Harding Administration.
4. That most collegiate jokes are written by people who wear slickers and balloon trousers and ride in collegiate flivvers.

Wisconsin Octopus

"He still works out: Needs Physical Ed. credit to graduate."

Thomas Merton/Columbia Jester

HE: I passed your house last night.
SHE: Thank you.

Northwestern Purple Parrot

▼

"There are four requisites to a good short story," explained the English prof to the story-writing class. "Brevity, a reference to religion, some association with the royalty, and an illustration of modesty. Now, with these four things in mind, I will give you thirty minutes to write a story."

Ten minutes later the hand of an ambitious young writer was raised.

"That is fine, Mr. White," she complimented him. "And now read your story to the class."

The student read: " 'My Gawd,' said the Countess, 'take your hand off my knee.' "

USC Wampus

Christmas Greetings

TO MUSSOLINI

We hail thee, Europe's only king;
You've tact and grace, for all your strife,
And sex-appeal, and everything.
But Lord, I'd hate to be your wife.

Williams Purple Cow

Men Only Read This!

Out of ninety thousand women there will be eighty-nine thousand nine hundred ninety-four who will read this. The other six will be blind.

Georgia Tech Yellow Jacket

▼

"How do you like your new girl friend?"
"Sofa, pretty good."

Brown Jug

"Know why I call my gal willow?"
"No, why?"
"Only God can make a tree."

Robert C. Ruark, Jr./*North Carolina Buccaneer*

▼

JAILER (to prisoner): You have an hour of grace.
PRISONER: OK. Bring her in.

Colgate Banter

▼

The husband who knows where his wife keeps her nickels has nothing on the husband who knows where the maid's quarters are.

Ohio Green Goat

▼

SENIOR: Freshman, pace nervously back and forth. I've been called to the Dean's Office.

Oklahoma Whirlwind

▼

"My boy, do you think you can love two girls at once?"
"Yes sir. Immediately."

Wisconsin Octopus

▼

Twinkle, twinkle, little star,
How I wonder where you are—
Way up in the sky so high,
Like a goddam electric light bulb.

Cornell Widow

▼

"Could you love me in spite of myopia?"
"Let's see your opia and I'll let you know."

Brown Jug

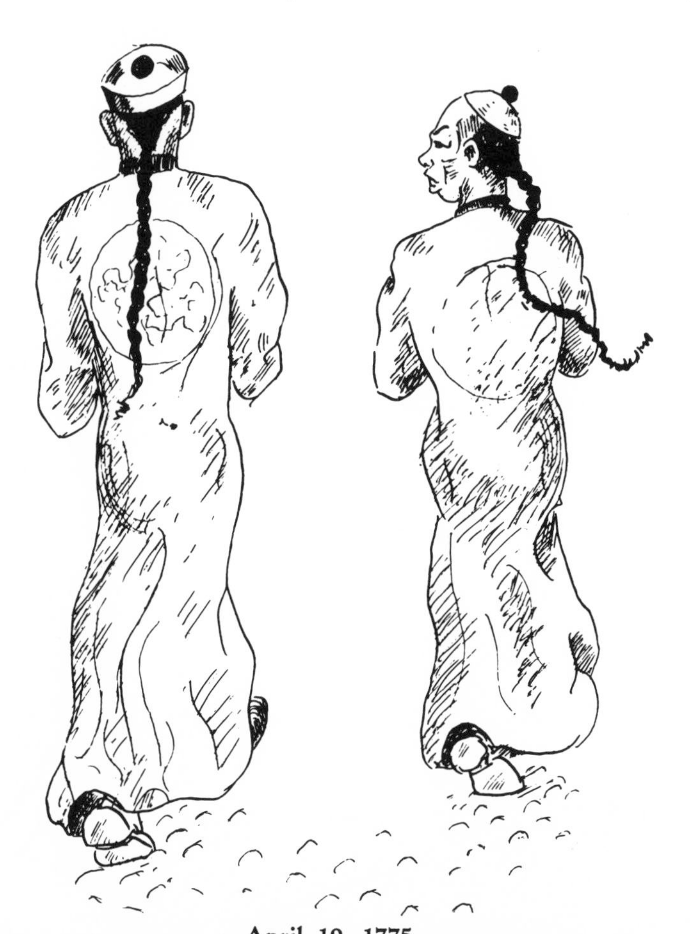

April 19, 1775
"Funny, I could've sworn I heard a shot."

Nathaniel Benchley/*Harvard Lampoon*

RASSLERS AND RUSSLERS

Gilman Gist, Jr./*Stanford Chaparral*

Professor Hart gets off a story about a young English teacher who began teaching in the grades. She opened her first class by laying down the law, telling the kids what would be expected of them, and above all, what would not be permitted. She said, "There are two words that I positively will not allow anyone to use in this class. They are 'lousy' and 'screwy'."

She paused a moment to let it sink in, but one little fellow got impatient and asked, "What are the words, teacher?"

California Pelican

▼

Household Hint

Left-handed teacups may be converted to right-handed ones by turning them around.

Virginia Polytechnic Institute Skipper

"I see by the paper that nine professors and one student were killed in a wreck."

"Poor chap."

St. John's Analyst

▼

ELDERLY LADY: Do you know my daughter, Mae?

STUDE: No, I don't. Thanks for the tip!

Wisconsin Octopus

"CHILDREN, LET US SPRAY!"

Ohio Ohioan

My parents told me not to smoke
—I don't.
Nor listen to a dirty joke
—I don't.
They make it clear I mustn't wink
At pretty girls or even think
Of an intoxicating drink
—I don't.
To flirt or dance is very wrong
—I don't.
Wild youth chases wine, women and song.
I kiss no girls, not even one.
I do not know how it is done.
You wouldn't think I had much fun.
—I DON'T!

Amherst Lord Jeff

▼

Beef stew:
Here today,
Here again tomorrow.

Harvard Lampoon

THROUGH THE WAR 1940 ★ 1949

HOME SWEET HOME

HERE's the set-up, which is common enough . . . A soldier returns home after three or more years in a faraway place and finds that his wife has a kid of two.

Let's see what would happen in Germany . . .

(The soldier steps through a hole in the wall of his house and embraces his wife.)

FRAU: Mein Gott! Liebchen! where have you been?

HANS: All over. I have so much to tell you . . . first we went to New Jersey, where I met Hans' brother-in-law. The Bund had me on the honorary committee . . .

FRAU: We don't think of politics any more around here, Liebchen. But what have you got in the bag?

HANS *(opening the bag):* Just a few little knick-knacks we were allowed to buy in the PX at Fort Monmouth . . . a Zippo lighter, officers' pinks, cigars, chocolate, cameras, electrically heated boots . . . we had a helluva time getting the boots . . . they was going to send them to their infantry in Italy but we went on a hunger strike and they let us have them so we'd eat.

FRAU: A fine mess you boys made of the fighting down in Africa.

HANS: We was robbed.

FRAU: Thank the Führer somebody in this household had sense enough to provide for the future. Look what I've got to show you! *(She produced a little extrancum.)*

HANS: What a front-line fighter he'll make! Look at that back!

FRAU: Over my dead body. My child's not going to be cannon fodder. He's going to have a career. He's going to use his head. I can see him now, sitting at the switchboard of a transatlantic rocket-bomb station.

HANS: Liebchen!

(Slow curtain)

So much for that. Now for the country of pleasure and adaptability, France. The wife, let's call her Josie, is rocking the baby in her lap and crooning *Alouette, Je te Plumerai*—a lullaby which instills aggressive gallantry in the Gallic male at a time when the Anglo-Saxon boy is trying to get away from women. A door opens, and here is Renard, back from the class of '39.

JOSIE: Cheri, embrasse-moi!

(They do this at length.)

RENARD: My cabbage, my soup of various sorts, my old bottle, embrasse-moi.

(The curtain falls and rises again after a decent interval)

RENARD: Mon Dieu! What's that? (He points to the child.)

JOSIE: A bagatelle. It is my infant. A nothing.

RENARD: How could you be so careless?

JOSIE: I don't know, Cheri. One weeps; one goes to Church; one despairs that France will rise again. Then the fine day dawns. Liberty! The feelings burst into flower. It is Spring. The stars shine on the Cathedral of Sacre Coeur; the Seine is singing . . . and there one finds oneself, with the rabbits, producing.

RENARD *(shrugging his shoulders):* Eh bien. Who can prevent love? What is the child's name?

JOSIE: I have name him simply, after his father.

RENARD: Alors?

JOSIE: The Four Fifty-fourth Infantry Regiment and Attached Units.

Let's see how one of His Majesty's Fusiliers, returning to the hamlet of Little Bundlemonley, Hants, England, might receive the news that his union had been blessed during his absence in Burma. Sally (half of the women in England are named Sally) is reading the newspaper the fish-and-chips were wrapped in as Hugh enters . . .

HUGH: I say old girl, bit of a surprise, what?

SALLY: You didn't 'arf give me a turn. So sudden like.

HUGH: Was in Burma, you know. Beastly place. Full of natives.

(Sally stirs a pot of tea on the stove. A faint wail comes from the nursery.)

SALLY: That must be Alf.

HUGH: Oh.

SALLY: 'E gets upset when 'e don't get 'is bitters regular like a tram. Though the vicar's wife she does say it does 'im no deal of 'arm.

HUGH: Oh, I see. It's a child. Whose is it?

SALLY: Yours. A little smasher 'e is, too.

HUGH: I say, that's rather thick, isn't it? I mean, after all?

SALLY: I suppose it's more mine, like.

HUGH: Well you know . . . I mean . . . you haven't exactly been playing cricket, have you?

SALLY: 'Ere, 'ave a cup of tay.

HUGH *(taking it):* I say, this is a bit of all right.

(Curtain)

And last, our own Jackson returns to the hearth, having done more than his share to make other men's wives happy. He finds that someone has done him a favor, too.

The heroic American male is not apt to take anything lying down. But there's the American female . . . that's the catch. In this case we've made her a Barnard graduate, which isn't fair to the millions of normal women in our Republic, but anyhow here goes . . .

JACKSON: If you don't get that blasted brat into a basket and over to the orphanage inside of two minutes, I'll break your goddamned neck!

MARY: You've really been acting so strangely since you got back, dear. Of course I knew what to expect from articles I read in the *Reader's Digest,* but it's difficult to be tolerant when you go out of your way deliberately to embarrass me.

JACKSON: Embarrass, hell! I ain't started yet. By God, I think I *will* break your-------neck. It costs a lot less than a divorce. Quicker, too.

MARY: Of course, your ego's been starved so long you simply must find a compensation factor. But this kind of bickering is on such a low animal level! I'm willing to forget everything you've said. I know you're tired. You feel insecure. You know it'll be years before you approximate my earning power. All this has unbalanced you. But I'm willing to treat the whole incident as closed.

(Jackson picks up a souvenir machine pistol.)

JACKSON:------*!!!!*

MARY: You've got to learn to be polite, darling. After all, we're civilized people, and just because you had some bad experiences over in Europe you can't expect life to stand still.

(He presses the trigger and keeps it down.)

MARY *(from the floor):* And don't get blood all over the walls! It's almost impossible to have the painters come up nowadays. Service is simply horrible. Of course, you wouldn't realize it, but . . .

(Curtain)

Louis Simpson/*Columbia Jester*

Are you
Maeb eht no*

You are, if you get tongue-tied when you meet a cute cookie! Or worse yet, if you stoop to "weather talk!" *Get on the beam* right, fellow! Start off from third base! Offer that choice bit of calico a yummy Life Saver. She'll be keen on them (and you).

*** "On the beam" backwards**

5¢

P. S. ***Just in case this friendship ripens—Life Savers keep your (and her) breath kissably fresh!***

Each month the makers of Life Savers award a carton of their yummy product to the winner of the Jester joke of the month contest. This month's lucky candy sucker is:

JASON EPSTEIN
1005 Livingston

A prominent Bishop was sitting in a box at the Opera House. The low cut of the women's gowns were extremely daring. After looking around the house through an opera glass, one of the ladies leaned over to the Bishop and said: "Honestly, Bishop, have you ever seen anything like it in your life?"

"Never, Madam, never since I was weaned," replied the Bishop gravely.

Jason Epstein / *Columbia Jester*

HIP HIP HURRAH

A SHORT PLAY TRANSLATED FROM THE OLD ENGLISH

DRAMATIS PERSONAE

JOHN BULL ....a Puritan
NELLIE BULL ....his wife, not a Puritan
MASTER PERCY SMELLWELL ....a gallant
ISABELLA BELLAFRONT ....a tumbler[1]

NEIGHBORS, FRIENDS, SERVANTS

The Scene—London[2]

Enter JOHN BULL followed by his wife, NELLIE, without shoes.[3]

JOHN: Fiddlesticks![4] What's the hour is it?[5]

NELLIE: Shall I ask Master Percy? He has a most excellent sun dial.[6] (She calls.)[7]

JOHN: That rogue![8] A plague o' his house.[9] Why only last weekend I saw him in northern London[10] with that hell-cat[11] of bad fame,[12] Isabella Bellafront. She's a wanton woman.[13]

Enter MASTER PERCY SMELLWELL smoking a pipe.[14]

PERCY: Hi, ho! What's new?[15] *(aside)* Sticks and fiddles,[16] what a pretty wench. I'll buss[17] her yet. *Bonjour, mes amis!*[18]

JOHN: Enough of that sweet tongue. Let's be Elizabethan here.[19] We would inquire of you the time of day.

PERCY: Oh, 'tis the feed-bag hour as the crow wings.[20]

JOHN: I must be gone for a moment to see a gallant about a canine for the hunt.[21] *(Exeunt.)*

PERCY: Is your tongue asleep in your mouth?[22]

NELLIE: Hello.[23]

PERCY: Ah! A voice from the wilderness.[24] *(aside)* My, she's a queen.[25]

NELLIE: Must you keep that infernal machine? 'Tis like a fish market in Bristol.[26] *(aside)* My, he's a sharp one.[27]

PERCY: I will it away.[28] Ah, Bess,[29] you are lovely. *Ouvrez la fenêtre! Fermez la porte.*[30] (He kisses her.)

NELLIE: Oh! What if someone saw you do that. More! More.[31]

(Enter NEIGHBORS, FRIENDS and SERVANTS making mocking gestures.)

PERCY: You peasants, flies[32] and hot-loined[33] foreigners[34]. Go to Hades![35] Go jump in the river.[36]

(Exeunt NEIGHBORS, FRIENDS and SERVANTS by several doors.[37])

PERCY: 'Tis too crowded here. Let us go to my rooms. I'll show you my Hogarth prints.[38]

(Exeunt PERCY and NELLIE by one door and enter JOHN and ISABELLA BELLAFRONT by another.[39])

JOHN: Ah! We are alone. *(aside)* This is duck soup.[40] (He kisses her.)

ISABELLA: More! More![41] (She begins to sing.)[42]

JOHN: Silence thy tongue.[43] Do you want people to hear you?

(Enter and exeunt FRIENDS, SERVANTS and NEIGHBORS making mocking gestures.)[44]

[1] A harlot.
[2] Probably northern London as later dialogue reveals.
[3] Milton adds a dress. This seems logical.
[4] A popular Elizabethan oath.
[5] I.e., What time is it?
[6] Probably a watch. Longfellow suggests that she may mean a Grandfather's clock.
[7] Probably through an open window as Alexander Graham Bell suggests.
[8] Ruffian.
[9] This carries a double meaning since the black plague was, at that time, sweeping through London.
[10] See note 2.
[11] Witch, hag.
[12] Reputation.
[13] I.e., she's not wanted in this house.
[14] Raleigh had just introduced this fad.
[15] A popular Elizabethan greeting.
[16] See note 4.
[17] Kiss.
[18] *Hello, my friends!* De Maupassant suggests that Percy was probably educated in France.
[19] I.e., Let's talk English in this house.
[20] I.e., It's time for lunch, 12 o'clock.
[21] I.e., I must go and see a man about a dog.
[22] I.e., Aren't you going to say hello?
[23] See note 15.
[24] Harry Emerson Fosdick suggests that Percy must have been a very religious man.
[25] Hussy or perhaps *a hot number,* as Thomas Manville suggests.
[26] I.e., Must you smoke that pipe? It stinks.
[27] A dandy.
[28] Kittredge adds *throw*.
[29] He probably means Nellie. Rodgers and Hart believe that he is referring to Queen Elizabeth. Because of rumors concerning the Spanish Armada, there was a great national feeling in England at this time.
[30] *Open the window! Close the door!* He probably does this in an effort to drive the tobacco smoke out. Cotton Mather suggests that he is so overcome by Nellie's beauty that he utters French, the romantic language.
[31] Sir Thomas More, famous English author *(Utopia)* during the reign of Henry VIII. Byron suggests that Nellie desired to have Percy repeat his previous action.
[32] Probably Spanish flies in this sense.
[33] Lustful. See note 32.
[34] A pun on the American colonists at Plymouth.
[35] Hell.
[36] Dr. Johnson suggests the Thames.
[37] Coleridge believes that some of them probably left by means of the open window. That seems unlikely since it was a sheer drop of twenty feet.
[38] Etchings.
[39] Keats adds *door*.

(Enter NELLIE and PERCY.)[45]

NELLIE: Oh, my husband, in the arms of that two-shilling[46] camp follower.[47] That woman of the streets.[48] How came she here?[49]

PERCY: *(aside)* This Isabella is with the illness of Venus.[50] How well I know. (To Master John) Come, sir, your lovely wife has missed you. Do not associate[51] with Isabella.

ISABELLA: Phi![52] I am as pure as Queen Bess.[53]

NELLIE: Come, husband, let us do the May dance.[54]

JOHN: Yes, let us dance.

ISABELLA: Oh, la, la![55]

PERCY: Roger![56] Thence to the Globe.[57]

(They all join hands and dance to the music of a hidden orchestra.)[58]

ISABELLA: More! More![59]

(Enter NEIGHBORS, FRIENDS and SERVANTS who join in the dance making mocking gestures.)[60]

CURTAIN[61]

[40]A stock expression. Although, according to Fannie Farmer, duck soup was not introduced into England until the time of Queen Victoria, who first served it at a banquet in honor of Disraeli.

[41]See note 31. The Byronic interpretation is accepted here since Isabella could not read.

[42]Probably *God Save the King,* but Emerson suggests that this could not be true since Elizabeth was then in power. He believed it to be a line from an obscene ditty.

[43]Shut up.

[44]Elizabethan audiences delighted in seeing their fellow citizens, hence the second appearance of these persons.

[45]She and Percy probably entered amid the confusion.

[46]About twenty-five cents or two bits as Mark Twain suggests.

[47]A popular occupation of Elizabethan women.

[48]Probably a prostitute. Louisa May Alcott suggests that this may mean she was a street dancer as prostitutes were women of houses.

[49]Harvard and Folger copies read, *How can she hear?* This seems unlikely in this case.

[50]A popular Elizabethan disease.

[51]Accented on the first syllable.

[52]A letter in the Greek alphabet. Banta suggests that this shows Isabella's great fraternal spirit.

[53]Here she refers to Queen Elizabeth, known to the British as "the virgin queen." This myth has been widely circulated in historical textbooks. According to the Earl of Essex it was entirely false. See note 29.

[54]A popular English dance usually performed on May day although it was popular throughout the year.

[55]I.e.,that's a good idea.

[56]This probably means yes. Edgar A. Guest suggests that he might have been referring to Sir Roger Mayfair, who originally composed the May dance.

[57]A local Elizabethan theatre. Probably some play by Shakespeare was there at the time.

[58]The 1620 folio does not mention a hidden orchestra. It was added by Warner brothers in the 1947 folio. James Petrillo suggests that the orchestra was hidden because it played so badly.

[59]This refers to the dance. See note 41.

[60]Evidently they did not exeunt through the window. See note 37.

[61]This was added by Macy.

Lafayette Marquis

"Hey, bud, which way to West Falmouth?"

Oliver E. Allen/*Harvard Lampoon*

MURDER

At 13 rue de Ditoot

HAMHOCK BONES and I were huddled in his study one night looking through some back issues of *Esquire*. Outside the wind was howling a melancholy song that sounded like a voice tearfully crying "Open the Door, Richard." The rain hammered the nails back into the roof, and the flashes of lightning made weird shadows on the Vargas girl. I wondered as I watched Hamhock puff on his pipe if the track would be muddy tomorrow.

"Hamhock," I said, "what is the strangest case you have ever been on?"

The great detective reluctantly looked up from his magazine and answered:

My dear Whatson, it's strange you should ask that, because I was saving the story for my next movie. But if you promise not to tell the Falcon, I'll relate it to you.

The crime took place at 13 rue de Ditoot. You're familiar with the street, no doubt. It's where all the ghost writers for college professors live. They eke out a bare existence writing textbooks. Instead of getting paid by the word, they get paid by the pound; and some of the books have been known to weigh between forty and fifty pounds.

Well, the crime took place in an old abandoned "U" car. When I forced my way in with the help of an acetylene torch and a street car token, I discovered the blighter hanging from the strap of the car. Immediately my suspicions were aroused because there were plenty of seats available.

His wrists were cut up to the elbows and there was a medium to medium-large sized bowie knife in his chest. I shouted, "General Studies '54," and when there was no response I surmised the poor chap was dead.

It really was an amazing crime. There were more clues than were necessary to solve the murder. As a matter of fact, I used some of the surplus clues for my next radio program, "The Hound of the Town and Gown."

I examined the body closely. On his chest, in red paint, were painted the words, "This was a Dirty Bruin." A stomach pump was lying on the floor with the inscription "Compliments of the Student Union" on it. Off in a corner I observed a book that had fallen to the floor. It was Seed and McRorkle's fascinating *Reading in Execution*. As I was riffling through the pages, a gray-haired old lady of at least seventy handed me a transfer and sat down.

"Aha, an old woman!" I exclaimed.

"Who'd you expect, the Yearling?" she spat back.

"What do you know of this crime?" I queried. But before she could answer, a man in a white jacket with the words "Good Humor" sewed on his hat came in and sat down.

"Does this here car go to Pershing Square?" he asked.

I was about to answer when a young, beautiful blonde elbowed her way past me and screamed when she saw the body.

"Oh, damn," she cried, "there goes my skiing date. It's just too, too awful. Missing the skiing and all. You just don't know."

There they were, Whatson. I knew one of them was the killer. Who was it? Was it Whistler's mother, or the popsicle man or the blonde? I studied them closely, observing every little detail. I concentrated particularly on the blonde —she looked very suspicious. She was the only one who seemed upset. But then I pointed to the old lady and said:

"You did it!"

She broke down and confessed.

"Sure I did it," she cried. "He gave me his fraternity pin, and when I saw him with another woman I flew into a jealous rage. I called him every name I could think of. I called him a non-org, and a journalism major, and names even worse than that. He raged back at me. He called me the Bag of the Month and the girl he'd like most to be seen dead with. But when he called me a second-semester pledge, that was going too far. I did it and I'm glad."

"But Bones," I asked, "how in the world did you know it was the old lady?"

Hamhock stroked his chin.

"It was very elementary, my dear Whatson," he said. "The streetcar transfer that she handed me was covered with crib notes for a Man and Civ test."

"And you reasoned . . ."

"That anyone who will cheat in a Man and Civ test will commit any crime, even murder. It was simple. She had a short trial; the jury was out only two minutes. The judge sentenced her to a full semester of English Literature 60b, but when the jury recommended clemency, he changed the sentence and sent her to the gas chamber.

"That's about all, Whatson, except that the 'U' car has now been put back into service."

Art Buchwald / *USC Wampus*

Father Jesse

(With apologies to Lewis Carroll and Professor Wrench)

"You are old, Father Jesse," the young man said,
"And ungiven to strenuous sports.
Do you think it quite right at your age to appear
Cutting grass, while clad only in shorts?"

"My boy," said the sage, "I'm a radical man,
of political patience bereft;
So why do you ask if my actions are right,
When you know that I tend to the left?"

"You are old," said the youth, "as I mentioned before,
And you wear both moustache and goatee.
Though a staunch whisker-lover, I cannot discover
Whatever their purpose might be."

"Young man, the inflation which saddles the nation
Makes purchasing luxuries tough;
I grew the moustache since it tickles my nose,
And saves me the price of my snuff."

"You are old, Father Jesse, and your stately white locks
Are worn in a net ornamentric.
Do you fear that the populace near
May consider you slightly eccentric?"

"Young man, your impertinence borders pervertinence!
I am shocked at your impolite ease!
So be gone! But remember the source of my acts
Is whether or not I damn please!"

Saul Gellerman and Flash Fairfield/*Missouri Showme*

HOLIDAY IN MEXICO

Produced by: Pobre Pictures
Written by: Arturo Buchwald
Technical adviser for Mexican scenes: Senor Alonzo Heex

Senors Tanquary, Unruh, and Flynn wait for the gran bull-throwing to begeen.

Eet ees the day of the gran bullfight. For many miles around the peons and pesos have come to the Ciudad de Troy to see the bulls and have wan beeg fiesta. The Ciudad de Troy ees known for eets bull throwers, an no wan wants to miss the big event.

All day long the Senors de Seegma Nu have been swallowing Tequila an having wan beeg time. The Bueno Humor man, he ees much busy, and so ees the speegots at the Nuevo o Uno, wheech has been running all day. Een the square many bonitas senoritas are walking around with their mantillas steecking out. Eet is wan beeg excitement.

Suddenly a fight breaks out between the senoritas from the Casa de Tri Delt and the Casa de Alpha Gam. Eet ees over a man and we hear them say:

"Peeg of a Phi Seeg, he ees ours."

To which the others spit back, "Dog of a Delt, we saw heem first."

"Swine of a Sae, he ees our."

"Toad of a Theta Xi, how can you say that?"

Tearfully the girls pull out each other's hair. The leetle fellow whom the senoritas are fighting over ees Don Juan Winn, a great bull thrower. Eet ees a fight to the end, and some of the mantillas have taken mucho beating.

The bull ring ees on the Calle e 28. Already the great and near great have arrived. In the gran box ees the Grande Presidente Senor Amigo Wildman. Senor Don Hillings, once the biggest bull thrower in all the Ciudad de Troy, ees shining the presidente's boots. But wait. Now the presidente ees shining Senor Hillings' boots.

Eeet ees custom of political party now in power, known as the Todo Notra Epsilona, to do thees to each other.

Een the boxes are many bonitas senoritas. Wan half of the arena has been reserved for the Casa de Delta Gamma pledges. Een other boxes are Casa de ADPi, Casa de AOPi, Casa de Delta Zeta, and Casa de O Mi Gawd. The best seats are for the Don Squires and the Don Knights. The peons are behind the gold posts.

The arena eet ees filled. The bull fighters have already sold their teekets for many centavos and are reech man. Eet ees sell-out crowd.

The gran presidente makes a speech weeshing everywan the best of luck especially the bull throwers from the Todo Notra Epsilon party. The senorita smiles at the happy peeple. Across from the gran presidente een a box seets the great bull thrower Senor Jose Unruh. To hees right seets Senor Jose Flynn who ees dressed een a checked sombrero, and to the right of heem ees Senor Tanquary who ees known as a revolutioniste. Every wan ees here to see what weel happen.

The bugle eet ees blown and the bull thrower Don Juan Winn enters the ring. He bows to the crowd and as he does so the bull comes from behind and gores heem een the pants. As they say een the Unido Estado, he could not make the grades.

Than wan by wan the bull throwers go down unteel the beeg bull fight ees about to take place. Eet ees between Don Juan Davis the great bull master and the great bullhead bull-loaded bull of the pampas Hynsonbiter. A long time ago Hynsonbiter had brains gored out, but he steel has beeg body an' all the fans boo heem. He ees meanest bull een all the pampas.

Don Juan Davis shakes a red sweater at Hynsonbiter. The bull rushes forward madly and dives at thee sweater. He meeses and a laugh goes up from the arena. Eet ees from Senor Anderson de La Prensa. The guards drag heem out. Eet ees against the law to laugh at bull fight.

Again Don Juan Davis taunts the bull. The bull he ees so stupid he runs straight eento cement wall. The bull he keeps banging hees head against the wall until he ees senseless. The victor ees Don Juan Davis King of the Bull Throwing Pampas. The senoritas throw heem flowers, and he eats them. The peecture ends as Senor Hillings jumps from the box and starts shining boots of Don Juan Davis.

Art Buchwald/*USC Wampus*

STORY FOR WEE ONES

Once upon a time in a land far, far away, there lived a little lad who wanted only one thing for Christmas. That thing was a sexy.

He had heard his brothers talking about sexies, and he had been led to believe a sexy was a very desirable thing. And so on the night before Christmas he sent a letter to Santa Claus saying: "Dear Mr. Claus, please, Mr. Claus, I have been a very good boy all year and there is nothing I would rather have for Christmas than a sexy. If you love me at all, Old Nick, oh boy, send me a sexy for Christmas—for God's sake."

Now when Mr. Claus received this letter he was deeply touched, and so he set all his little gnomes to work making the finest sexy in the world for this little boy. They painted the sexy in all sorts of bright colors with lipstick and pancake and leg make-up and eye shadow and eyebrow pencil. Then Mr. Claus put the sexy in his bag and hopped in his sled and went tearing off over the roof tops like dammit.

When he got to the little boy's house he popped down the chimney, and what should he find but two stockings hung up over the fireplace. Santa placed his finger aside of his nose and remarked, "Not such a dumb kid." So he put the sexy into the two stockings and popped up the chimney quick as a flash.

The next day the dawn broke a steely gray, but this did not bother the small boy at all. He went tearing downstairs. When he saw his sexy he let out a joyous squeal, and started to tear his sexy apart to find out how it was put together. After he had it all apart he could not find out how to put it back together; so he threw it away. All of which goes to prove that a sexy does one no good unless one knows how it is made.

Bob Symons/*Stanford Chaparral*

Harvard Lampoon

LITTLE JOHN: I don't like Suzie. Her neck's dirty.
LITTLE JIM: Her does?

Purdue Rivet

Lamentations

OF THE TIMES AND CUSTOMS

On Monday he started to talk about what's coming up on the test:
Osmosis, hypnosis,
Psychosis, neurosis,
We're keenly awaiting the rest.

On Tuesday he mentioned a few salient facts that he thought we should know:
Machine-gun ballistics,
Insurance statistics,
And homework to do as we go.

By Wednesday we've wrestled with all forty questions and problems he gave:
Gyration, vibration,
Amelioration,
It sounds like he's starting to rave.

On Thursday, he covered a number of various figures and odd little facts:
The Belt of Orion,
The Nemean lion,
And India's property tax.

On Friday, he lectured on everything east of the Realm of Siam,
Convection corrections,
Ejection, dissections,
Now bring on your simple exam!

On Saturday what do you think the professor had asked on the quiz?
Osmosis, hypnosis,
Psychosis, neurosis,
Machine-gun ballistics
Or vital statistics?
Gyration, vibration,
Amelioration,
The Belt of Orion,
The Nemean lion?
Convection corrections,
Ejection, dissections?
He did not.
He quizzed about:
Hand-painted ceramics,
And thermodynamics,
Organic detectors,
Mechanical vectors,
Agenda, errata,
Addenda and data,
Transmuting, polluting,
Disputing, refuting,
Exponents of x's
And why are there sexes.

And any number of other topics not even remotely hinted at during the previous week.

Georgia Tech Yellow Jacket

This

This is not very interesting
But if
You have read this far already
You will
Probably
Read as far as this:
And still
Not really accomplishing
Anything at all

You might
Even read on
Which brings you to
The line you are reading now
And after all that you are still
Probably dumb enough to keep
Right on making
A dope of yourself
By reading
As far down
The page as this.

Princeton Tiger

"Honey, ah loves yo' bathin' suit!"
"Sho' nuff?"
"Man, it sho' sho' does!"

Penn State Froth

PROSECUTING ATTORNEY: It's my duty to warn you that everything you say will be held against you.
DEFENDANT: Jane Russell, Jane Russell, Jane Russell...

Penn State Froth

"I think these Econ classes are getting out of hand."

Missouri Showme

Me Mudder

"M" is for the million drinks she brought me.
Who makes a daily grind seem bearable?
Me Mudder.
Who helps me over de bumps?
Me Mudder.
When life's chorus
Makes me hoarse,
Who soothes me pantin' lil liddle t'roat?
Me Mudder.
When all de woild's a stage
And I feel de coise of age,
Who raises me cane?
Me Mudder.
When udder dames are frilly,
Who's me tiger lily?
Me Mudder.
Life is just burlesque
And humoresque
But who's for real?
Me Mudder.
When I'm bad,
Who's glad?
Me.
Who's a cool Mudder?
Mudder.

Purdue Rivet

*"Oh, while you're at it—
Now is the time for all good men
to come to the aid of the party."*

Coles H. Phinizy/*Harvard Lampoon*

A beauty, by name Henrietta,
Just loved to wear a tight sweater.
Three reasons she had:
To keep warm wasn't bad,
But her two other reasons were better.

Colorado Dodo

FIRST FROSH: Next to a beautiful girl, sleep is the most wonderful thing in the world.
SECOND FROSH: I don't get it.

Harvard Lampoon

"Vidi, vici, veni."

Princeton Tiger

SONGS FOR THE TENDER HEARTED LIBERAL

"Pass The Biscuits Pappy" O'Daniel

A study of the votes
Of Texas' Pappy O'Daniel
Will show he has the brains
Of an intelligent cocker-spaniel.

Rep. Gordon Canfield (Mine Own Dear Congressman)

Canfield votes like a
Typical politician,
Guided strictly by
November Intuition.
For Canfield is
But half a man—
The other half
Republican.

Allen Ginsberg/*Columbia Jester*

POSITIVELY COLOSSAL!

"Plans are being discussed at Metro to make a picture combining Andy Hardy and Dr. Kildare." News item in *Variety*.

NEVER IN ALL HISTORY has so much literary talent sat around a single table. There is Ernest Hemingway smelling of good tobacco and Martha Gellhorn. There is sage, bewhiskered George Bernard Shaw. There is John Steinbeck squatting on his heels and drawing with a stick in the thick nap of the Oriental rug. There is William Faulkner mounted on a white stallion hitting a sharecropper across the face with his riding crop. There is Ben Hecht, Charles MacArthur, Robert Nathan, Erskine Caldwell, Dalton Trumbo, Margaret Mitchell, John O'Hara, James Farrell, Sinclair Lewis, William Saroyan, Robert Sherwood, Archibald MacLeish, Pearl Buck, Vincent Sheean, and Thomas Wolfe (posthumously).

The door is locked. The story conference begins. For forty days and forty nights the writers sit in solemn conclave. No one goes in or out. Hollywood holds its alcoholic breath.

Finally it is ready. While flash bulbs pop and newsreel cameras grind, the writers file out, weary, smiling, triumphant.

The screen play has been completed for *Dr. Kildare Performs a Very Delicate Operation on Andy Hardy!*

The story concerns the parallel and involved adventures of Andy Hardy and Dr. Kildare. Andy impales his father to a hall tree during a darts game and flees to escape arrest. While hiding out in a waterfront flophouse, he gets into an argument with his landlady, who implies that he is not a normal American boy. He stabs her four times in the groin and flees to escape arrest.

She is rushed to the hospital, and Dr. Kildare is called in to operate on her. He takes a quick look at her and says, "This is a cinch. Nurse, hand me my dull scalpel." During the operation Jap bombers fly over the city and bomb the power plant. All the lights go out. Dr. Kildare, operating in the dark, miscalculates. He cuts off both of the woman's legs.

When she comes out of the ether, she is furious. Dr. Kildare pleads with her. "Jeez, shorty," he says, "I couldn't help it." But she is unmollified. She calls the police, and he flees to escape arrest.

Meanwhile Andy joins the navy. He is on a battleship steaming across the Pacific. The crew puts on a show one night on the ship. Andy does imitations, and he is so funny that the man who steers the ship dies laughing. This is a tough spot. The captain asks if anybody knows how to steer a ship. Andy, thinking the captain has asked if anyone knows how to ship a steer, says "I do" because he has had some experience in shipping steers when he was on a ranch in Texas.

The captain turns the wheel over to Andy who immediately runs the ship up on a reef and rips off the bottom. Everybody is drowned except Andy, who clings to the first mate's wooden leg for three days until he is picked up by a coast guard cutter named Sam.

They ask him what happened. He knows that he will catch hell if he tells the truth, so he makes up a story about how they were attacked by a pack of submarines. He says he sank four submarines himself by diving under the sea and punching holes in their sides with a dirk.

When the President of the United States hears about it, he makes Andy commander-in-chief of the Pacific fleet.

Dr. Kildare, meanwhile, falls upon evil days. He is hiding out in the underworld making a precarious living by doing plastic surgery on criminals who are wanted by the law. One day two hundred Japanese spies come into his office and ask him to straighten their eyes so people won't be able to tell that they are Japs.

Dr. Kildare says all right, but instead of straightening their eyes, he cuts their noses off. Then he gets J. (for Jerque) Edgar Hoover on the phone. "There are 200 Japanese spies around here," he says, "and they're easy to identify."

"How do you identify them?" says J. Edgar Hoover.

"They haven't got no noses."

"No noses!" exclaims J. Edgar Hoover. "How do they smell?"

"Terrible," says Dr. Kildare.

When the President of the United States hears about it, he makes Dr. Kildare the commander-in-chief of the Far Eastern army.

Andy and Dr. Kildare meet in Honolulu to discuss war strategy. They talk for a long time, and finally hit upon a plan so daring that it is almost unbelievable. They decide that the way to beat Japan is to send a bomber over the crater of Fujiyama and drop bombs into it. That will cause the volcano to erupt, and all of Japan will be buried under lava.

Their plan is so risky that they don't think it fair to ask anyone to undertake it except themselves. They agree that in the morning the two of them will take a bomber and carry out the dangerous mission.

They shake hands solemnly. "This calls for a drink," says Andy.

"No, thanks," says Dr. Kildare, "I never touch it. But you go ahead."

So Andy calls in his orderly and tells him to bring up a bottle of Benedictine. The orderly, unfortunately, is hard of hearing, and brings Andy a bottle of benzine. Andy, who has no taste buds, drinks the whole bottle and goes to bed.

In the morning when Dr. Kildare comes to call for him, Andy is lying on the floor screaming with pain. There is no time to waste; Dr. Kildare has to operate at once. With a pipe reamer and an old pair of shears, Dr. Kildare removes Andy's stomach.

Andy immediately feels better. They jump in a bomber, fly over Fujiyama, drop a bomb dead center, and blow up the whole island.

When the President of the United States hears about it, he resigns and makes Andy and Dr. Kildare co-presidents.

Max Shulman / *Minnesota Ski-U-Mah*

To a Certain Professor Who Has a Profuse Admiration For Extraneous Facts

DEAR SIR: You may as well abandon hope.
Not all these months have forced into my mind
The date of birth of such-and-such a Pope,
Or why the pygmy culture fell behind.
Details you will not let be blurred by trends
Have hid the trends and burdened down my thought
With fascinating small-talk for my friends
Or just how long Anaximander taught.
Original great books, which I devour,
You find of little import, and instead
On commentaries dote, which I abhor,
To learn just what it was that Plato said.
More learned now I don't believe I am;
And frankly, sir, I do not give a damn.

Michigan Gargoyle

Could Have Called Him Finis

The new colored parson, calling for the first time on Mandy, was puzzled to hear her call the children Eenie, Meenie, Minie, and Henry.

"Why did you name him Henry?"

Mandy replied: "We didn't want no Mo'."

Pomona Sage Hen

"Mirage or no mirage. I'm going up to investigate."

Tom Goldberg / *Pomona Sage Hen*

PREFIX FIXER

A Funny Story That Will Enlarge Your Vocabulary

REPORTER: MR. OGLETHORPE, I understand that you believe that the English language is not making full use of all its words. Would you mind answering a few questions?

OGLETHORPE: Go ahead. I'm hibited.

R: That's fine. I hope you don't think that some of my questions are silly.

O: I'm sure that anything you will ask me is sipid.

R: Thank you. Naturally my paper will pay you for this exclusive interview.

O: That isn't necessary. I want to be demnified.

R: That's awfully decent of you. I warn you, some of my questions may offend you.

O: Don't be silly. I'm always dignant.

R: All right. My first question is very personal. Is it true that you have left your wife?

O: Yes. I'm fatuated with her.

R: I see. Now, how about that crime you are supposed to have committed in New York? Did you do it?

O: Well, some people thought I was nocent, but the jury dicted me.

R: Then you didn't go to jail.

O: No, I was carcerated.

R: And now you are writing a book. Are you going to put all your theories about the English language into your book?

O: No, I am going to clude some of them.

R: How about your private life? Is that going to be in your book?

O: No, I am going to sert that.

R: I see. By the way, Mr. Oglethorpe, would you care for a cigarette?

O: No, I dulge.

R: Don't you ever smoke?

O: Occasionally. But I hale, so what's the use of smoking?

R: I admire your strength of purpose. You must lead a well-ordered life.

O: On the contrary. I cipline myself.

R: Do you mind if I smoke?

O: Go right ahead. That turbs me.

R: Don't you think it is rather dark in here, Mr. Oglethorpe?

O: Yes it is. That light is candescent.

R: Well, no matter. Would you like to tell me something of your life?

O: I will if you want me to, but I am afraid that it is teresting.

R: Nonsense, I know it is fascinating. I heard that you were a fireman once.

O: Yes, I was a cendiary.

R: Why did you quit? Weren't you good at it?

O: Oh, I was ept enough, but I got tired of it.

R: Then you ran a chick hatchery. What became of that?

O: The chicks all cubated.

R: Gee, that's tough. Can you tell me any more about your life?

O: No, it was very tinguished.

R: What do you think of the foreign situation, Mr. Oglethorpe? Do you think the war will come to America soon?

O: No, I think it is minent. But we should not make the mistake of fending ourselves.

R: You must have thought that over carefully, Mr. Oglethorpe.

O: Yes. I always think before making a statement. I am very petuous.

R: Then you don't believe in lightning decisions.

O: No, I think they are telligent.

R: Do you believe that personal appearance is a valuable asset for a young man?

O: Yes. I always try to keep couth and kempt.

R: Well, that's about all. Have you any message to give to the youth of America before we conclude?

O: Yes, I have. I have always followed this rule and I think it can help everyone. Be imical and you will be jured.

Max Shulman / Minnesota Ski-U-Mah

Yes, sir! She certainly is!

Utah Unique

"Is Mr. O'Neill at home?"

Michigan State Spartan

STEAL AWAY, STEAL AWAY; OR, WHERE THE HELL HAVE I SEEN THAT BEFORE?

AH HAH! there, Wits of Colgate, Cornell, West Point, Williams, Dartmouth, Wisconsin, Duke, Alabama, and sundry others including St. Mary's.
Speaking on behalf of my confreres,
I should like to inquire, are your consciences quite clear and clean, or are they cloudy and checkered?
Did you devise that uproarious cartoon and that sidesplitting anecdote all by yourselves, or did you pilfer it from the *Yale Record?*
Now, slowly, restrain that outburst, and pray do not so wrathfully blanch; Oh
Am I not aware that humor is a universal sense, alike in the Gaucho ranching on his rancho
And the Eskimo iggling in his igloo? Must you say to us what matter the origin
As long as in these troubled times people everywhere have some haven of humor to forage in?
My reply is that your statements are excellent in principle, but mechanically sloppy—
Because we are not interested in the universality of humor half so much as the universality of the *Yale Record,* selling at 25c the copy.
After all, let's call a crumpet a crumpet;
If your partner lays out a good ace you certainly are not going to trump it;
So instead of reprinting all our old gems and then having these conniptions,
Maybe you would like to invest in some subscriptions?
Once serves the purpose, of course, but if you insist—now mind you, I cast no aspersions—
I suggest that you alter your versions of our versions;
I imply that you could be subtler,
For what fool openly covets his neighbor's ass or even his butler?
And in conclusion, allow me to state, if I may be so crass,
That this shall probably come to pass:
While your erstwhile wits and persifleurs are merely soldierizing, we will be colonelizing and majorizing,
For Yale usually leads the way, and when she does not she is very particular from whom she is plagiarizing,
Since she desires to maintain those high standards of individuality and originality, democracy's precious symbols;
And to sum the whole affair up in a nutshell, I refer you to somebody's apt statement, viz., "Does Macy's tell Gimbels?"

H. Berger / *Yale Record*

EDITORIAL

In the first place the whole thing is sort of a mistake.

I wandered into room 403 in the Student Union one day a couple of weeks ago to repair the steam radiator (I'm a plumbing major, and that counts as part of my lab work), and a real worried-looking gal, who was sitting at the desk cutting paper dolls out of old magazines, said:

"How would you like two redheads from Abilene?"

(I later figured out that she must have said, "How would you like to edit a magazine?")

At the time it sounded like a good deal; so I said:

"Sure."

Right away things began to happen. She lost her worried expression, jumped up from the desk with a happy little squeal, kissed me once on the forehead, and handing me a key to the office, she ran out of the room. Over her shoulder she shouted:

"Don't worry about what you write in your editorials. Nobody ever reads 'em anyway."

Well, I got to hanging out in this room 403, which had a sign saying WAMPUS on the door, and some of the oddest-looking characters wandered in and out of the place. A few

A girl shock of wheat went and sleeped
By a boy shock of wheat that was heaped.
On waking, 'tis said,
She found herself bread
And shouted, "My Gawd, I've been reaped."

Washington and Lee Southern Collegian

"Hey, Joe! A new student agency!"

Lyman/*Yale Record*

continued from Editorial, page 135

of them left cartoons or stories or pictures, but most of them just came in to talk, or bum cigarettes, or help themselves to things from the desk.

Finally a fellow came in who said he was the business manager and he wanted to know when the next issue was coming out. I asked him what next issue, and he explained that I was the editor of a magazine called *Wampus* and that I was supposed to take the stories and stuff that people had brought in and put them together for a January issue.

Well, I'm more familiar with tissues than with issues; so I got in touch with another plumbing major who once wrote an article called "Sewers I Have Known" for the *Plumbers Journal,* and he helped me get this issue out.

Now that I got it all together, I'm kinda pleased with it, only my friend says next time I should use what he calls the "editorial we" when I write on this page.

Sounds sorta silly to *us,* but *we*'ll try it next month.

—THE NEW EDITOR.

Al Hix / *USC Wampus*

NURSE in maternity ward to MR. DRACULA: Congratulations, it's a boy! Do you want to take him home with you?

MR. DRACULA: No, thanks. I'll just eat him right here.

Bob Wilbur/ *Washington & Lee Southern Collegian*

Trees

(If it had been written by a certain modern poet)

It often strikes me as being queer and unusual and really quite odd
that nobody in the whole world, with the definite exception of God,
can make a tree. Anybody can make pomes.
Anyone can make ashcans, automobiles, crêpes suzette, or homes,
but a tree is different; a horse of another color, something else again.
A tree that may, for all you or I know, or imagine, or care,
be wearing a nest of robins in its hair.
Who (meaning the tree) has a bosom on which snow has lain
and who has been kept by, or at least lived intimately with, the rain.
Now pomes, in brief, are made by fools like you, or more frequently, like me.
But I don't suppose you'll ever catch either one of us going around
dashing off a tree.

Oklahoma Covered Wagon

An American was sitting on the couch with a French girl in a drafty room.
"Je t'adore," said the American.
"Shut it yourself, you lazee Yangkee," replied mademoiselle.

Alabama Rammer-Jammer

Who comforts me in moments of despair?
Who runs fingers lightly through my hair?
Who cooks my meals and darns my hose?
Squeezes nose drops in my nose?
Who always has a word of praise?
Sets out my rubbers on rainy days?

Who scrubs my back when in a shower?
And wakes me up at the proper hour?
Who helps keep me on the beam?
And figures in my every dream?
I do.

Colorado Flatiron

"Dear Student,
It has been brought to my attention that you have been cutting an excessive number of classes. This is a reminder that if you continue to disregard the University rules of attendance, we will be forced to place you on probation for the remainder of the college term.
Yours very sincerely,
WILLIAM C. DEVANE,
Dean of Yale College"

J. Julien Dedman/*Yale Record*

the sub-deb

EDITED by JAN WILD

Okay, Honey It's your first date

So many sub-debs write me asking for information on what to wear, how to look, how to act and what to do on a first date that I thought I'd just sit down here at my rusty old typewriter and answer those questions right here and now. Before I get specific, let me give you innocents a few general words of wisdom.

Girls, good looks count. There is just no sense in denying that. Sure, boys are interested in your mental ability and your personality. But first (and may I say: foremost) they are interested in your physical attractiveness. And to be even more blunt: your body. There! Now I've said it. The fat's in the fire now. (If you'll pardon my pun.) If you are not a raving beauty play up your good points, like your Marlene Dietrich legs or your lovely chestnut hair. Take me for instance—and all the boys do, don't kid yourself on that score. Now I have an interesting chest; some say it's a deformity; I say it's a chest. Now, my chest (and forgive me, girls, if I am prone to boast, but being prone is one of my incurable weaknesses) is interesting, real dreamy, outstanding. I play that particular thing(s) up to advantage. And believe me the boys appreciate it. But, my dears, don't overdo the thing. For instance, you don't see me going around stripped to the waist. Not if you are a Sub-deb, you don't. So, like I say, play up your advantages. Think of your particular virtue like merchandise. Take a lesson from the shopkeeper: if he has a good piece of stuff he puts it on display, lays the goods on the line, so to speak. So be it with you. And then, sweets, that first date will be upon you, literally, before you know it. Or better: before you know it, literally. Or better . . . well, let's get on the question box.

How old should a girl be before she dates?

Before she dates what? Let's say men. Well, we feel that she should at least be in the fifth grade. By the fifth grade you've got something to talk about. You've studied algebra and geography and American History. After all, you can't talk spelling, can you now?

Do boys like girls to wear makeup?

Boys like girls to wear nothing.

Should a girl kiss a boy good-night on a first date?

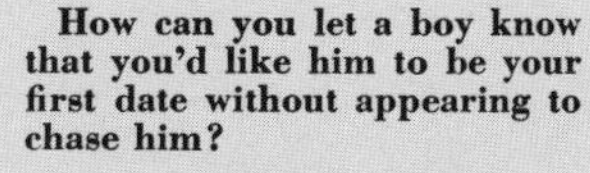

How can you let a boy know that you'd like him to be your first date without appearing to chase him?

Tell your best friend to hint subtly to the boy: "Sally's a sweet girl, have you had a chance to talk to her?" Or, "Why not take Sally out sometime? She's got her own apartment."

If you don't have a best friend to serve as cupid, you can try a more direct approach. Look up the boy's schedule of classes and make it a point to be where he is. He's bound to catch on after seeing you around so much. Or if he works in the local drugstore, you could start getting your hypodermics there. But really, the best way is to find out those things that he likes and then casually ask him questions about them without letting him know you found out beforehand. Say, "Hi, Elmer. What's new with the ceramics of the Papauan element of the Southern Malayan Archipelago?"

What should I do when my first date comes to pick me up?

He's on time, and so are you. Boys are as shy as girls, especially when they've got to meet your parents. He'll appreciate your show of confidence when you calmly introduce him to the door and slam your parents. Here's an easy rule to remember on those introductions: the man is presented to the woman unless the woman happens to be your date in which case he would be a man and that would mean that you'd have to decide whether you should introduce to your mother or your father first. Say, "Mother, I'd like you to meet Dad." When you get around to introducing him to your sister say, "Nancy, this is Don." Yes, that's much better, except that this happens to be Elmer, remember?

Since this is your first date with Elmer, invite him into the living room. This gives your parents a chance to find out he's as nice as you say he is and it prevents him from trying to neck with you in the kitchen. To get the conversation rolling, throw dad a line —"Elmer thinks winters are getting milder each year." Or "Elmer thinks Nick Kenny is the greatest living American poet." Watch that one rock dad back on his heels! Or, rather than start a controversy, appeal to dad's ego with "Elmer has been dying to meet you since you got your new glass eye." This starts a gabfest between the two men. But remember you are responsible for getting Elmer away and off on the date. So after ten minutes or so say, "Elmer, you'd better give dad back his eye, it's getting late. The dance begins at eight-thirty."

What can a girl do if she is taller than her date?

You may be a bit taller than your date because you are wearing high heels. If you continue to wear high heels your date will develop what is known in the trade as a "Shortie Complex" (or technically a Teenius Weenius Mentis-corpus psychos.) Girls who are dating short boys definitely should not wear high heels. BUT, on further consideration, if the girl does NOT wear high heels perhaps the boy will think she is not wearing them because he is so short (and that's a fact) so he will develop as strong a shortie complex as if his date were wearing high heels. This leaves you up a tree, barefoot.

Of course if you, without shoes, are still taller than your date, then there is a more ticklish problem. You can send your date home and wait until the boy grows a little taller (boys mature later than girls) but this will take time. In the intervening years you can develop your mind. And there is nothing a boy likes better than a cultured girl. No siree.

If you are impatient you can slice off the lower part of your feet, but this, we warn you, is messy. And, anyway, you'll look like hell in a bathing suit.

For the present? First concentrate on your posture, tall gals. If you walk around all slouched over with your hands trailing on the ground this will only *accentuate* your height. Then, too, try to dress smartly rather than prettily. Well-tailored, conservative, easy-to-get-off clothes. After all, you can't help it if you are a great big slob of a girl. STAND ERECT. Straight as an arrow, with your chin held high. Be *proud* you're eight feet tall.

There are other questions that you may want answered, really. Some of these will be answered if you send us $1.00 in cash for our little booklet which will be sent to you in plain, brown paper wrapping. (You must be at least over twenty-one.) Anyway, if it isn't necessary, please don't call. Where there's a will, there's a way.

The World' Most Sluggish Circulation
Fifteen Limp Copies

The Reader's Dijest

A JESTER PARODY 35¢

ARTICLES OF LASTING INSIGNIFICANCE • 28TH YEAR OF PUB.

The Truth About Joseph Stalin . . *Calling All Girls* 1
A Faith for Our Time . . . *Women's Wear Daily* 5
Are We Us . . . . *DeWitt Wallace* 6
Gotham's Growling Bus Driver . . . . *Hygeia* 9
New Hope for Something or Other . . . *Downbeat* 12
Are Comics Corrupting Our Parents? . *A Symposium* 15
Poverty—Life's Cheapest Blessing . . . *Fortune* 18
Victory Through Bird-Power . . . . *Field & Stream* 21
The Most Unforgettable Character I've Met *John Gunther* 24
How to Be a Parlor Psychologist . . *Havelock Ellis* 27
Breathe 24 Hours a Day . . . . *Kiwanis Magazine* 29
Children *Can* Be Taught Sacrifice . *Good Housekeeping* 32
Life in These Here States . . . . . . *A Feature* 35
The Liver—Vicious and Depraved Organ . *Seventeen* 37
Homemade Help for the Jobless 40
Uncle Oliphant—Canada's Champion Tosspot *Recreation* 43
It Pays to Decrease Your Word Power 47
How to Stop Living and Start Worrying *From the Book* 49
What We Believe . . . . *Compressed Air* 52
Animal Wisdom 53
America's Profiteer Patriot . . . . *Martin Bormann* 55
The Miracle of Fear . . . . *Boy's Life* 58
Grandma is a Jet Pilot . . . . . *Smart Knitting* 70
Pleasantville Cleans House . . . . . . *Oral Hygiene* 74
I'm Nursing My Baby . . . . *Eric Johnston* 80
Detroit's Fighting Milkman . . . . *Civil Service Leader* 85
Serve Yourself Sunny Side Up . *Ladies Home Journal* 87
God's Double-Entry Bookkeeping . . . . . *Wings* 93
What About Petting? . . . . *Elsa Maxwell* 97
Well, What About it? . . . . *Country Gentleman* 103
Why Truman Didn't Win . *Kiplinger's News Letter* 104
Henry Ford Looks at Birth Control . . . . *Power* 120

Book Section The Encyclopædia Britannica *Clifton Fadiman* 59

Sliced Tongue, 84 — Wild Wild Wisdom, 104

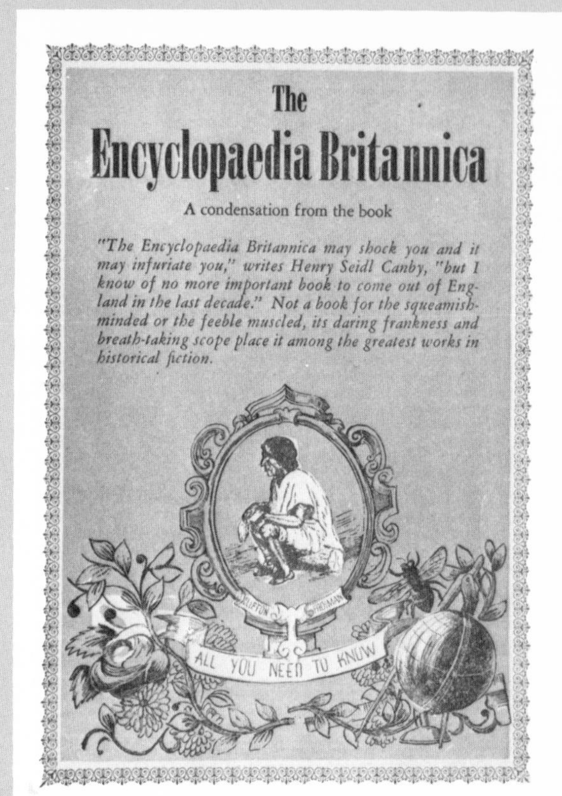
The
Encyclopaedia Britannica

A condensation from the book

"The Encyclopaedia Britannica may shock you and it may infuriate you," writes Henry Seidl Canby, "but I know of no more important book to come out of England in the last decade." Not a book for the squeamish-minded or the feeble muscled, its daring frankness and breath-taking scope place it among the greatest works in historical fiction.

The Encyclopaedia Britannica

VOL. I, A TO ANNO

A long time ago, back along about the days the Aardvark (small animal) was evolved, a sinister group of people at what is now Aachen (Aix-la-Ghent) were noted for the practice of such rites as the worship of Ammon-Ra. This is hardly possible, since Ammon-Ra was worshipped in Egypt. Anyhow, these people (or some others) invented the Adze, the Alphabet, and numbered among themselves several Anchorites. Living on the shores of Lake Absaroka, they were naturally Amphibians and had resort to Ablatives (small boats) and Albatrosses (you know what *they* are!) for transportation, and, in case of need, to Ambulances for transporting those wounded fighting the dread Afflatus. Their main diseases were Ambivalence and Angst. They died out about Anno (see v. 7 for Domini) 416.

VOL. II, ANNO-BALT

Annually, (founded perhaps at the turn of 1929) is perhaps best known for his best work "Blatehorn," 1923-25. Considered by many authorities the most definitive study of the subject of Annuities (see Metropolitan Life vii,6) it dealt with the life story of Annubis the Dark, dean of American Humor for fifty years.

VOLUME III, BALT TO BRAI

Castle—a word, actually belonging in another volume, but lost through the carelessness of a roving editor. Colloquially: a three room apartment containing kitchen, bedroom, and salle á manger. It is a unit of family life in Western civilization. Baboons have been known to have possessed castles containing father, mother, and hordes of children. These castles have rocky walls without room divisions. During ancient times there were no castles, as they are of quite recent origin.

VOL. VI, COL TO DANA

A corruption of the Old Phrase, "From Dan to Beersheba."

(N.B. Alert readers will have noticed that Volumes IV and V are missing. While the editors do not ordinarily believe in Bowdlerizing the text, they feel that in view of the extremely licentious nature of the material this omission is advisable.)

VOL. VII, DANA TO EDUC

Dana Burgess, dean of American Humor for fifty years, lived until Darryl Zan—(vii,6) uck (vi,5) of film fame intervened in the building of Dams. These trace back to the Detroit Tigers, (won 35, lost 3) an ancient fraternal organization, (latitude 36°E, 34°W) dedicated to Dande-

lion admirers. First president of the order was Demosthenes who spoke into a microphone with sea-shells in his mouth. Despite Democratic hopes, (see "hopes" in any undigested version) the Devil (discovered 1947 by Mr. Niebuhr, a writer for Mr. Luce) all but stopped disarmament, (no dove of peace, he).

VOL. VIII, EDUC TO EXTR

(Editor's Note: Sometimes we find it impossible to dijest a whole volume. But we never give up. As our founder's said: "If'n ya cain't cut, tellum a story.")

Educ—Founded in 1756, it was the first American University to institute a "beat Russia" rally as part of its extra-curriculum. Plans to include this at Extr., a New Hampshire telephone booth, (founded by Mary Baker Eddy) have been laid. This is directly due to the agitation of the Boston Red Sox, a Harvard Alumni association (1564 and as long as the deah endowment holds.)

VOL. X, GAME TO GUN

(Note: For some time there has been sharp academic debate over the authenticity of Volume IX, "Extr to Gamb", a number of authorities preferring to class it among the apocrypha. Now, thanks to Prof. Barzun's definitive monograph, "Extr to Gamb, Hoax or Gospel?", scholars are generally willing to agree that the document is spurious, having been added in the late 13th century by Hucbald the Fat.)

Game to the last, the Gallant General "Chinese" Gordon (famed as the inventor of the Gordon Knot and other Chinese puzzles) refused to surrender his Grenadier Guards to the Gamle Schmo (Old Man of the Mountains) in the Gobi Campaign of 1869. For this defiance of the Gamle Schmo and his fierce sect of Geriatrics, the Guards have since been permitted to wear Gray Gloves gaily. Shortly after the campaign had Genug, (stopped) the war (of the Glasses) was arbitrated by Gandalf (1776-1923), who pleaded that the Old Man was suffering from Gummata, the deadly chicle disease. On the return home of the Glorious troops, they found that the Works (see Vol. XXIII) has been effectually Gummed up. Rising in Groups of Gninety, they Ganged up on the officials, the failure of whose Gilt-edged Bonds (see Vol. III) had caused the collapse. Unable to Gauge the results of this Gouge, the Gladstone Government was forced to Genug (stop) at the point of a Gun.

VOL. XI, GUNN TO HYDR

At the Grocery store I used to meet a quiet, middle-aged lady who was the thriftiest shopper I had ever seen, and one day I told her so. "I suppose it runs in the family," she said. "My grandmother brought me up on a farm in Vermont, and she would never cut the lettuce on a Sunday till she returned from Church."

"Why?" I asked in surprise.

Granny paused, smiled and replied: "Oh, just for the Hell of it."

VOL. XII, HYDR TO JERE

Hydrophobia means fear of water, and is the basis of many neuroses, since the human body is 90 per cent water. Thus from Hydrophobia can come agoraphobia (fear of Greek markets), acrophobia (fear of quarrels) and inferiority complexes. In extreme cases, it becomes Impossible to use India Ink, or to drink anything but Iced Pomegranate Juice. Iardella (1928-et Seq.) was the first to analyse this cure in enough detail to be at all useful. The letter "I" (just to mention it in Passing's monumental history on the subject) has a long and diverting history. Nothing is known of it, however. It is the ninth letter of the Ilphabet, and so (according to numeralogy, the Numbers Racket) the most important. Hence it was Chosen (see Korea) to indicate personality. Reform has been proposed in this matter, but these matters drag on, and never do come to a head. You know how it is. It, by the way, is what is put to people in cross examinations—"I put it to you." The content of It in this usage has never been determined, but the best authorities assume a link with prehistoric Druidic rites, when whatever the object was that was put, or more probably *stuck into,* the sacrificial victim, was too holy to be naumed. It may have been a knife made of Jasper (994-1073) or other precious material. In any case, it is not a nice thing to do (or put). This same Jasper (surnamed De la Nuit) is supposed to have started the first Jehad, in conjunction with Jehu, the Traction Magnate. The scandals resulting from this crooked deal, brought on several Jeremiads from the stockholders.

VOL. XIII, JEREZ TO LIBER

Jerez my little dog gone? That was the question the entire civilised world (4 square miles in diameter) was asking in the Renaissance. It was more of a rhetorical question, so to speak, since no one could possible answer it. The Clergy tried to stop its being propounded by the so-called Jocular laws, but this did not succeed. People had stopped asking it long before, which made the lawmakers feel pretty foolish. It is supposed to be on account of this controversy that the fierce Jugular tribesmen revolted, and, in the historic Burning of the Jugs (their infamous badges of Servitude) declared their Jingoist sentiments, in Jingles. Bells were banned in the reign of the Baron Janglars because they were held to interfere with the Jongleurs, (at the instigation of Jongleur Jim). Somewhat Later than this (equivalent to Never, and *much* better), Lamination set in, and civilization as we knew it was in a fair way of being destroyed. Never happens, though. We always get by. It seems to be due to the Lassitude, or some other feature of the climate. Naturally, so world-shaking an event could not take place without a good deal of hard feeling, and Lawsuits were constantly being instituted. It seems hard in these less troubled times to believe all this, and in fact it is.

Very.

In mid-August, the Liberation of Paris was complete, and once away from the enervating influence of Helen, he soon regained his old Snap and Tingle, favorite to us of his childhood days.

VOL. XIV, LIBI TO MARY

The licentiousness of the times is illustrated in lively fashion by the following anecdote of the Emperor and the Lictors. The Emperor (Livius), wishing to gain control of the toll-gates on the Via Licata because he needed some ready money, is presumed to have employed three Low-

lifes (a dissenting sect of Lunch-wagons) to murder anyone he objected to, or who objected to him. This was in some ways a good thing, as it promoted Unity. From here on, the story is a little confused. Since there is a strong (though by no means well-founded) supposition that Lions (Light Blue ones) come into it some place, we may assume there was Lots of blood shed. As an interesting (if you have that sort of mind) footnote to this era (456-789), we note the origin of the phrase "left in the Lurch" . . . The left wing of the Senate was generally out of favor, and was so seated in the less fashionable section of the arenas. The seats in this section had a tendency to sag, and it became known as the Lurch Perch. The rest is only too obvious.

Concurrent with these developments, the Mabinogions (fairy-worshippers) were s p r e a d i n g their creed throughout Andalusia and Northumberland. Maddeningly enough, they were successful in defeating the Empire's picked troupes in the annual Malagueñas (theatrical contests) which enhanced their prestige no end. Their Queen, Mab, was their greatest asset, as she could play a large variety of tunes on the Marplot, a confused stringed instrument. Just at the point when it seemed Rome was to Fall (down), the Mabbies (as they were called) were destroyed by a plague of Marmosets, from down the road.

Thus the Markets of the Empire were made safe for trade. Marriages could be once again performed, and the ground was laid for Marx. Mary Queen of Scots had nothing to do with this, no matter what you think.

VOL. XV, MARY TO MUZ

October 29, 1929
Miss Spence's

Dear Muz,

Well! You'll never guess what happened *Yesterday!*

Hal (You remember Hal, he was the one you were so crazy over in the Fall) came down to see Jim yesterday, Jim's the current, or was, until —Well, anyhow, Hal came down from New Haven to see Jim, and of course Jim said he had a date with me. Because he did, you see. Anyhow since Hal had come all that long way —"Had quite a spell on the cars," he said—he's a *scream,* really—Jim felt he ought to ask him along, and could I dig up another girl for him. Well, I was going to, but I remembered how Hal was—you sure were crazy over him, you remember, and I don't blame you—but more of that later, or, as Miss Palmer used to say, "Plus en retard," ha ha.

So anyway, I told Jim I thought it would be nice if we went out on a threesome, and, as luck would have it, no sooner had we arrived at the Plaza than Jim came all over funny, I guess it might have been the vermouth alexanders he kept drinking all morning. Anyhow, he had to leave, and there was I with Hal. Naturally, he took me home, and—

There's Hal now, I must rush, all I can say now is, don't feel too badly no matter what you hear and

all my love,
Mary

VOL. XVIII, PLAN TO RAYN

The Best Laid (see vol. vii, 6) plans of mice and men (look it up yourself) gang aft agley. Poverty is

no disgrace. Rave and the world raves with you (see vols. xx-xxii, or your neighborhood mirror).

Plane Plant Planter's Punch Plattdeutsch Pores Poor-boxes Prattfall Pungs Punjab Punk Pure Purr Rasp Rare Rank Raynbow	Gentlemen of the court of Verona

VOL. XXI, SORD TO TEXT

(Due to a fire in our offices it will be impossible to present XVI-XVII and XIX-XX as planned. A portion of Volume XXI, slightly charred, was salvaged from the flames by Mr. Max Eastman, one of our Roving Editors who happened to be roving through the building at the time of the fire, and is presented below. The book, that is, not Mr. Eastman.)

But it was not until 1653 that the Sordids, a no-account tribe from the Inner Desserts of W— (including Sorghum), under their leader, Sordello (El 5-2100) burst from their confines and laid waste to the Surrounding countryside with fire and Sord. Sordello's motives were mysterious; as he himself said, "Only God and I know what I meant."

The effects of all this were incalculable, and it is therefore pointless to say anything about them here, however interesting they be. We deal in facts, Sir (Sorr: Ir. Colloq), and more facts. Opinions have No place here. You want to know, we tell you. Do your own speculating.

But to return to our muttons. Once the things referred to in para. 1 had been Squelched, Squashed, &c, on account of someone's Squealing, most probably Stephano the Butler, the Sordids were heard from no more. I expect they became extinct. Seems rather a pity, but that's how it goes. Makes you realize.

Their only lasting contributions to civilization (as we know it today) was the introduction of Sweets as a regular part of the meal. Tactically speaking, this was a mistake all around, since it is believed to have been this innovation (537-693) that led to the fall of the Roman Vampire (as the Emperor Draculus was called) and the final dissolution of the Sugar beet. The Rayn of Terror which replaced this was largely considered to be a Test of good government (Fusion) and the governors became known as Testators because of their excessively Testy behavior. At this period Texas (as we know it today) emerged from its Triassic silt, and led all the civilized world in Textual power.

(Volumes XXII and XXIII cover approximately the same ground as the earlier and more memorable "Game to Gun." As so often happens, the author, having written himself out, has attempted to rework old material.)

VOL. XXIV ATLAS and INDEX

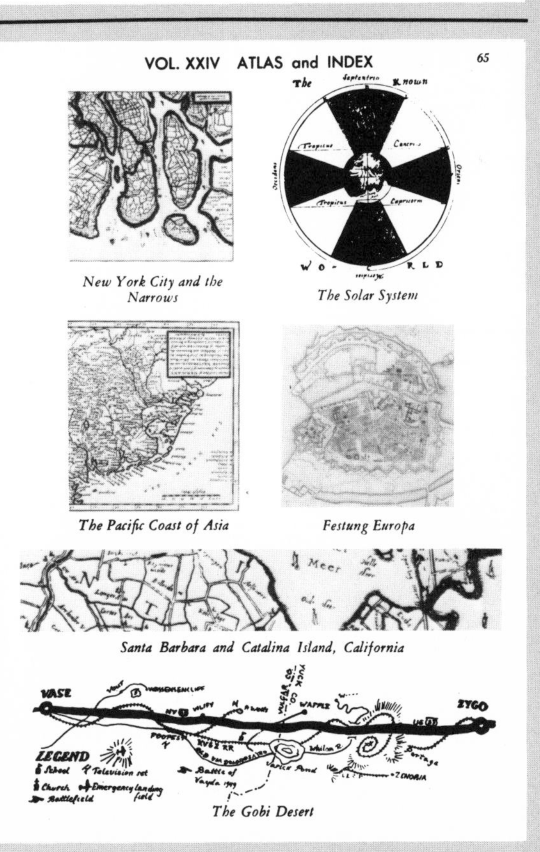

New York City and the Narrows

The Solar System

The Pacific Coast of Asia

Festung Europa

Santa Barbara and Catalina Island, California

The Gobi Desert

BOOKS

BIG MAN IN HOLLYWOOD

THE LIFE OF PHIL KAPLANSKY (814 pp.)—Jean Peters—Simon & Shuster ($5).

On May 14, 1933, Phil Kaplansky was born at the age of seven in a log cabin on the outskirts of Canton, Ohio. The son of Nancy Hanks Kaplansky and Dad Kaplansky, young Phil displayed great erudition and learned to write by scribbling diligently on a wooden fire shovel with a ball-point pen.

No account can make the story of Phil Kaplansky seem dull, nor has any account, including this one, quite seemed to do it justice.

KAPLANSKY
Promoter

Miss Peters, a Midwest coed—turned Miss Ohio State—turned actress, has picked her subject well. Her writing shows traces of amateurishness, and in places the verbiage is a bit strained, as if she were heaving mightily to turn over a flat rock. On the whole, however, the book is delightfully refreshing. Miss Peters writes:

"It was back in Canton that I first got to know Phil. I mean, to really *know* him. I wanted to be a school teacher in those days, and Phil was such a wonderful help. All the kids used to come over to my house and we'd sit out on my back porch and play school.

"I was the teacher, of course, and it always seemed to happen that Phil was a bad boy and had to stay after school when all the others went home. I suppose it was just fate.

"But sometimes, when we were all alone, Phil would say a naughty word, and I'd have him write 'BMOC' on the blackboard a thousand times.

"We got to be such good friends that way, just Phil and I. He used to tell me of his ambitions to grow up and write great things for the Lantern and the Citizen. He was so modest, and so shy —even then.

"But it was really Phil Kaplansky who made me, Jean Peters—the actress that I am today. During those long months I used to grope uncertainly around the studio. And then Phil hit town and BANG!—he gave me a nudge and I shot straight into Howard's heart. It was really a terrific boost to my career. I owe it all to Phil."

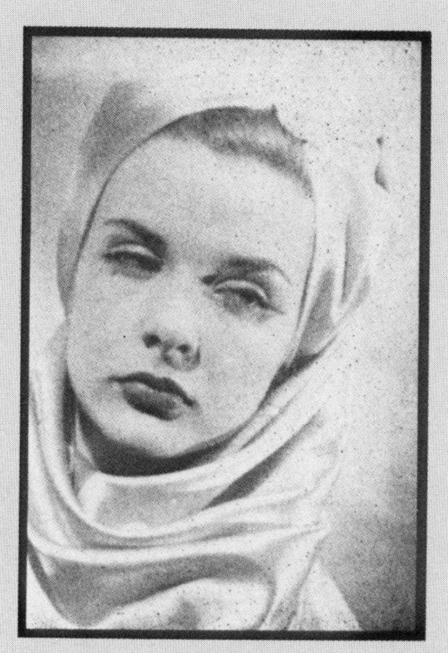

PETERS
Promoted

"I think I'll always remember Phil best for the time when he walked in the front door unexpectedly and caught Howard and me curled up on the love seat. Phil was so manly and masterful and everything. He just sat down on the love seat beside us and started talking as if nothing had happened.

"Phil is really so talented. Even Howard was amazed when Phil told him how he was making a mistake trying to build that big Hercules flying boat. Phil was telling Howard that he ought to sell it to Ohio State for a floating dormitory on Mirror Lake.

"And Phil even told Howard what he was doing wrong making his movies. After the success of Jane Russell in *The Outlaw*, there ought to be a sequel called *The Outhouse*. Phil confessed shyly that he has had some experience along these lines and might, with a little coaxing be persuaded to take the job of technical director.

"Howard was so impressed that he jumped up off the love seat and grabbed Phil by the hand. He wanted Phil to stay on in Hollywood to look after his interests in case there's another Congressional investigation. Phil just shook his head and sailed gazelle-like out the window. He's so modest."

Ugly Goslings

MOTHER GOOSE (664 pp.)
Compiled by Clement Wood—Haldeman-Julius ($0.05).

MOTHER GOOSE (CENSORED) (30 pp.)
Copyrighted by Kendall Banning—Mother Goose ($1.00).

Were the old nursery rhymes crawling with double entendre? This question had long baffled experts. Last week the experts had something to honk about; two literary ugly goslings had been hatched, and Mother Goose hung high.

The two slender, cynical volumes cleared up a lot of things. Nursemaids got goosepimples as they read new meanings into the old familiar rhymes. Publishers began to look for new markets as rumors spread that Mother Goose, as a children's book, was cooked.

What was the effect of all this anserine agitation on the kindergarten set, who had long had the controversial ditties all to themselves? Many felt that the effect amounted to a goose egg.

Less Rhyme than Reason. Mother Goose had laid a golden egg on the doorstep of obscure, aptly-named Mother Goose Press, mother of the first ugly gosling. The work had seemed innocent enough; its contribution to the general goosiness was probably accidental. Banning's device was simple; with an eye on the college market, he had struek out strategic works from several of the rhymes and marketed the product. The words were left for the reader's morbid imagination to fill in. The results were startling; where the meaning had been ambiguous or nonsensical, it now became painfully clear.

The moral imbecility of Simple Simon; the psychological abnormality of Robin and Richard, the "two pretty men"; the nefarious goings-on in the corrupt royal household; the rationale of the shoe-dwelling old woman; the loose morality of the lower aristocracy:

Goosey, goosey gander,
Where do you wander?
Upstairs and downstairs,
And in my lady's chamber.
There I met an old man,
Who would not ....
I took him by the ....
And ....

Such were the skeletons, exhumed at last from their medieval closets. As the author comments, there is "less rhyme than reason" in many of his censorial efforts.

Delightfully Immoral. The second ugly gosling first saw the light of day in the dingy offices of Haldeman-Julius, whose versatile, eccentric "Little Blue Books" (variously colored) usually leave readers with the impression that they have got their money's ($.05) worth.

Critic Clement Wood shows, in the introduction to his little blue and yellow volume, that he has been taking a gander at the same situation; says he: "Some of the rhymes are very, very moral . . . Some are delightfully immoral . . . The sovereign state of Louisiana has just dismissed quaint old Mother Goose (from) its . . . school readings . . . This action would have brought ribald joy to the spirit of Mother Goose, who did not hesitate to write, 'Q was a queen, who was fond of good flip.'"

Wood's own ribald joy was probably not justified; "flip," as defined by Webster, is merely "a spiced and sweetened drink consisting of ale, beer, cider, . . . and containing an egg or eggs . . ."

GROUND WATER IN THE BALTIMORE INDUSTRIAL AREA (299 pp.)— John C. Geyer—Maryland State Planning Commission ($)

"Ground water is water
contained in the zone of saturated voids
in the rocks of the earth's crust
and in the saturated mantel rock and soil . . ."

To some, Geyer's dank, sodden lines seemed to ooze a poetic insight which put him on a level with T. S. Eliot or Edgar A. Guest; others maintained stoutly that "Ground Water" was not poetry at all, a suspicion strengthened by the fact that it is written in prose.

Whether prose or poetry, the work held a morbid fascination for a tiny circle of initiates, who were studiously absorbed in "Ground Water" last week. The literary squall was not without reverberations in publishing circles; there were rumors that persnickety, detestable, old Haphazard House was "out to get" Geyer. The author himself was not available for comment; he had gone to look at some wells.

Geyer's stodgy, statistic-spangled tome achieves a certain humid atmosphere, but the frequent charts, graphs, and enumerations of wells will strike many readers as needless bad taste.

Michigan State Spartan

THE MAJOR PEDAGOGICAL

(Modified, with sincere apologies to Messrs. Gilbert and Sullivan, from "The Pirates of Penzance")

I am the very pattern of a major pedagogical.
I've taken all the courses (none of which are very logical)
That do the job of giving me my credits distributional,
But which, by way of protest, I declare unconstitutional.
I'm very well acquainted, for example, with World History,
Though how I ever passed it still remains a total mystery.
Regarding English usage I am bursting with proficiency . . .
Proficiency . . . Proficiency? . . . Ah!
But I've never learned to use the doggoned language with efficiency!
I've suffered through the obstacles of Kilby's text so physical,
My attitude toward Chemistry is anything but quizzical,
But actually in all these many subjects cosmological,
I am the very model of a major pedagogical.

I know Ammurican History, both Southern and Colonial;
My German's of a quality Miss Helmrich terms demonial;
I started French, but dropped it, thinking Greek would be much easier,
And wound up in the chorus, dancing hard and breathing wheezier!
Religion kept me up all night and left me stunned and groggy, O!
And my training in Philosophy was arduous, but foggy, O!
Then on some kind friend's suggestion I signed up for Sociology . . .
Sociology . . . Sociology? . . . Whew! . . . Aah!
Just recently she's made me the most abject an apology . . .
Just recently she's made me the most groveling apology!
I understand the nature of the Democratic primary;
I learned what ancient Roman matrons thought was ladies' finery . . .
In short, in all these very many matters cosmological,
I am the very pattern of a major pedagogical.

I fear from Mathematics what I learned was problematical;
I cannot solve equations, neither simple nor quadratical;
I'm wholly lost in integral and differential calculus;
I couldn't learn the names of all those beings animalculous;
And when it comes to bird trips at the daylight's early dawning, sir,
I never got to see the birds . . . I was far too busy yawning, sir!.
What I obtained from taking Psych was, frankly, a psychosis, O!
Psychosis . . . Richosis? . . . Lycosis? Dychosis? Blychosis? . . .
Ah, I've got it!
My record in my major work surprisingly like those is, O!
My record in my major work surprisingly like those is, O!
Yes, my knowledge in my major is at best but rudimentary,
And has only been brought down to the beginning of the century.
But still, when you consider all these subjects cosmological,
I am the very model of a major pedagogical!
I am the very model of a major pedagogical.

Randolph-Macon Woman's College Old Maid

"I don't give a damn what I am. I'm thirsty."
Pittsburgh Panther

I've never been dated.
I've never been kissed.
They said if I waited,
No man could resist
The lure of a pure and innocent miss.
The trouble is this—
I'm *fifty*.

Princeton Tiger

She was peeved and called him "Mr."
Not because he went and kr.
But because just before,
As she opened the door,
The same Mr. kr. sr.

Utah Unique

She's such a pretty little wench
Sitting there upon the bench,
Looking very coy and shy
At every passing college guy.
Such thrilling eyes,
Concentric thighs—
It's too bad
She's bald.

Penn State Froth

Oh, that's an Econ prof who tried the stock market.
Missouri Showme

¿Quién fué la dama con quien te vi anoche?
No fué dama. Fué mi esposa.

Yale Record

TESSIE: He's a nice guy, but he knows the worst songs.
MARY: Does he sing them to you?
TESSIE: No, he whistles them.

Princeton Tiger

"Uncle, what's a bachelor?"
"Junior, a bachelor is a man who didn't have a car when he was in college."

Penn State Froth

SHE'S LOVELY....
SHE'S ENGAGED...
SHE USES AIR-WICK

AIR-WICK because...

Cornell Widow

Cinderella

FROM TIME TO TIME we are fortunate to acquire material submitted from other countries. *Voo Doo* is pleased to present, directly from France, a work by the well-known teller of children's stories, Henri de la Desqui. Monsieur de la Desqui will relate the beloved fairy tale, *Cinderella.*

Bonjour, mes enfants. Today we tell ze storee of Cinderella. Cinderella, she ees a young girl. Gorgeous! But she ees veree poor. She always wears rags. But veree form-fitting.

Cinderella, she have two stepsistaires. Zey are ugly, but not *too* bad. Ze one, she have a beeg nose weeth a wart on ze end, and ze othaire have long stringy hair and a scar ovaire her ear, but still, zey are *girls.*

Also, there ees ze stepmothaire. Not bad for an old woman. She's fat and she's nastee and she has a terrible tempeur. But sometimes zeese old ladies weeth hot tempeurs—I remembaire one time in Marseilles there was—there was—

Well, anyhow, one night there ees a beeg partee in the castle. Ze ugly stepsistaires and ze ugly stepmothaire zey go. But lovely Cinderella, she don't go. Imagine—beautiful girl ees home and ze partee ees full of ugly women. Aah, zeese British.

Anyhow, Cinderella ees home crying, when, all of a sudden, *pouf. Voilà,* there ees her fairee godmothaire. Gorgeous! She wave zee wand and *sacrebleu,* Cinderella have beautiful dress and glass slippaires. Ze reason she geeves her glass slippaires—zey are not comfortable—but everybodee can see zat her feet are *clean.*

Ze fairee godmothaire, she send Cinderella to party. But she must be home by twelve o'clock. These fairee godmothaires, zey mean well, but what do zey know about parties?

Anyway, Cinderella go to zee

partee and right away she see ze handsome preence, who ees ze ruleur of ze whole land. He ees Preence Sharming. He ees ze son of King Sharming. He ees ze brothaire of Joe Sharming. He ees gorgeous!

Ze preence, when he see Cinderella, he fall in love weeth her. But just then, ze clock strike twelve. Bong, bong, bong, and nine more.

Cinderella run and drop ze glass slippaire. She care *more* about being home on time than about ze *romance*. Aah, zeese British.

Ze next day, Preence Sharming carry ze glass slippaire around ze town and ees looking for a girl who have ze foot een wheech ze slippaire of eet—ze foot weel feet een eet—ah, een eet. He will marry such a girl whose foot feet een eet. *Oui,* een eet. Ze foot. This foolish man, he fall in love with a *foot*. He do not care about ze othaire end. Aah, zeese Breetish.

Finally, he come to ze home of Cinderella. Cinderella, she put on glass slippaire and eet feet like a glove. Well, naturally, she put her hand een eet. But then she put her foot een eet, eet feet perfect—her foot—een—eet. Een eet.

So at ze end of ze storee, Preence Sharming, he ees veree hapee and he asks for Cinderella's foot in marriage. *Au revoir.*

MIT Voo Doo

"Quit worryin', Nick. I tell ya this babe's a queen."

Missouri Showme

"Who gave the bride away?"
"I could have, but I kept my mouth shut."

Wisconsin Octopus

Oh, Mother, may I go out to swim?
Why not, my darling daughter?
You're so damned near naked anyhow
You'd be safer in the water.

Penn State Froth

STUDE: What did your professor give you in math?
STEWED: I flunked. He said I didn't know math from a hole in the ground.

Texas Ranger

pas ce soir
PARFUM
PRONOUNCED "NAW"
MEANS "IS THAT ALL YOU EVER THINK ABOUT?"

Yale Record

ODE TO A ZO 3 PIG FOETUS

Hail to thee, pink foetus!
Pig thou never wert.
Fourth-floor Silsby you greet us
On laboratory bench,
Wafting fumes of unprecedented stench.

Foetus, foetus, lying limply,
With your skin all-over dimply,
What eager hand with callous pride
Plunked you in formaldehyde?

From what lady pig or sow
Did they take you? Why and how?
Why must I, a harmless youth,
Cut you up? (It seems uncouth.)

Your mother's womb
Became your tomb.
Your world is now celestine,
But *Zo 3* lab
To me is drab,
Dissecting your intestine.

They say your pharynx
Meets your larynx,
And while I wonder whither,
Your fibia
And tibia
Have got me in a dither.

O foetus, my foetus, the dreaded slits and slit.
I have severed every cell, your cerebrum is split.
My knife so keen has seen your spleen,
You're really, I confess,
(From my mauling
Overhauling)
A dank, ungodly mess.

Well, back to your formaldehyde,
Piglet, I will plunk thee,
Something tells me, here, inside,
That, foetus, you will flunk me.

Sigmund Lophauser/*Dartmouth Jack O' Lantern*

Mort Walker/*Missouri Showme*

"Have a Coke"

It's the
friendly
high-sign

BOTTLED UNDER AUTHORITY OF THE COCA-COLA COMPANY BY

COCA-COLA BOTTLING CO. OF UTAH

SALT LAKE CITY

COASTING 1950–1959

Everything WONDERFUL happens in APRIL LOVE!
PAT
BOONE
and
SHIRLEY
JONES
in
April Love
CINEMASCOPE
COLOR BY DE LUXE
starring
DOLORES
MICHAELS
ARTHUR
O'CONNELL
Hear Pat and Shirley sing and fall in love to
"April Love"
"Clover In The Meadow"
"Do It Yourself"
"Give Me A Gentle Girl"
"Bentonville Fair"
SEE IT AT YOUR FAVORITE NEIGHBORHOOD THEATRE!

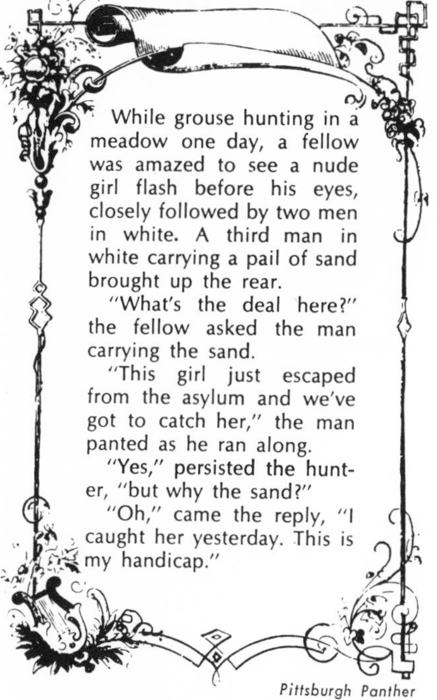

While grouse hunting in a meadow one day, a fellow was amazed to see a nude girl flash before his eyes, closely followed by two men in white. A third man in white carrying a pail of sand brought up the rear.

"What's the deal here?" the fellow asked the man carrying the sand.

"This girl just escaped from the asylum and we've got to catch her," the man panted as he ran along.

"Yes," persisted the hunter, "but why the sand?"

"Oh," came the reply, "I caught her yesterday. This is my handicap."

Pittsburgh Panther

Responding to a knock on the door, a housewife found a man standing apologetically before her.

"I just ran over your cat," he told her, "and I'd like to replace her."

"Well, get busy," snapped the housewife. "There's a mouse in the pantry."

American University Bald Eagle

D. Roberts/*Texas Ranger*

Page Brownton/*San Jose State Lyke*

AND A PARTRIDGE IN A PEAR TREE

850 Park Ave.
New York, N. Y.
The First Day of Christmas

Jimmy Darling!

Oh, you *precious* thing! Of all the absolutely *adorable* things to send me—I mean it was simply *perfect!* That *huge* big box had us all simply *dying* of curiosity until this morning when I opened it—and then all those *tons* of paper covering up that *darling* pear tree! Daddy and Mummie helped me lift it out of the box, and then we found that dear, sweet little bird hiding behind one of the pears. It was just like two presents in one. Honestly! It was just *divine* of you to send me such an original gift—I'm so tired of getting furs and jewelry and that sort of thing. I can't *wait* to get back to Poughkeepsie and show all the girls! Thank you with all my heart, sweetie.

All my love,
Margot

(Excerpt from letter, Third Day of Christmas)

. . . the turtle doves are so nice—they sit up there on the chandelier and just coo their little hearts out. Of course, Mummie is a bit worried about the rug, but I'm sure she'll get over it. And those French hens, Jim! They're so *big!* I don't mean that they're not gorgeous or anything like that—but the maid *was* rather upset when one lit on her head this afternoon. But anyhow, I'm getting to love all my little feathered friends very dearly. Thank you so much.

Love,
Margot

(Excerpt from letter, Fifth Day of Christmas)

. . . unfortunately, Jimmy, Daddy finds those calling birds kind of annoying. Actually, he says they're just plain old crows, and they *are* rather loud. Also, the maid quit because they kept pecking her legs all the time. And the French hens have gotten somewhat out of hand—we keep finding eggs in the *strangest* places. Feathers too. On the other hand, the rings are quite handsome. But why five? And I'm *sure* it's my imagination, but my fingers do look just the teensiest bit green . . .

Sincerely,
Margot

850 Park Ave.
New York, N. Y.
The Seventh Day of Christmas

The New York State
Employment Service

Gentlemen:

Recent happenings have made it necessary that I procure as soon as possible an expert in the handling of birds. All types of birds, I might add. It would be helpful but not essential if he could also serve as cook, maid and butler.

Yours truly,
Potter A. Smythe-White

(The Tenth Day of Christmas)

Jim—

Hasn't this gone far enough? I mean *really!* It's not that I don't appreciate the thought, but all these *birds!* Father was positively *livid* when two of those swans beat him to the bathtub this morning, and Mother has polished off two bottles of APC's since yesterday morning because of those milking maids out in the kitchen.

Regards,
Margot

(Telegram, Twelfth Day of Christmas)

MR. JAMES BARTON
BOSTON, MASS.

SIR: EXPECT LORDS, LADIES FLIGHT 401; PIPERS, DRUMMERS, MAIDS TEN O'CLOCK TRAIN; SWANS, GEESE, COWS, BIRDS, HENS, DOVES, PARTRIDGE RAILWAY EXPRESS; RINGS, TREE REGISTERED MAIL. ALL COLLECT. TRY CONTACT ME AGAIN AND WILL HAVE YOU ARRESTED.

MARGOT SMYTHE-WHITE

H. Snee/*Yale Record*

Florida State Smoke Signals

THE SEX LIFE OF A HEDGEHOG

One of the things I want to discover
Is how the hedgehog takes a lover.
Maybe he practices
On cactuses.

UCLA Scop

"How old are you?"
"I'm five. How old are you?"
"I'm either four or five. I don't know which."
"Do women bother you?"
"No."
"You're four."

Colorado Flatiron

Scene in an English barroom—
LIMEY: 'Allo, Mary. Are you 'aving one?
MARY: No, it's just the cut o' me coat.

Pomona Sage Hen

"Was that your best girl I saw you with last night?"
"No, necks best."

Princeton Tiger

"Heard you were moving a piano so I came over to help."
"Thanks, but I've already got it moved upstairs."
"Alone?"
"Nope, hitched the cat to it and drug it up."
"You mean your cat hauled that piano up two flights of stairs? How could a cat pull a heavy piano?"
"Used a whip."

Florida State Smoke Signals

READ THIS

It's something new! Never before has such an offer been possible. No buckles, straps or other clumsy devices. Comes in a variety of beautiful shapes. You'll love the full selection of beautiful colors—rust, pink, brown, light red, brown, pinkish-rose and brown. Order yours today. If not completely delighted and satisfied, we will refund your used postage stamp.

UCLA Scop

It has been recounted to us that a reporter once called on Bertrand Russell for an interview. Greeted at the door by Russell's daughter, age seven, and seeing her stark naked, the reporter stepped back. "My God!" he exclaimed.

"Oh!" the nude young thing chirped, "there is no God. Won't you come in?"

Columbia Jester

HE: What would you say if I stole a kiss?
SHE: What would you say to a guy who had a chance to steal an automobile but only took the windshield wiper?

Pittsburgh Panther

Greta Garbo, star of *Camille*, was, perhaps, an eccentric. She once, so the story goes, sprinkled grass seed in her hair. When asked why she performed this stunt, the elusive Swede replied, "I vant to be a lawn."

Texas Ranger

An up and coming South American government decided to get new uniforms. The official tailor was called in and shown the design. It included blue trousers, red boots, a green jacket and gold epaulets.

"Is this the uniform for the President's palace guard?" inquired the tailor.

"No," said the officer, "it's for the Secret Police."

Florida State Smoke Signals

I'M HOT FOR YOU, BABY

"I'm hot for you, baby!" he bellowed through smoky breath, seizing her roughly somewhere between the waist and chin and hurling her viciously to the bed. With a precise motion, he ripped her flimsy dress.

(How do you like this story so far? Good, huh? Just as I figured. You know what I should do right now? I should stop. You know why? Because sometimes you make me sick. But don't worry, I won't. Not while I have you eating out of the palm of my hand. And I do, you know. How many people, after seeing the above title, and first paragraph, skipped this story? How many would dare? Show me one, and I'll show you a liar.

(You know, you're all good kids, but sometimes you make me so mad! Month after month we courageously attempt to sublimate our literary efforts. We try to foment the intelligent capacity of a supposedly high level of humanity. And what happens? We get letters—tear-smeared letters. Not enough sex. Give us more sex. SEX! SEX! Aaah, you make me sick!)

"Bruno!" she shouted, dropping her shoes to the floor and making herself comfortable. "You don't have to treat me like this, because I'm hot for you too!"

(Getting better, now, isn't it? Here's a girl who—well, who might possibly flunk or get a very low C on her convent entrance examination. But a girl, nevertheless, who is a victim of environment. Underneath—if you want to dig—you'll probably find she's pure. Why, she could be your . . . sister. Well, she could! But do you care? Nah. You're just sitting there chewing this up, swallowing it, and crying for more. All you want to see is——Aaah, sometimes I get so fed up!)

"Malvina!" he roared. "Malvina baby! Don't torture me like this when I'm so hot for you!"

"Who's torturing you?" she asked, leaning back and loosening—well, whatever she wanted to loosen.

(Who's torturing you? Who's torturing you? Did you hear what that horrid girl said? That—that —— Did you hear what your sister said? But, no, you won't go home and tell your mother. Oh no, you're really beginning to enjoy this. Aaah!

(Do you know what I had originally planned to write? A brief account of merchandising before and after the Middle Ages. What are you twisting your face like that for? It would have done you some good.)

Princeton Tiger

Deftly Bruno divested himself of his shirt and revealed a hairy chest, which rose and fell in the accelerated tide of passion. Eagerly she helped him off with his shoes. "Baby," he said, "I'm so ——"

"So stop talking already!" she shouted.

(So stop talking already! So stop talking already! Listen to her moan. Your own flesh and blood. Would you help her? Do you care? Naah. You're just squirming because I'm delaying this.

(I suppose you think you know all there is to know about merchandising before and after the Middle Ages.)

Gently Bruno took her into his hairy arms and crushed her to his heaving bosom.

"Oooh!" she squealed.

With his right hand he——

(I'll bet you think it's easy to turn out a college humor magazine every month and please everybody. Sure, you say, and put plenty of sex into it. It's easy to say. Put sex into it. Of course, you forget that we writers are conscientious, clean-living people who are making an earnest attempt to lay the groundwork for future, sober endeavors.

(My God, we're just Americans like the rest of you. We like picnics, hay rides, Coney Island, and Bing Crosby. We hate to see that evening sun go down. We like to wrap sandwiches in old Chicago Tribunes and go fishing. Give us a break. How far can we get writing stuff like this?)

With his right hand he seized her left shoulder, and with his left arm he seized her right shoulder. Only her quick, uneven breath, which started from her nose and came out from her mouth—except when it was vice versa—interrupted the stillness of the room. Suddenly something dropped to the floor.

(In a recent poll conducted by

Thomas Trot, George Gallop, and Eddie Canter, it was revealed that out of the three hundred branches of the W.C.T.U. which are located in the area between Des Moines and Dobbs Ferry, not one—I'll repeat—not one subscribes to Shaft.

(And do you know why? Do I have to tell you? Not enough sex.

(Well, I tell you, I'm sick of it. I hate sex. I'll get it out of the homes. I'll take it off the campuses. On the blackboards of sex-hygiene classes I'll write, "It ain't fitten to talk about."

(We could have had fun, you and I. You know, merchandising before and after the Middle Ages isn't anywhere near merchandising DURING the Middle Ages.)

"What dropped to the floor, Bruno?" Malvina asked, disengaging herself from him.

A surge of crimson enveloped his face. "It was . . ." he stammered. "It was . . ."

(Look at her now! Look! Look! Look at Malvina! Hah, Malvina! I only call her that. She could be anybody. She could be . . . well, you know who she could be; I told you before. Look at her! Disgusting! Look how she's dressed! What would your father say? What do you say? Listen to her; she wants to know what dropped on the floor. That's all that's important to her right now. Nothing else on earth matters. Schools, studies, the future, Russia; they're unimportant. And what about you—a blood relation? What about you? You want to know what dropped on the floor, too. To tell you the truth so do I. But you can ask her when she comes home, I can't. That's one of the reasons I get so fed up. Sex. Baah!)

NEXT MONTH—DEFINITELY: A DISCUSSION ON MERCHANDISING BEFORE AND AFTER THE MIDDLE AGES; OR MAYBE—A LITTLE TALK ON WHAT DROPPED ON THE FLOOR.

"Sparks" Siegel/*Illinois Shaft*

"Oh, he just does that to attract attention."

Princeton Tiger

The bee is such a busy soul
It has no time for birth control,
And that is why in times like these
There are so many sons of bees.

Anonymous/*Columbia Jester*

Jack be quick; Jack be nimble;
Jack jump over the phallic symbol.

Columbia Jester

PROF: What is the difference between a little boy and a dwarf?
STUDENT: There might be a lot of difference.
PROF: For instance?
STUDENT: The dwarf might be a girl.

Missouri Showme

COMIC STRIP

"Explain sex," she said,
On the sofa with me.
I figured I should—
She was past twenty-three.
"My dear," I declared,
"I shall do as you bid,
But you'll have to bear with me—"
And (bless her) she did.

Ivan Gold/*Columbia Jester*

POEM

Preacher Ben despite adversity
Saved a southern university;
Said his nephew: "Ain't that nice?
Uncle Ben's converted Rice."

Louis Anthony/*Columbia Jester*

THE RE-EVALUATION OF EXTRACURRICULAR ACTIVITIES

TRANSCRIPT OF THE FIRST SESSION

(The meeting was called to order at 3:15 P.M.)

SECRETARY FOR PROTOCOL: Hear ye, hear ye, hear ye! Student Board is now in session, please refrain from conversation. Everyone rise. His excellency, the Chairman.

(The Chairman took his place on the dais.)

SECRETARY FOR PROTOCOL: Be seated.

CHAIRMAN: In an attempt to alleviate the chronic and pervasive apathy of the student body, and in its desire to fulfill its obligation to encourage, regulate, control, direct, and periodically evaluate and re-evaluate the extra-curricular activities of the Columbia College community, the Board of Student Representatives will now proceed to examine the position of these activities within the general framework of the College, taken as a socio-psychological whole. The success of our venture rests not only on the punitive and regulatory powers of Student Board as defined in Article XLV, Section 47A of the University Charter, which reads —and I quote—"But if you will not obey the voice of Student Board, then all these curses shall come upon you and overtake you. Cursed shall you be in the city, and cursed shall you be in the field. Cursed shall be your basket and your kneading-trough. Cursed shall be the fruit of your body, and the fruit of your ground, the increase of your cattle, and the young of your flock. Student Board will send upon you curses, confusion, and frustration in all that you undertake to do, until your activity is destroyed and perishes quickly, on account of the evil of your doings, because you have forsaken its tenets"—no, the success of our venture rests also on the cooperation given to it by the respective activities. Call the first witness.

His excellency, the chairman

PROTOCOL SECRETARY: President of the Chess Club to the stand.

(The President of the Chess Club took the stand.)

PROTOCOL SECRETARY: Do you swear to tell the whole truth and nothing but the truth so help you God?

PRESIDENT: P-K4.

PROTOCOL SECRETARY: Be seated.

CHAIRMAN: Mr. Alekhine, would you tell us something about your activity? What are its aims and purposes? What is its Ultimate Goal?

PRESIDENT: P-K4.

CHAIRMAN: I'm sorry, Mr. Alekhine, but that doesn't really answer my question. Perhaps you don't really understand, and are not in sympathy with, the purposes of this investigation. If this is so, then you are unadjusted to the broader socio-political currents of the College community.

PRESIDENT: Kn-KB3.

CHAIRMAN: Mr. Alekhine, won't you listen to Reason? Once more I will clarify the general framework-area of this re-examination. As I said in a letter to our campus newspaper, "Our 'investigation,' or 're-evaluation,' or perhaps 're-appraisal,' which is really a much better term except maybe for perhaps 're-study,' is a well-meant attempt to improve the academic atmosphere of the extra-curricular community, which has been shirking its responsibilities, although we will not at the moment define the sphere-context of this shirking."

". . . PK4"

PRESIDENT: Kn-QB3.

CHAIRMAN: Mr. Alekhine, I beg you: please don't forget that Student Board has the constitutional power to exercise control over and make regulations for all—

PRESIDENT: B-Kn5. P-QR3. B-R4. Kn-KB3. Castles.

CHAIRMAN: Ah, Mr. Alekhine, the lot of a Student Board Chairman is difficult, indeed. Ah, yes. Will the Recording Secretary strike the Chess Club from the roster of the extra-curricular community?

RECORDING SECRETARY: It has been so stricken.

CHAIRMAN: You are excused, Mr. Alekhine. Call the next witness.

SECRETARY FOR PROTOCOL: Editor-in-Chief of *Spectator* to the stand.

(The Editor-in-Chief of Spectator *took the stand.)*

SECRETARY FOR PROTOCOL: Do you swear to tell the whole truth and nothing but the truth so help you God?

EDITOR: Check.

SECRETARY FOR PROTOCOL: Be seated.

CHAIRMAN: Mr. Nussbern, could you give us some idea of what your activity is accomplishing within the sociological framework-context of the extra-curricular community? Do you think you could sum this up for us, as succinctly as possible?

EDITOR: Gotcha. Now here's the deal. Story breaks, we get man out on it. Man comes back, bangs out copy, flips to copy desk. Copy proofed, flipped to city ed, down to plant. Check. Proofs rolled, nite eds read. Slugs pulled, typos reset. Check.

CHAIRMAN: Mr. Nussbern, could you speak a little slower, please? Now I lost you when you said—

EDITOR: Gotcha. Yes, sometimes hit snag. Chem Club elections come through, got to tear up front page. Call plant. Yell "Tear up front page!" Sometimes big edit controversy or nite ed drunk. Sometimes bad headline. Sometimes—

CHAIRMAN: Yes, Mr. Nussbern, but I don't quite understand—

EDITOR: Gotcha. We got on-ball reporters what know business.

CHAIRMAN: Yes, Mr. Nussbern. That will be all.

EDITOR: All news what fits we print is motto. We got big exposé coming up. We got hairy-chicken story from Lions' Den—

"We got big sports story. Cantabs rout Mermen."

"Being a product[8] of the New Capitalism,[9] you could scarcely be expected to."[10]

CHAIRMAN: Yes, Mr. Nussbern, yes. Won't someone please escort Mr. Nussbern out?

EDITOR: We got big sports story. Cantabs rout Mermen. We got—

(Mr. Nussbern was escorted out.)

CHAIRMAN: Will the Recording Secretary extirpate *Spectator* from the roll-call of the extra-curricular community?

RECORDING SECRETARY: It has been so extirpated.

CHAIRMAN: The life of a Student Leader is a hard one, isn't it, Harvey?

VICE-CHAIRMAN: You said it, Stan. Yes, sir.

CHAIRMAN: Wouldn't you say so, too, Bob?

SECRETARY FOR PROTOCOL: Oh, you bet, Stan. You said it.

CHAIRMAN: It's good to see you boys have the right slant on things. Call the next witness.

SECRETARY FOR PROTOCOL: Editor-in-Chief of *King's Crown Essays* to the stand.

(The Editor-in-Chief of King's Crown Essays *took the stand.)*

SECRETARY FOR PROTOCOL: Do you swear to tell the whole truth and nothing but the truth so help you God?

EDITOR: I do.[1]

SECRETARY FOR PROTOCOL: Be seated.

CHAIRMAN: Sir, as you have no doubt observed, the psychosomatic factors making for community unadjustment have indeed wreaked an obverse effect on the extra-curricular community at Columbia. I trust that you will comport yourself in such a manner as to obviate the drasticity it has been my sad duty already to exercise against your colleagues.

EDITOR: I think[2] Bryan made a similar point[3] when he was howled[4] down[5] by the St. Louis Hegelians.[6]

CHAIRMAN: I'm afraid I don't understand.

EDITOR: Neither did McKinley.[7]

CHAIRMAN: I'm afraid that I still don't understand.

EDITOR: Being a product[8] of the New Capitalism,[9] you could scarcely be expected to.[10]

CHAIRMAN: Very well, then. You force me to exercise extremitism I abhor. Your activity will be disbanded.

EDITOR: You realize,[11] of course, that *Freenwitch vs. Porkel Fertilizer Corp.*[12] renders your decision[13] unconstitutional?

CHAIRMAN: Before this tribunal, *I* am the Constitution. Will the Recording Secretary eradicate *King's Crown Essays* from the call-list of the extra-curricular community?

RECORDING SECRETARY: It has been so eradicated.

CHAIRMAN: You are excused. Call the next witness.

SECRETARY FOR PROTOCOL: Dean of the College to the stand.

(There was a stir in the audience. The Dean of the College was escorted in by a squad of student leaders and was brought to the stand.)

SECRETARY FOR PROTOCOL: Do you swear to tell the whole truth and nothing but the truth so help you God?

DEAN OF THE COLLEGE: This is ridiculous. Take these handcuffs off me.

SECRETARY FOR PROTOCOL: Be seated.

CHAIRMAN: Well, Dean—

DEAN: This is ridiculous. You have no right to do this.

CHAIRMAN: Dean Chamber, as you no doubt are aware of, we of the Board are conducting a re-evaluation of the extra-curricular community—

DEAN: But I'm *not* extra-curricular! I'm the Dean!

CHAIRMAN: I will read from the University Charter, Article CXVIII, Section 76C: "All those activities which, by definition, do not fall directly within the academic context of the College shall be designated as "extra-curricular."

DEAN: But—

CHAIRMAN: Do you teach, Dean Chamber?

DEAN: No, but—

CHAIRMAN: Do you play any direct role in any of the departments of study of the College?

DEAN: Well, in a manner of speaking—

CHAIRMAN: Then you are an extra-curricular activity. Now would you tell us, please, just what you are doing to further the aims of the Columbia College community within the contextual sphere of your activity?

DEAN: I refuse to recognize the legality of this farce! I refuse to answer any more of these questions! I am the Dean! The Dean, do you hear? The Dean! The Dean!

CHAIRMAN: Escort the Dean out, please.

DEAN: The Dean! The Dean! I'm the Dean!

(The Dean was escorted out.)

CHAIRMAN: I move that we adjourn until 3:15 tomorrow.

VICE-CHAIRMAN AND SECRETARY FOR PROTOCOL: Seconded, Stan!

(The court-room was cleared.)

Henry Ebel and David A. Rosand/*Columbia Jester*

"But I'm not extracurricular! I'm the Dean!"

"Well, Miss Bentley, it looks like the time has finally come to transfer you to the hat-check room."

Yale Record

LIMERICKEY

"Buford, there is a fourth-year poultry major"
Rowland Wilson/*Texas Ranger*

Another Charles Van Doren story which has come to us second-hand (who knows?—perhaps this will be the last) concerns one of his lesser known but strongest skills—pedagogy. It seems, we are told, that the major portion of his Humanities A1 class last year was avidly preparing for his midterm examination with the help of the standard pony for the course. The question was to be centered about the inevitable comparison between Herodotus and Thucydides, one which has plagued students from the time the course began. As we all know, the pony contains a ready-made summary of such a comparison, and this outline was dutifully committed to memory by the mass of grateful culture-gatherers.

On the day of the exam, Mr. Van Doren's disciples filed confidently into their lecture room. Their instructor greeted them and proceeded to outline the vital question on the blackboard. Before the incredulous eyes of the twenty-odd students seated in the room, the pony analysis began to appear, word for word, upon the board. No one could properly understand what was happening until the final, and decisive, command appeared in writing at the bottom. It stated simply: "Disprove the above."

Columbia Jester

Howie was a good man, it was just that he didn't like to pass up opportunities to get something for nothing. He went out of his way to find sneak previews, had in his library the *A-Ames* volume of every encyclopedia ever offered through the mail, and had developed an absolute mania for little piles of assorted miscellany entitled "take one." Otherwise, as I say, Howie was a good man.

Then he discovered the limerick contest.

It happened one evening on his way back from the Waldorf Cafeteria. He had picked up a copy of the New York *Daily Mirror*, because of its "Lucky Buck" listings, and was glancing through it by the dim light of the streetlamps on Chapel Street. Howie suddenly stopped. There before him was a full-page ad describing how easy it was to win an oil well. *AN OIL WELL!* All he had to do was finish, in rhyme, the sentence, "I'm glad I use Dial. . . ." Well, Howie was a pretty good man, but he wasn't absolutely celebrated as the cleanest guy around. He had never even heard of Dial soap. Nevertheless, he was determined, and walked back to his room counting barrels.

After a few pencil-chewing minutes, Howie came up with

"I'm glad I use Dial whenever I wash;
I've used it to clean me since I was a frosh."

Howie's roommate Earl looked up from his prone position studying on the floor, raised an eyebrow, slowly shook his head from side to side, and went back to reading. Howie thought for a while, scribbling a bit, and read

"I'm glad I use Dial, its lather's so creamy;
When I use it the girls think I'm really quite dreamy."

Earl sat up straight. "Just wait a second," he said. "I suppose you're trying to win something, but you'll never do it with *that*. You need something different—even bizarre." That was Earl all over, always looking for the *macabre*, like the skull he used for an ashtray in his bedroom. "How about

I'm glad I use Dial, made from glycerine and lye—
The last time I used it I burned out my eye.

—or even better—" by this time there was a decided gleam in Earl's eye. "How's this:

I'm glad I use Dial, said Queen Cleopatra
As she carved off her leg with a blade from Sumatra."

The door to one of the bedrooms was slowly opened, and Paul stepped out and lit a cigarette.

"I'm glad I use Dial, because then I won't smell
And then my friends will think I'm swell,"

he offered.

"Not quite," Earl said. But Paul was not one to be discouraged by so slight a rejection, and suggested

"I'm glad I use Dial soap, it makes me feel so homey,
Because when I put it in water it gets all lathery and foamy."

"Good God, man!" shouted Walt from the bedroom. He bounded into the room nearly ready to throttle his roommate Paul, who was, after all, trying.

"You have no sense of poetry WHATSOEVER, man!" Walt was an English major and took things like this pretty seriously. "You need something like a literary tradition. You could satire, well, Kipling, for example.

I'm glad I use Dial, it cleanses my skin.
A much better soap than I'm Gunga Din!
or show your knowledge of early prose form something like
I'm glad I ufe Dial foap, faid Tyndale to Wyclif;
Because if I do fo I'm not quite fo tycklif."

By this time it was obvious that no one was listening to anyone else—each of them was writing furiously.

"I'm glad I use Dial, it's so wonderfully sweet;
It cleanses my arms and my legs and my feet,"
said Howie, who was beginning to catch on.
"I'm glad I use Dial, but too much don't scrub;
A friend rubbed too hard and dissolved in the tub!"
shouted Earl.

Paul blew a smoke ring into the air and suggested
"I'm glad I use Dial, it's really swell
So please go to Hell."
This pleased him so much that he was about to repeat it when Walt started jumping up and down. "Listen, T. S. Eliot! Listen!
I'm glad I use Dial, I'm so glad you see—
Datta Damyatim Dayadvam—Shan—Ti!"

Sandy from across the hall, a serious sort of boy with a calculated cleverness, had strolled into the room about five minutes before to see what the commotion was all about. At last he could stand it no longer.
"I'm glad I use Dial. From senile sterility
It's borne me to heights of exceptional virility."

The entire room was now in high gear, everyone enthusiastically interposing his latest in a louder voice than the last.
I'm glad I use Dial—give birth my long locks.
It burns at the stake, shrieked the opera box!"
said Walt. Howie shouted—
"I'm glad I use Dial, said the bird to the bee.
It saves much explaining to children, you see."
Earl intoned—
"I'm glad I use Dial, it not only kills germs,
But rids my whole body of maggots and worms."
For a brief moment Sandy's voice could be heard above the rest.
"I'm glad I use Dial, it's so Machiavellian.
It cleanses my arms and my legs and my bellian."

The room reached fever pitch. Faction faced faction. Instead of words, books and ashtrays soon became missiles. From an open window across the courtyard came two more gems:
"I'm glad I use Dial, the octopus said.
Or else, with eight arm pits, I'd be better off dead."
and
"I'm glad I use Dial; the rats in the wall
Inhale of it, pale of it, and die away all."

The sound apparently had reached all the way to the office of Fred the college guard, who strode triumphantly into the room, held up his arms, and dramatically recited:
"I'm glad I use Dial, for filth is a sin;
But if you don't hit the sack, I'll turn you all in."

Slowly, grudgingly, the noise abated. Apologies were made, lights were turned off, and everyone found his way to bed, mumbling in rhythmic fashion.

Unfortunately, the next morning Howie could remember none of the limericks composed the night before. It didn't make much difference, though. Two weeks later Howie's Texas uncle died and left him seventeen oil wells in Dallas. Howie was rather pleased—especially since he never had to use Dial soap.

J. S. Stevenson/*Yale Record*

"You're upside-down"
Rowland Wilson/*Texas Ranger*

The student passed the classics professor in the corridor of Hamilton Hall, and greeted him with a cheery "Hello, sir; what's new?"

The professor stopped, turned, and replied: "*Nu* is the thirteenth letter of the Greek alphabet, following *mu* and preceding *xi*. Its capital form is similar to the English upper case N, its lower case form is like the English small *v*. It is sounded like the English 'N.' "

They parted in silence.

Columbia Jester

While motoring through scenic Vermont one day we stopped to ask directions from a lanky old farmer who looked as if he might say something witty.

"Say, Grandpa, where does this road go to?" we asked.

"Wal," he drawled, scratching his head with a hoe, "the way I look at it is, if you don't plant 'taters, they won't grow."

Chuckling over the fellow's homely philosophy, we dumped all our trash on his property and drove on.

Cornell *Widow*

TWENTY THOUSAND LEAGUES 'NEATH THE SEA Or GLUB GLUB

A THREE-ACT FARCE IN TWO ACTS

LIFE MAGAZINE CAME OUT RECENTLY WITH THEIR LIST OF THE BEST movies of the year. *Spectator*, too, has selected the best movie of the year . . . which was shown in the town of Charlottesville. The poll showed the following facts.

156 students were asked: Which movie, of all those shown here in Charlottesville during the last year, did you like best?

153 have never been to a movie.

100 of these spend their time at the library.

53 of these are in fraternities.

3 of those polled go to the movies only to see the newsreels.

Conclusion:

153% of the students do not attend movies.

3% of the students see only newsreels.

156% of the students have not seen any full-length movies.

In view of the following poll, *Spectator* thought it best not only to give the name of the year's best movie but also to print the script of the said movie. The following was shown at the Jefferson Theatre . . .

Act I, Scene I

SCENE I: *Twenty thousand leagues below the sea.*

TIME: *1:35 P.M.*

Mary is imprisoned in the castle of the Green-Eyed Monster twenty thousand leagues below the surface of the Pacific Ocean.

Mary speaks: "Help! Help!"

Act I, Scene II

SCENE: *New York office building in the center of Manhattan.*

TIME: *1:35 P.M.*

John is dictating a letter to his secretary and hears Mary's scream.

JOHN: Quick! Turn off the pencil sharpener; I thought I heard my true love Mary.

MARY: You did.

JOHN: That's what I thought. *(He jumps from his chair and leaps out of the window. Landing nimbly on his feet, he whistles three times for his faithful horse.)*

HORSE: Heh?

JOHN: Hurry, faithful horse. My true love Mary is imprisoned by the Green-Eyed Monster in his castle twenty thousand leagues below the sea.

HORSE: How far?

JOHN: Twenty thousand leagues!

HORSE: Gawd! Let's take a cab.

(John whistles three times and the horse whistles once. John can whistle much louder than the horse. A cab, driven by John's father, pulls to the curb. John and the horse get in.)

CABBIE: Where to, boss? "You call, we haul, das all."

JOHN: To Mary, who is imprisoned by the Green-Eyed Monster in his castle twenty thousand leagues below the sea, and hurry!

(The cabbie turns on the meter and the horse turns it off and the cabbie turns it back on and the horse turns it back off and the cabbie turns it back on and the horse turns it back off and the cabbie . . .)

Act II, Scene I

SCENE: *Twenty thousand leagues below the sea.*

TIME: *1:35 P.M.*

(Monster and Mary in his castle.)

MONSTER *(angrily)*: Did you yell "help!"?

MARY: No, I yelled "help, help!"

MONSTER: Oh!

(The cab, containing John and the horse, drives up.)

MONSTER: I didn't call a cab.

CABBIE: Oh! *(The cab drives off.)*

JOHN: Stop, fool, stop! You've left the castle of the Green-Eyed Monster who has my true love Mary imprisoned twenty thousand leagues below the sea. *(The cabbie stops and turns the meter back on and the horse turns it back off and the cabbie leaves it off and the horse turns it back on . . .)*

JOHN: Enough, stupid! We're here now.

Act II, Scene II

SCENE: *In the dining room of the Green-Eyed Monster in his castle twenty thousand leagues below the sea.*

TIME: *1:35 P.M.*

(The Monster and Mary are seated at the table eating, in the dining room of the Green-Eyed Monster, in the castle twenty thousand leagues below the sea. John dashes into the room, followed by his faithful horse, followed by the cabbie, followed by the cab.)

JOHN: Ahoy there, varmit!
MARY: Who, me?
JOHN: No, stupid. Ahoy there, varmit!
MONSTER: Ahoy there, yourself!
JOHN: Ahoy there, John!
MONSTER: Have you come to do battle with me in order to rescue your true love Mary?
JOHN: Yeah!
MONSTER: Oh!
JOHN: En garde ! ! !
(Monster en gardes.)
JOHN: Grr . . . Take that! And that . . . and that.
(Monster takes that and falls back on the floor.)
MONSTER: Ohhhhh! You've done me in. *(The Monster slyly draws John's sword from his body and stabs John with it.)*
MARY: Ohhh! Poor John, who is my true love. *(She weeps.)*
MONSTER: Do not cry, true love, for I am really John and John is the Monster. *(He unzips his monster suit and reveals himself as John.)*
MARY: Ah, true love. *(She rushes to John's arms.)*
CABBIE: Stop, true love Mary. I am your true love John. *(He rips the John suit from the Monster and unzips his cabbie suit, revealing himself as John.)*
MARY: Ah, John, my true love. *(She rushes to his arms.)*
MONSTER *(from the floor)*: Stop, true love Mary. I am your true love John. *(He jumps from the floor revealing himself as John, and John as the Monster.)*
MARY: Ah, my true love John. *(She rushes to his arms.)*
HORSE: Stop, Monster, I am John.
CAB: Stop, I am the horse.
JOHN: Stop, I am the Monster.
MARY *(sitting in the cab's arms)*: This is all so confusing. *(She unzips her Mary suit, revealing herself as the Monster and kills them all.)*

FAST exit. Finis!

Rex Gatten and Mark Friedlander/
Virginia Spectator

Ted Robins/ *Florida State Smoke Signals*

Gilbert Shelton/Texas Ranger

"Let's see that map again."
Princeton Tiger

"What's your problem, Shorty?"
Walt Kraemer and Fred Sellers/American University Bald Eagle

"It seems that Mr. Hollenbeck doesn't agree with my last point."
Don Peterson/Florida State Smoke Signals

California Pelican

"You sweaty son of a bitch!"

Princeton Tiger

Gilbert Shelton/Texas Ranger

"It's that man from the telephone office."

John Frazer/Texas Ranger

"It's good, Amedeo, but is it really me?!"

Paul T. Nagano/Columbia Jester

BARNARD TILSON: "THIS IS MY BEST"

(Reading time: 12:5 seconds.)

EVERY organization that amounts to anything these days has a poll. When a friend of ours who works for *Mechanics Diagrammed* asked us to help him test a new, minute recording device, we perceived our opportunity to take a survey of what subjects occupy the conversational time of average Cornellians. We placed these recorders in representative places about the campus, and collected them the following day. Below are the literal remarks of speakers near the microphones at the places indicated.

2:00 *A.M. Behind a wad of gum, under a fraternity bar.*

Feminine voice: "I want to go home in the worst possible way."

He: "Take the Lehigh Valley . . . or better still, may I take you home? I like to take experienced girls home."

"I'm not experienced."

"You're not home yet. . . ."

9:00 *A.M. Inside a Puffed-Rice Sparkie at The Johnny Parsons Club.*

". . . Did you get home all right last night, after you took me home?"

"Yes, thanks, except that just as I was turning the corner someone stepped on my fingers. But say, speaking of last night," he went on, "I had to come clear across the room to kiss you!"

"I'm glad you didn't come from the next block! By the way, when you come here, do you always flirt with the waitress?"

"I'm playing for big steaks!" he exclaimed in a triumphant tone.

"Ooh . . . Say, would you have the man put some more chocolate syrup on my sundae?"

"Sure, I'll have him goo the limit for you."

7:00 *P.M. Under a couch in a modern downtown office.*

". . . Let's play air-mail."

"What's that?"

"Post-office on a higher plane. . . ." (*At this point a low feminine groan is heard—Ed.*)

"All right, then, let's play Morse Code. . . ."

"I suppose that's post-office on a touchier basis!"

"You're too smart . . . we'd better play pony express."

"Let's stop being subtle, I can think of quicker ways to get my male."

"OK, then, kiss me!"

"Make me!"

"Oh, can't I kiss you . . . please may I kiss you?"

"Say, are you paralyzed?"

"Hey, just a minute," he said, "I thought I heard something break."

"Never mind, that was just my promise to mother."

8:00 *P.M. Clara Dickson waiting room . . . in an ash tray.*

"It's about time you got here, shall we sit in the parlor?"

"No, I'm too tired. Let's go skiing."

"Oh, better yet, Bobbie was just married, we're giving the bride a shower . . . like to come?"

"Sure, count me in, I'll bring the soap."

"Speaking of brides, Betsy, would you get angry if I proposed to you?"

"It depends on what you propose."

"Oh, dearest, where's your heart?"

"Straight down my throat, first turn to the left."

"It certainly is cool in here all of a sudden. . . . I don't see what keeps you girls from freezing."

"Silly, you're not supposed to."

10:10 *P.M. In the ignition of a car that has just pulled up outside Balch.*

"I've got to be in by 10:30. . . . Say, are there any couples that don't neck in cars?"

"Yeah, the woods are full of them. Oh, darling, I could sit here and look at you forever . . ."

"That's what I'm beginning to think."

"All right then, may I kiss your hand?"

"What's the matter, is my mouth dirty?"

"Well . . . did you take a shower?"

"No, is there one missing?" (*Sounds of a struggle*—Ed.)

"(Gasp) Where did you learn to kiss like that?"

"From eating spaghetti."

"How about one more kiss before I go in."

"I couldn't take another one on an empty stomach."

"Certainly not! On the mouth!"

"Oh, one last thing, how do you know that people can see me dressing through the window?"

"I went to some pane to find out."

"Well, let's call it a day."

(In distance) "What if it's a girl?"

Barnard Tilson/*Cornell Widow*

"God, I'm horny!"

Yale Record

CROSSING THE DELAWARE

I realize someone is going to catch hell for this article, but it so happens I don't much care. Of course, this is not the kind of attitude that will get you very far, but some things just have to be said. Now you take this business about Washington crossing the Delaware. Good stuff, you may say. Well, I have it on reputable authority that American youth are getting taken for a ride when it comes to this guy Washington. He had some good qualities, I'll admit, but on the night of December 25, 1776, he was registering very low on the old herometer. But don't take my word for it. Decide for yourself.

WASHINGTON: God damn it! Stop rocking the boat. My head is killing me.

GEN. GREENE: Well, get away from the bow and stop waving that flag. Every time you get fried you have to ham it up.

WASHINGTON: The people love me.

GEN. GREENE: All right, the people love you. Now sit down.

WASHINGTON: What river is this?

ADJUTANT: The Delaware, sir.

WASHINGTON: The Delaware! What are we doing on the Delaware? Who gave this order?

ADJUTANT: You did, sir.

WASHINGTON: Why did you let me do it? I'll have you drummed out of camp for this. You, there! Don't row so hard. Can't you see my head is splitting open? How did this happen, Greene?

GEN. GREENE: Don't you remember? We were having our Christmas party and the liquor ran out. Someone told you the Hessians were having a big blowout across the river and you got the bright idea to come over and join the party.

WASHINGTON: Oh, my God! . . . What are these other boats doing here?

GEN. GREENE: You invited the rest of the army along.

WASHINGTON: The whole army! Greene, we're dished!

LAFAYETTE: Ha, ha, ha. *C'est drôle.*

WASHINGTON: What did the brat say?

GEN. GREENE: He says the whole thing is good for laughs.

WASHINGTON: Oh, he did, did he? Well, you can tell him to take the first ship for France in the morning. He's done nothing but gum up the works ever since he's been over here. I can't figure what Martha sees in him.

GEN. GREENE: The Continental Congress is going to raise hell about this. We'd better think of something fast.

WASHINGTON: They've got a lot of nerve. Trying to palm off those phony bills on me.

LAFAYETTE: Ha, ha, ha. *C'est très comique.*

WASHINGTON: What did he say?

GEN. GREENE: He says he thinks you're funny.

WASHINGTON: Everything's funny to him. That's all he says, *"Oui, oui,* ha, ha, ha. *C'est drôle. C'est comique.* Ha, ha, ha. *Oui, oui."* What a bonehead!

ADJUTANT: Lights, sir! The Hessian camp!

WASHINGTON: Where?

ADJUTANT: Dead ahead, sir! Don't you see them?

WASHINGTON: Stop shouting. Now look what you've done. I've dropped my teeth. Everybody look for my teeth.

GEN. GREENE: Which ones?

WASHINGTON: Damn it! The mahogany ones.

LAFAYETTE: *Reportez-moi à la vieille Virginie. C'est où le—"*

WASHINGTON: For the last time, shut up!

ADJUTANT: Sir, we are about to land. What shall we do?

WASHINGTON: Do? There's nothing we can do but surrender. But first find my teeth! They cost $150 and they're all I got in the world.

I know what you're saying. You're saying the whole thing is ridiculous. That we won a victory at Trenton. But just remember this. The Hessians were pretty tanked that night, too. Just how tanked you'll find in the history books. Ha, ha, ha. *C'est drôle, eh?*

Yale Record

"You know, he looks just like an evening spread out against the sky."

Mitchell Gruber/Columbia Jester

Visit the beautiful red hills of serene North Korea. Gaze at the sublime beauty and tranquil serenity of this ancient vista that spreads itself before your eyes.

Now you, too, can afford that trip to KOREA for an ... unlimited peroid

All Expenses

PAID

Luxurious staterooms. A congenial club lounge on the lower deck.

Don't hesitate. You will enjoy the beautiful fall weather. Investigate at once this pre-arranged, all expense tour of the fascinating Orient.

Sign up in a group or by yourself. Just ask your local recruiting agent for further details.

Reservations at each stop are guaranteed!

No waits between airports

Pomona New Sage Hen

US ARMY World's Most Experienced Airline

FEATURE!

ALMOST A PAGE OF RAUNCHY LIMERICKS

There was a young maid from La
Jolla
Who had an affair with her lolla;
Since her boudoir, though regal,
Smacked of the illegal,
Their meetings were held in the
folla.

There was a young myth named
Medusa,
Whose morals were something
quite loosa,
But the snakes in her hair
Didn't like being there,
Which played hab with Medusa's
seduca.

Do you ever put on rayon scanties?
When they crackle electrical
chanties?
Don't worry, my dear,
The reason is clear,
You simply have amps in your
panties!

There was an old couple from Say-
ville
Whose habits were quite medieval;
They would strip to the skin,
Then each take a pin
And pick lint from the other one's
navel.

An amoeba named Joe and his
brotha,
Were drinking toasts to each otha;
In the midst of their quaffing,
They split themselves laughing—
Now each of them is a motha.

There once was a moron named
Moe,
Who misunderstood mistletoe.
He thought it for luck,
So he carefully stuck
A big sprig in his hip pocket. Ho!

Stanford Chaparral,
Pomona Sage Hen,
Iowa State Green Gander,
Colorado Flatiron

Ed Koren/*Columbia Jester*

"Do you have any funny cards for an elderly lady with pleurisy?"
Walt Kraemer/American University Bald Eagle

Tom Roberts/California Pelican

CRUEL ???

"Hey Mrs. Jones. Hey Mrs. Jones, can Johnny come out and play baseball?"

"Now Elmer, you know very well Johnny has no arms and legs."

"That's all right Mrs. Jones, we just wanta use him for third base."

• • •

"Mommy, Mommy, why can't I go swimming with the other kids?"

"Shut up, you little monster. You know your iron lung won't float."

• • •

"Mommy, Mommy, can I help wash the dishes?"

"No, dear. You know it'd rust your hooks!"

• • •

"Daddy, Daddy, can I please play with Grandpa?"

"No! You've already dug him up three times this week."

• • •

"Haircut, Mr. Anastasia?"

• • •

"How'd you like the play, Mrs. Lincoln?"

Florida State Smoke Signals

SIGNATURE OF A MEDIEVAL ILLITERATE

Frederick W. Umminger, Jr./*Yale Record*

The Longhorns have returned to the two-platoon system this year —one team to play football, and the other one to attend class.

Texas Ranger

Two roosters were caught in a rain storm; one ran for the barn, the other made a duck under the porch.

Then there was the wren who only did it for a lark.

Occidental Fang

I said Pheasant, you fool, Pheasant.

Arizona Kitty Kat

Good grief, man. Is nothing sacred!?!

Bill West/*Texas Ranger*

"Governor, disa my boy Mario. He lika to work
for da State next summer. O.K.?"

Massachusetts Yahoo

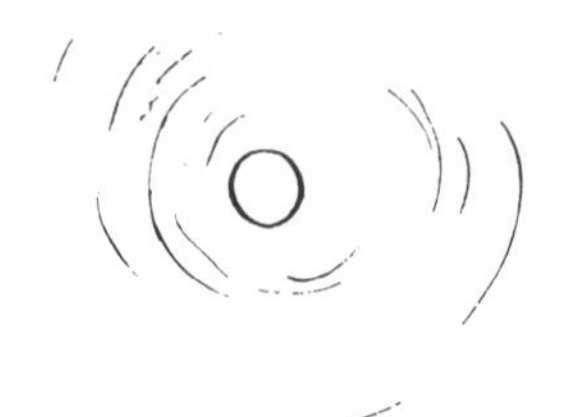

HUTCH

Princeton Tiger

Said a duffer, a fella named Lee,
After scoring a 73,
"It's not skill, it was haste;
I just thought of the taste
Of the Schaefer that's waiting for me!"
18
alphonse normandia

What makes Schaefer taste so good? Flavor . . . flavor that's light and lively, exciting and satisfying. Next time you're looking for the best in beer, pour some real enjoyment—Schaefer.

For real enjoyment–real beer!

THE F. & M. SCHAEFER BREWING CO., NEW YORK

FREEDOM & THE FADEOUT 1960-1969

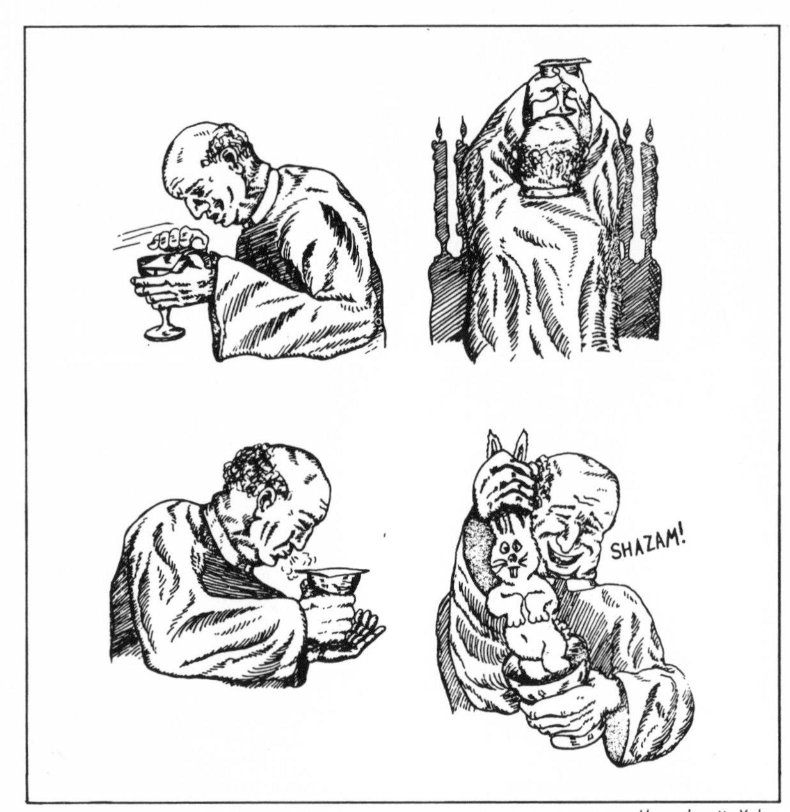

Massachusetts Yahoo

At the exclusive Union Club, where more wasps congregate for a drink and good company than in all of Darien, Rheingold Beer is not the favorite beverage. However, in the rest of New York which has more Wops, Chinks, Japs, Spics, Kikes, Polacks, Turks, Dagos, Niggers, VC, Hindus, Krauts, Ricans, Hunkies, Squareheads, Slavs, Frogs, Greasers, Micks, Arabs, and Wetbacks than any other major city in the country, Rheingold is the workingman's beer, brewed for the masses! How unfortunate that the members of the Union Club insist on only imported beers. But then wasps will be wasps.

Columbia Jester

The best to you each Mourning

FAREAST LAWN Cemetery

BEAUTY THAT COSTS

Occidental Fang

Dial "N" For Nothing

Boston 1961 Telephone Directory, by N. E. Tatco *(publ. by The New England Telephone and Telegraph Co., 1379 pp. Free.)*

AS IN past years Mr. Tatco has provided a brilliant and engaging piece of documentary adventure. One can say, without fear of contradiction, that he has once again run the gamut of characters, actions and emotions from A to Z. And he has done so in a triumphantly ordered progression. Never once does the lightning pace falter. Never once does this unique and brilliant stylist evade or bewilder his reader, and always there is passion, romance and a variety of subjects never before attained in one single paperback volume.

The main character of this rambling pageant is Stanley K Griganavicius of 699 E. Seventh St., whose telephone number is ANdrew 8-5351. Flanked by his henchmen, John and Adolph Grigalus, Victor Grigalunas and A C Grigas, Griganavicius proceeds undaunted through the rank and file of the Great Unwashed, all the while pursued by six hundred Griffins. I tell you it is a veritable pilgrim's progress as Stan fights his courageous way through Halls over Hills down Valleys and such like. It doesn't really matter to the avid reader that our man Stan did the very same thing in Tatco's previous novel. It is all done this time in the spirit of the New.

In addition to the classic heroism of the book there is a good deal of spicy down-to-earth humor. Take for instance the incident mentioned on page 610 in which Wm B Horsey of Topsfield perches lasciviously over Miss Norah J Horsfield. Perhaps he is just being coy.

But even so, I feel there is nothing to equal this breathtaking moment in all of modern literature. It has energy, suggested by the two surnames. It has unity in the similarity of the names and their animal quality. The intensity increases to a climax as we come to the addresses. Mr. Horsey could live on no other than Kinsman's Lane, and Mr. Tatco has done the only thing possible with Miss Horsfield. He has put her at 149 Hancock Street. Again, coy, but for the sake of decency, the reading public must make a small sacrifice.

And there is more. Much more. Two thousand four hundred Murphys to contend with. Stanley Griganivicius very nearly meets his doom here, but fortunately an onrushing force of thirty-one hundred Smiths intervenes.

It is blood, sweat, toil, and tears, and every name is fictitious. Any similarities between actual persons living or dead is to be expected in this, Mr. Tatco's slice-of-life technique.

It is our considered opinion that this year Mr. Tatco has outdone himself. The sheer beauty of his prose, the delicate and tasteful use of number, and the adroit juxtaposition of exchanges become more enchanting as the piece gains momentum. There is an unmistakable feeling of catharsis (and I do not mean Miss Rona Katharsis of 243 Bay State Road . . . KE 6-5868) when one finally reaches the Zzzzyx Club; in other words, the end.

John Berendt/*Harvard Lampoon*

Ned Bayrd/*Dartmouth Jack O' Lantern*

Joel Beck/*California Pelican*

Vassar and Smith:
Don't bother with;
Wellesley and Conn:
They're bad for you, son;
Wheaton and Hood:
More harm than they're good.
No matter what place,
No matter what name,
If it's crawling with women
You'll end up the same:
They'll drink all your booze
And spend all your money,
And all you'll get back
Is a small dab of honey,
Which looks pretty good
In Saturday's light,
But loses it's charm
Come around Sunday night,
When you've totaled the score
And looked all around
At your deflated pockets
And a heart that's shot down,
And a pile of papers
All due the next day,
Which you'd never get done
If you had till next May.
So stick with your books
And you'll really go far.
(By the way, pal o' mine,
Can I borrow your car?)

Yale Record

Then there was the geneticist who crossed an intersection with a convertible and got a blond.

Brevard Engineering College Pelican

Two small mice were crouched under a table in the chorus girls' dressing room of a big broadway show.

"Wow," exclaimed the first mouse, "have you ever seen so many gorgeous legs in your life?"

"Means nothing to me," said the second. "I'm a titmouse."

Texas Ranger

Clive Cochran/*Texas (El Paso) El Burro*

OUT OF THE STIMULATING PAST,
RIDING ON A CONSERVATIVE GRAY CHARGER,
COMES THE MAMMOTH PARTY'S OWN . . .

B. G.

Notre Dame Leprechaun

DID YOU EVER GET THE IDEA THAT THAT ALL-AMERICAN MEDIUM, THE COMIC STRIP, IS NO LONGER REPRESENTATIVE OF THESE HARD TIMES? THAT THE CHARACTERS JUST DON'T ACT LIKE THE REAL AMERICAN? TRY THESE.

REALISTIC COMIC STRIPS

Massachusetts Yahoo

New Mexico Juggler

How We Got Goddamn

(An Exercise in Epistemology)

BY HEWETT JOINER, Ph.D. (Fenway's Barber College, 1939)

The *Phoenix* is pleased to present an excerpt from an impressive new example of Emory's exceptionally valuable historical scholarship. *A Child's Garden of the Origins of Popular English Words of Filthy, Nasty and Obscene Natures.* This remarkable book, called by the author the most important contribution to the history of semantics and language since the publication of Dr. George Cuttino's *Reconsideration of Strayer's Re-evaluation of Toynbee's Consideration of the Significance of "Gee Whiz" in English Constitutional History*, is the product of fourteen years research in English collegiate and monastic libraries.

Perhaps the most popular of truly serious oaths (the reader will doubtless recall the distinction drawn between "Truly serious oaths," "nearly serious oaths," "kind-of-serious oaths," "old ordinary every-day oaths," "socially popular oaths," and "oaths your mother likes to hear," which I discussed in detail in the first 654 pages of this work) is the perennially popular "God damn." Probably this is the most universally occurring oath today; it is found not only in all English-speaking areas, but even in many sections of the globe where English is very uncommon. Swartzengelber records, for example, that the fierce Bandar pygmies of central Africa employ the steady chant "goddamgoddamgoddamgoddam"[1] in their hunting ceremony, which precedes the quest for the legendary great white mongoose. Swartzengelber believes that these natives learned the chant from a late 19th-century Protestant missionary, who is reputed to have used the oath upon discovering that the contributions left by the Bandar in his collection plate were non-negotiable in more civilized monetary systems. This, I trust, will serve as sufficient example of the universality of the expression.

See? They always land on their feet.

RPI Bachelor

Contemporary thought on the subject is almost completely in agreement that this oath results from the juxtaposition of two autonomously meaningful words, i.e., "god" and "damn." The evidence I have unearthed proves conclusively that this supposition, however widespread, is false. In order to gain an accurate understanding of the origin of this oath we must move back in time to the day when England was undergoing the linguistic transition from Latin to the English vernacular. First, in the time of almost complete Latin predominance we discover that, as in every historical epoch, the name of the Deity was, in popular usage, a leading epithet. The Latin form in general usage for this purpose was "*Deum.*" The instances of this word's occurrence are quite numerous in the surviving records of the period. In the little known diary of William of Ockham, dating from the 12th century, we discover that Ockham's cook, upon discovering a large blue and orange lizard in a hasty pudding she was preparing, was heard to run off down the street screaming, "*Deum, Deum, Deum, Lizardus in Puddingum Hastum.*"[2] Even earlier, we discover a similar usage in the records of the ninth century in England. Fred of Limerick-on-Shaftsnifstraffing writes in his diary for the year 837 A.D. of the reaction of a neighbor to the discovery that Fred had seduced his eleven-year-old daughter. The neighbor is said to have yelled up at the window of Fred's monastic cell, saying, "*Seducerum monastum. Deum infinitum unum!*"[3]

(There follows in the book the author's listing in minute detail seven hundred and forty-six examples to support his point, which for sake of space—we don't have 279 pages to spare—we have been forced to omit.)

But, as we all know, the English vernacular was destined to succeed Latin, and this process necessitated a re-evaluation of the oath-structure of the popular language. But the language of the people, ever flexible, adjusted to the transition. The transition period itself is, however, the period in which our modern "God damn" developed. It is easy to understand the profound difficulty of communication concomitant with such a basic linguistic transition. When you met a friend in

"Pssst! . . . Or not to be!!"

Tom Cornelius and Jack Auspitz/*Columbia Jester*

the street you could never be sure whether or not he had been converted to use of the vernacular. Should one use the greeting "hello, friend" or *"ave, frater?"* This question produced real problems for a period stretching over two and one half centuries and produced many important results. Erasmus, in his recently translated correspondence with Jennifer Quigby-Ashcroft, an itinerant Welsh prostitute of the 16th century, indicates that the problem of vernacular vs. Latin would prove the basis for the separation of the English Church from the Catholic Church.[4]

But what is important for the question under consideration in this work is the inability of the Englishman of the day to be sure of the correct language to employ in attempting to communicate with the people he met. The problem was most pressing among the rising class of merchants gaining economic, social, and political predominance in this period. Since so much of their contact was with people they did not know, the question of what language to use was of great importance. Equally important for these merchants was the necessity of being able to impress the persons with whom they traded with their displeasure if the price quoted was not satisfactory. Obviously the force of "God!" would be lost if one were trading with a man who used Latin. The same was of course equally true for the Latin merchant who contacted exponents of the vernacular. So among this class, whose mobility made them the most important transporters of language development, there developed the practice of juxtaposing the vernacular "God" and the Latin equivalent, *"Deum."* In actual use, the words were expressed as "God! *Deum!*" In the records of the travels of one Pinckney Twattbottom of Salisbury, a traveling dealer in amber rectal suppositories "whyche wee guarantee wille prevente thee Blacke Dethe,"[5] we hear of a customer who complained to Twattbottom that his suppositories "hayve indede prevented the dred disease, but prevente as welle the natural flow offe waste matters, and are therefore note worthe a God! *Deum!*"[6] The records kept by the cathedral chapter at Canterbury reveal that the archbishop of the diocese remarked upon hearing the results of a papal election, "God! *Deum!* That goddeum Italian won!"[7]

Long after the vernacular was so widely accepted that few people bothered with knowing both it and Latin, the importance of making oneself understood when swearing dictated that the two words still be used together, just on the outside chance that your listener might still use Latin. Gradually *Deum* underwent alteration and became the single syllable, "damn," which stands today as the accompanying word for "God" in the most used oath in the modern English language. But even today there are living sources of the heritage of this expression. The noted cultural anthropologist, W. F. Buckely, recently discovered an English lumber and fur trading camp near the north shores of Hudson Bay. This camp has been isolated from the outside world since a great ice storm of the winter of 1701; its inhabitants were unaware of current events such as the American Revolution, the Boer War, or Mahandes Ghandi, and still used the late medieval English dialect. When Buckely questioned the leader of the camp, Sir Nelson Thistledown, concerning his reaction to the many events which had occurred in a world that had passed the little community by, Thistledown replied, "I reckone as howe wee doe nott give a goddeum."[8]

[1]Haargaard Swartzengelber, *The Phantom* (King Features, 1962), p. 34.
[2]William of Ockham, *Selected Post Cards,* ed. Leroy Leomker (Atlanta, 1925), p. 987.
[3]Fred of Limerick-on-Shaftsnifstraffing, *Diary of an Oversexed Medieval Monk* (New Directions Paperbooks, 1961), p. 87.
[4]Erasmus, *Love Letters to the Strand* (Phallic Press, 1962), p. 26.
[5]Harvey Young, *The Toadstool Millionaires* (New York, 1961), p. 78.
[6]*Ibid,* p. 79.
[7]Canterbury Records for the years 1106-1398.
[8]W. F. Buckely, *God and Man at Hudson Bay* (Oshkosh, 1960), p. 332.

William Hedgepeth/*Emory Phoenix*

"Remember the real meaning of Christmas this year. Attend the church or synagogue of your choice."

Harvard-Radcliffe Gargoyle

Me·ri'no (mĕ·rē'nō; mĕ), *n; pl.* -NOS (*-nōz*). [Sp.; cf. Sp. *merino* moving from pasture to pasture, *merino* a royal judge and superintendent or inspector of sheep walks, ML. *merinus,* fr. *majorinus,* i.e., major villae, fr. L. *major* greater. See MAYOR.] 1. a A hardy gregarious breed of fine wooled white sheep, originating in Spain, widely popular, esp. on the ranges in America and Australia. The rams have heavy spirally twisted horns; the ewes are hornless. The wool covers the head, often obscuring the eyes. In the better varieties the skin hangs in heavy folds, esp. about the breast, shoulders, and thighs. The breed excels all others in the weight and quality of its fleece, but does not rank high as a mutton producer. **b** [*not cap.*] An animal of this breed.
2. A fine soft fabric resembling cashmere, made originally of merino wool.
3. A fine wool yarn used in hosiery, knit underwear etc.

See the Merino Standing There, With His Long, Shaggy Hair

See the merino standing there,
With his long, shaggy hair.

See the merino standing there,
With his long, shaggy hair.

See the merino standing there,
With his long, shaggy hare.

See the merino standing there,
With his long, shaggy Eyre.

See the merino standing there,
With his long, shaggy Eire.

See the merino standing there,
With his long, shaggy air.

See the merino standing there,
With his long, shaggy hayer.

See the merino standing there,
With his long, shaggy heir.

See the merino, Stan Ding, there,
With his long, shaggy hair.

See the merino-standing, there,
With its long, shaggy hair.

"C", the merino, standing there,
With his long, shaggy hair.

See the marino standing there,
With his long, shaggy hair.

See the Marinos standing there,
With their long, shaggy hair.

See the merino standing . . . .
Therewith his long, shaggy hair.

See thumber Enos standing there,
With his long, shaggy hair.

Seethe the merinos, standing there,
With their long, shaggy hair.

Jack M. Winter, Christopher B. Cerf, and Michael K. Frith/*Harvard Lampoon*

Who's Afraid of Vagina Woolf?

A Parody of the Play

THE PLAYERS

MARSHA: A bulbous, corpulent woman, 52, looking somewhat like Elizabeth looks when she thinks no one is looking.
GORGE: Her husband, 46, thinnish, perishing slowly due to lack of publication.
HORNY: 26, a petite blond girl, drab as a bowl of wax.
DICK: 30, her husband, a stud, hung like a bison.

THE SCENE

The living room of a smallish garret somewhere on Parker between College and Piedmont.

ACT ONE
SIMPLE OBSCENITY

(Set in darkness. Crash against front door, which topples inward. MARSHA's laugher heard as front door is replaced on hinges and gas lanterns are turned up. MARSHA stumbles in, followed by GORGE.)

MARSHA: #$%&!¼@?/¢#!!!
GORGE: For God's sake, it's two in the morning!
MARSHA: Oh, Gorge.
GORGE: Christ, it's *late*, you know.
MARSHA: *J*esus Christ, Gorge . . . what a cluck! What a *cluck* you are.
GORGE: *Cluck?* Is that the best you can do? For God's sake, Marsha, try to remember: this is an inflammatory, biting social drama we're doing. Call me a Pr-ck, or an Assh-le, or something with guts in it.
MARSHA: Oh, Gorge . . . *can it!* Just *can it* for awhile. Take it slow, baby, we have to start out slow. (Looking around the room disparagingly.) What a *dump!* What a dump this is. Hey, what's that from—"What a dump" —what's it from, Gorge?
GORGE: What . . . What? What's what from?
MARSHA: "What a dump." What's it from?
GORGE: (Musing.) "What a dump." I don't think . . . I think . . .
MARSHA: You don't think! You think? *"You think."* That's the trouble with you Gorge . . . *"you think"* . . . that's what got us in hot water with the Regents . . . you *thinking* all the time.
GORGE: Marsha, please . . .
MARSHA: My little Gorgy-porgy . . . think think think . . . you almost lost your Goddam *job*, thinking. You don't see old Professor Mulcavy thinking, do you?
GORGE: Marsha . . . Mulcavy has been dead for three years.
MARSHA: So what . . . they made him department head last August, didn't they? Well . . . didn't they?
GORGE: I don't know . . . I don't know, Marsha . . . it's so late. Let's have a nightcap and go to bed.
MARSHA: Can't, Gorge . . . company's coming.
GORGE: Who in the hell is coming to visit at two in the frigging morning?
MARSHA: Oh . . . some new literature professor and his wife . . . you know . . . the skinny blond with no breasts.
GORGE: Well . . . after all, Marsha . . . he'd really look ridiculous if he had brea . . .
MARSHA: Oh, for Christ's sake, Gorge . . . you stupid b-stard . . . I mean his *wife* didn't have any breasts . . .
GORGE: Now Marsha, remember the social outrage. The skinny blond with no tits! *Tits*, Marsha . . . let's keep it meaty for the sociologists.
MARSHA: (Furious.) Listen, sh-t mouth . . .
GORGE: *Wonderful*, Marsha . . . truly spirited . . .
MARSHA: Gorge . . . you c-cksu . . .
GORGE: What a fantastic *Meter Maid* you'd make, Marsha . . .
(A sudden knocking at the door interrupts them.)

MARSHA: Go answer the damn door, Gorge . . . that's our company.
GORGE: I don't think I'll answer your damn door, lover.
MARSHA: SHOVE THE DAMN DOOR UP YOUR -SS, Gorge.

(At this juncture, the door topples open again, revealing DICK and HORNY, slightly abashed on the front steps. GORGE is pleased at his timing in embarrassing MARSHA, and greets them with overplayed warmth.)

GORGE: Well I'll be h-sed . . . you must be . . .
DICK: Dick . . .
GORGE: How very apt . . . Oh, Marsha, sweetie . . . there's a Dick here to see you . . .
DICK: Listen, it's late, maybe we should . . .
GORGE: Nonsense . . . *nonsense* . . . Marsha's been ready to go all evening . . . can't let her go to waste . . . ahh, and this must be your little wifey.
HORNY: Yes . . . I'm Horny . . .
GORGE: Yess . . . I'm sure you are . . . yes . . . BREAK OUT THE GIN, LOVER!

(Marsha enters with the gin and they all down it in one breath. This is merely the beginning to an epic drinking bout, which—if you bother to count the drinks consumed—is absolutely physically impossible.)

GORGE: (Now settled.) Well, listen . . . shall we quietly insult you and your wife . . . aspersions on her femininity . . . slandering your general inanity . . . or shall we . . .
DICK: Why don't we just . . .
GORGE: . . . get to the Games? *Perfect!* Now . . . that's perfect . . .
MARSHA: *No . . . no, not yet.* I want to insult Horny about her lack of tits for a while. Tell me, Horny, how are you fixed for fixations? Hung up on Dickie's member, are you . . . scared of having kids . . . come on, you can tell old mama Marsha.
GORGE: And make it good. We've got the audience for four-fifty a shot, and they're not here for "Pinnochio." Come on with me, Dick, and I'll show you the cr-pper . . . never know when you'll get some of Marsha on you and want to wash up . . .
MARSHA: (Gaily.) Up yours, sweetie.

Who's Afraid of Virginia Censor?

A Parody of the Play

(A playlet in One Act, after the Code of Television Propriety got hold of the Shooting Script.)
(Set in darkness. Crash against the door. MARSHA's lilting young giggle is heard, then the door opens and lights go on.)

MARSHA: Shucks . . .
JOHN: Shhhhh . . .
MARSHA: Gosh . . .
JOHN: For pity's *sake*, Marsha, it's ten o'clock at night!
MARSHA: Oh, *John!* What an old stick-in-the-mud you are.
JOHN: Well it *is* ten o'clock. The neighbors are probably asleep, and . . .
MARSHA: (Looks about the room. Imitates Judy Garland.) We're off to see the Wizard . . . Hey, what's that from? "We're off to see the Wizard!"
JOHN: What's *what* from, chickie-fluff?
MARSHA: We're off to see the Wizard!" It's from some flap-doodle old motion picture . . . this little girl has a dream where she goes off to this strange country and all kinds of nifty stuff and . . .
JOHN: "Pinnochio!" It's from Pinnochio, right?
MARSHA: Oh, John, you old stuff. That's not right!
JOHN: Well, *I* can't think right *now,* lovey-lamb. I'm tired, and . . .
MARSHA: Tired! But Johnnie-wonnie, we've got guests coming over.
JOHN: Guests!? Land-a-goshen, Marshie-poo, it's almost ten-fifteen!!
MARSHA: Oh, come on, Johnnie-duckie—let's live it up . . . just tonight! Straighten your ittie-bittie tie, and make mommy-wommy a drinkie-poo.
JOHN: (Going to the bar.) The usual?
MARSHA: That's right, lovey, straight Kool-Aid on the rocks.
JOHN: By the way, who's coming over?
MARSHA: Oh *you* know . . . that young English professor, with the graduate course on the *Saturday Evening Post.* And his pretty young wife, the one with no earlobes.

(A knock on the door.)

MARSHA: Answer the door, lovey-pie.
JOHN: It's your turn, lambkin. I answered it *last* week.
MARSHA: But I'm afraid you're wrong, sweetie-sugar . . . It's *your* turn!
JOHN: No no no, baby-poopsie, its your turn . . .
MARSHA: (Miffed.) Johnniekins . . . *You answer that door . . .*
JOHN: (In a pout.) No I *won't!*
MARSHA: Oh . . . oh . . . oh . . . HORSEFEATHERS!
JOHN: (Falls back against the wall, grasping his ears.) OH! WHAT YOU SAID!!!
(Just then, the door swings open, and BUNNY and NED stand embarrassed in the door frame.)

JOHN: Well, *Shoot-a-mile,* come right *in.* Put your things any place—we're just folks around here.
BUNNY: Pshaw, Neddy, we shouldn't have come. It's so late.
MARSHA: Oh fudge! Don't worry about *that.*
JOHN: *Golly sakes,* no. Uh, pardon my language, folks, but it is Saturday night, and the party and all . . .
BUNNY: Yes. We noticed you were putting the iced tea away at a pretty good clip tonight . . .
NED: Bunny-*wunny!* What a thing to say to our host.
BUNNY: Oh Neddy, I've gone and done it *again.* Boo hoo *hoo.*
MARSHA: Oh, bosh! What's a little spicey talk among friends?
JOHN: Yes, indeedy. (Winks, and aside to NED.) It's like I always say, "Here today, gone tomorrow!"

(JOHN and NED both break into raucous laughter.)

BUNNY: Oh my, I can tell *this* is going to be *some party!*

(They all sit around a central coffee table.)

JOHN: This reminds me of a time, long ago, when I was just a boy. A bunch of us chums had gone off to a little cafe outside of town . . . It was during the war, you see, and it was the only place you could get coffee with cream. Ration books, and all.
BUNNY: Oh, John . . . you *didn't!*
JOHN: (Shrugging) Well, we were just lads, then . . . innocent and frisky and . . .
NED: We understand, John. Boys will be boys.
MARSHA: *Oh Ned!* What a way with words. I sure wish *I'd* said that.
JOHN: Anyway, a waiter came over . . . and one of us . . . the very youngest boy . . . said, give me some Pills Brothers and cream, please, Well, we all laughed, and then everyone in the place began to laugh.
BUNNY: (Laughing hysterically.) Oh, that's simply *hilarious.*
NED: Boy, that's a knee-slapper, *I'll say.*
BUNNY: (Cautioning NED.) Now Neddy, no *body-words.*
NED: Sorry, bunny-poo. Anyway, what finally happened, John?
JOHN: We were raided. The boy was charged with illegal possession of Pasteurized Milk.
NED: Holy *moley.*
MARSHA: Oh Jonnie-wonnie—you're spoiling the party. Come on, now, how about a little game. How about a little game of . . . let's see . . . Tickle the Guests!
JOHN: (Shocked, gasps.) MAR-SHA!!
NED: (Shocked, embarrassed.) Well! Maybe we had better leave.
BUNNY: Ooh . . . ooh . . . ooh . . .
MARSHA: Oh please! I didn't mean *really* tickle. I just thought we might sit around and tell some *funnies,* and be *happy-wappy.*

Bob Wieder/*California Pelican*

–*Give me a "G"* . . .

Florida State Smoke Signals

An 8-foot-tall, 500-pound Texan died, and they couldn't find a coffin big enough for him. A Northerner, an expert in such matters, was called in. "I know Texans," he said, and ordered an enema. They buried the Texan in a shoebox.

Georgia Tech Rambler

It was high noon at the Mosque. The high priest was intoning, "There is no God but Allah, and Mohammed is his prophet."

A voice broke in: "He is not!"

The congregation turned, and among the sea of brown faces was a small yellow face.

The priest straightened up and said, "There seems to be a little Confucian here."

Annapolis Log

Have you heard about the Jewish guy who marries into a Gypsy family? As a wedding gift her father sets him up with a chain of empty stores. It's the truth.

MIT Voo Doo

King Arthur

King Arthur wasn't always a brave king.[1] His father, Arthur Sr., wrote books, and he wanted his son to be an Arthur, too. One day, Arthur pulled the sword Excalibur from a bounder,[2] and he won himself his very own kingdom.

Then Arthur was called "King" because he owned a kingdom. He was very fond of animals, so he developed a large collection and kept the animals in huge lots. He had a dog lot, a horse lot, a bear lot, and a goat lot; but his favorite was his camel lot.[3]

Lady Gwinanbere was to come to Camelot to marry Arthur. This was an unpleasant thought to the bachelor.[4]

One day, the king was knocked from his horse by another knight with a lance. The stranger didn't know whom he had contested with.[5] He hurt the king's pride.[6]

The king stood up, re-established his cool, and sarcastically said "Thanxalot." The king replied, "Yes, I am he."[7]

Thanxalot won the next joust, too. For a long time it looked like a draw.[8]

Thanxalot fell in love with Lady Gwinanbere. The feeling was mutual. They kissed on the mouth and did so behind Arthur's back,[9] keeping their secret in their heads.[10]

Arthur had many parties and he made the rounds, so it was rare that he had a (k)night alone.

One day Dreadmore, the illegitimate son of the king visited his father.[11] Dreadmore was very impressed by his father's kingdom. He loved castles, very much. As a matter of fact, he loved all kinds of buildings.[12]

Dreadmore knew that Gwinanbere had cheated on the king, so he decided to show proof of his theory of her disloyalty.[13] He plotted to catch Thanxalot and Gwinanbere together. To convince Arthur of the verity of his idea, he sent the latter to the woods for the night (without his dinner).

Meanwhile, back at the castle, Thanxalot and Gwinanbere were kissing on the mouth. They felt strongly about each other and recited love odes.[14] Dreadmore burst in, and, seeing the sin, he said "Gwinanbere, you're my step-mother, Ooh!"

When Arthur returned, he said cuttingly, "The only alternative would be for all of us to split up."[15] Arthur loved Thanxalot and Gwinanbere, although they hurt him so much. He was really a fine person.[16] Many years later, Gwinanbere joined a convent.[17] Arthur bought a (k)night club in New York City. He finally got his round table.[18]

Footnotes

1. When he was born he was a big baby.
2. He realized that he couldn't have done it if it weren't for his having been stoned.
3. Hence, the name of his kingdom.
4. But he decided to Gwinanbere it!
5. So he was joustified in doing what he did.
6. That's not all he hurt!
7. He was an English major.
8. Finally knight fell, followed by daze.
9. Arthur had never learned his "about-faces."
10. What an odd place to put deodorant.
11. When Arthur was kissing the mother she said, "Stop!" but Arthur went father.
12. He was known to have an edifice complex.
13. He was a geometry major.
14. They both studied oral interpretation.
15. Then they all went to pieces.
16. No relation to the author of this piece.
17. Nun-the-less, she was happy.
18. I bet you're wondering about Thanxalot. You're welcome.

Elaine S. Person/Montclair State Galumph

There has been great consternation lately in the higher stratas of the UCLA administration concerning the current trend among high school graduates to ignore the wonders that are Westwood in favor of the smaller, Eastern colleges. Solutions to this problem are flying around like IBM cards to a Mickey Mouse course, but we at SATYR believe that UCLA, like all large factories, can solve this problem through use of modern advertising techniques . . .

WHAT IF U. C. L. A. USED MADISON AVENUE TECHNIQUES TO ADVERTISE ITSELF?

by Mike O'Connell

Now Entering
UCLA COUNTRY
A Thinking Man's Factory
A Walking Man's School
FOSTER-KLEISER & MURPHY

TRAVEL POSTERS WOULD BE CIRCULATED, INVITING TEEN-AGERS TO VISIT *UCLA* AND SEE *WHAT* LIFE IN COLLEGE IS *REALLY LIKE*...

VISIT GIGANTIC UCLA

LARGER THAN EUROPE!
MORE red-tape than Russia!
MANY MORE coupons than Disneyland!

NOW—FOR A LIMITED TIME ONLY (FOUR YEARS OR A 1-A CLASSIFICATION)—YOU CAN VISIT THE SCHOOL EVERYONE TALKS ABOUT (BECAUSE EVERYONE GOES THERE!)

See these famous landmarks:

The UCLA Dorms—See these fantastic locker rooms with beds built to house the horny student body. Built at great expense, great distance from campus.

The Med Center—Gasp at this fantastic psychological experiment where humans replace rats in an endless maze. Built at no expense, as the contractor is still trying to get out.

Motherhood Row—Don't step on a crack as you walk down the sidewalk in front of the sorority houses—built from public contributions from citizens who thought they were giving to a home for unwed mothers . . .

AND MANY MORE STIMULATING, EXPENSIVE THINGS TO RAISE YOUR INCIDENTAL FEE FARE...

ENROLL NOW!! JOIN FRANKLIN SURFEY'S ONE-MAN WAR ON POVERTY—ASK ABOUT "OUR WALK NOW, PAY AND PAY AND PAY LATER PLAN"

TO FURTHER UCLA'S PUBLIC IMAGE, CHANCELLOR FRANKLIN D. SURFEY, WESTWOOD'S ONE-MAN SHOW, WOULD GO ON AN ENTERTAINMENT TOUR OF THE UNITED STATES . . .

The New York Exhibition Center is Pleased to Present:

LAUGHABLE, LOVABLE, LECHEROUS

one-year only! *Frankie Surfey* in person!!

America's Latest Sensation-Seeker!!!

SEE UCLA's one-man bag of tricks sing, explain, perform feats of budgetary magic, turn tables . . .

Hear these new song hits:
The Pile Driver Stomp * Don't Bend, Spindle, or Mutilate My Blue Suede Reg Packet * Indecision * We Shall Overcharge.

Thrill as Frankie does these amazing feats of magic:

☞ SEE FRANKIE TRANSFORM ENTIRE PARKING LOTS INTO BASKETBALL AND FOOTBALL STADIUMS . . .

How does he do it? Only the Regents know for sure!

☞ SEE FRANKIE TEAM UP WITH WALT DISNEY IN THE CREATION OF NEW COURSES FOR THE BIG U . . .

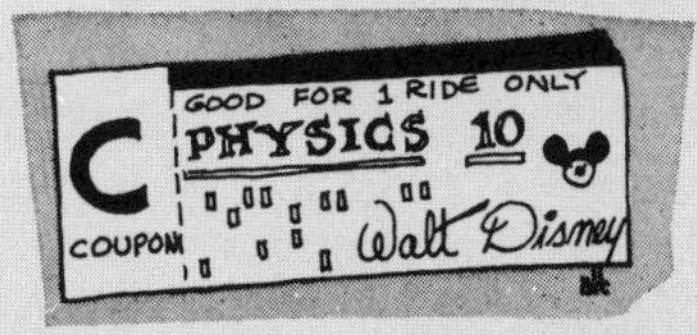

☞ SEE FRANKIE TURN MOM'S HAPPY HOURS INTO A THREE UNIT COURSE FOR THE PHYS. ED DEPARTMENT . . .

Don't Miss this exciting new entertainer—Admission free with UCLA Reg. Card or $121, plus increments.

BE ON TIME!!!—$10 LATE FEE

BIGGER Than the Beatles— GREATER Than Cassius Clay— MORE EXPENSIVE Than an IBM Computer!!

Annapolis Log

There was a pitcher with the Giants named Mel Famie. He was a lousy pitcher and spent the game drinking beer in the bullpen. By the end of the game he was always dead drunk.

One day the Giants and Dodgers were locked in a tie, 18-18, going into the last of the ninth. Mel Famie was the only Giant pitcher available to pitch this all-important inning. He was so surprised to see the manager beckon toward him that he just stuck his beer can into his back pocket and trudged to the mound. He walked the first three men on 12 straight pitches. Bearing down, he struck out the next two. The crowd was tense, the players were tense—that is all except Mel Famie, who was pretty loose. The count went to 3 and 2 and then Mel Famie threw the fourth ball that lost the game.

As he was walking off the field, one Dodger asked another, "Hey! What's that beer can in Famie's pocket?"

"Don't you know?" was the reply. "That's the beer that made Mel Famie walk us."

Ohio State Sundial

ADVERTISEMENTS WOULD APPEAR IN NATIONAL MAGAZINES GEARED FOR CHILDREN AGES 6-16, SUCH AS *PLAYBOY*, *RAMPARTS*, AND *LIFE*.

ARE YOU A-DULT ENOUGH FOR UCLA?

Yes!! Now YOU can attend the school that flattens your wallet while fatiguing your mind!!

THE ONLY SCHOOL WITH METERED DESKS

FEATURING:

The only Theatre Arts Dept. where the boys play women's roles—on and off stage.

27,000 Libraries scattered strategically across campus—one per student—guaranteed never to have the book you need.

A fantastic Student Union building containing restaurants, rest rooms, an ambulance service if the rest rooms won't do, and—most important for the UCLA student—a complete psychiatric service and rest home.

Rushing for classes—that unique experience for college students where they discover that, even with fee raises, they still have a chance to take classes at 4 a.m. and 11 p.m.

Harold's, Tony's, and Mom's; three after-hours spas where UCLA students can grow to love wonderful UCLA—in the only way possible.

DESIGNED FOR THE DISCRIMINATING MAN—THE MAN FOR WHOM SECOND BEST WON'T DO, BUT WHO CAN'T AFFORD THE BEST!!

NATURALLY, A SERIES OF TELEVISION COMMERCIALS WOULD BE CREATED FOR NETWORK TELEVISION SHOWS, EXTOLLING THE VIRTUES OF UCLA IN LAYMAN'S TERMS . . .

"Today we are speaking to the world-famous mother of 27 children, Mrs. Patience Beardsly. Mrs. Beardsly, would you tell us about the test you and your family participated in?"

"Yes, Bob, you see, we divided our 27 kids in half and sent one half to UCLA and the other half to an inferior college."

"And the Results?"

"Well, Bob, after 4 years of testing, the group that went to the great Westwood factory had 30% few brain cavaties than the inferior college."

"Great; That's proof-positive that UCLA . . ."

"Wait! I'm not finished—the UCLA group also had 99% more mental breakdowns, held 69% more inferior jobs, were 99 44/100% less individual, had IBM-itis, brushed without Crest, drove Edsels, voted for Goldwater, worshiped material values . . ."

To smell as if you're . . .
arrivée

PISSOIR PETIT BOURGEOIS SUEUR

Columbia Jester

AN APPEAL WOULD GO OUT TO THE PEOPLE WHO LOVE TRUE-LIFE DRAMA—IT WOULD APPEAR IN SUCH MAGAZINES AS *READER'S DIGEST* AND *AWAKE!*

TRUE-LIFE ADVENTURES PRESENTS:

The CHARGE of the *UNI-COPS!!*

Episode #cu 07734 6014Q of the UCLA Story

SEE FOR THE FIRST TIME IN THE MASS MEDIA, THE HEART-WARMING SAGA OF THE STALWART MEN IN FADED GRAY!

THRILL AT THESE COURAGEOUS SOLDIERS-OF-FORTUNE, AS THEY BRAVE THE PERILS OF SADDLE-SORENESS AND WRITER'S CRAMP!

GET SICK AS YOU DISCOVER A $15 TICKET ON YOUR CAR FOR PARKING IN A "No Parking from 1:34 to 1:35 p.m. Tues., Thurs., or Chanukah" ZONE!

Read about such thrilling episodes as:

— *3* aged, pot-bellied Uni-cops charging pell-mell down Dormitory Hill after their scooters!!

— *400* fear-crazed students rushing to move their cars!!

— *1* sobbing Uni-cop losing his badge and crying towel for not getting his quota of student cars, and exceeding his quota of Cadillacs!!

— *1* "No Parking" sign creator going crazy from getting a ticket in one of his own zones!!

DON'T MISS THE NEW MOVIE ABOUT THESE NEW HEROES OF AMERICANA, SOON TO BE RELEASED!!!

Starring:

FRANKLIN SURFEY, as a Uni-cop
CLARK CUR, as a parking ticket
THE PSYCHE DEPT., as a "No Parking" maze.

Taken from the novel *"How to Lose $4,000 a year, Without Using a Drop of Gas."*

OF COURSE, ONE AD WOULD HAVE TO BE DIRECTED AT THE SOCIAL SIDE OF THE AMERICAN TEEN-AGER, PRAISING UCLA's FANTASTIC SOCIAL LIFE . . .

U.C.L.A. WHERE THE ACTION IS!!

DON'T THINK COLLEGE IS ALL STUDY, HIPPIES! COLLEGE—AT UCLA—IS FAR MORE!!! UCLA IS . . .

—Dancing with an ugly girl at a Student Union dance!
—Finding love in the bushes behind Hedrick!
—Going to a Beer bust and being used to tap the keg!

WOWEE GANG!—BURN YOUR DRAFT CARD, QUIT THE BOY SCOUTS, AND FIND OUT WHAT "BRUIN" REALLY MEANS . . .

SEE Snake dances down Janss Steps celebrating victories of our necking, drinking, and Mahh Jong teams!

See Great entertainers like Oral Roberts and Lenny Bruce in UCLA's dramatic presentations!

SEE thousands of coeds earning their MrS Degree on the darkened campus at night!

DON'T MISS THE LSD PARTIES IN THE DORMS, THE DRUNKEN ORGIES PUT ON BY THE BRUIN YOUNG DEMOCRATS, THE FRANK RELIGIOUS TALKS BY LYNDA BYRD, THE PORNOGRAPHIC LITERATURE PUBLISHED BY THE DAILY BRUIN, THE GREAT LITERATURE PUBLISHED BY THE CHANCELLOR'S COMMITTEE ON STUDENT FERMENT, DON'T MISS ANY OF IT . . . ENROLL IN UCLA NOW!

YOUR REG. CARD GETS YOU ALL THIS PLUS MORE!

If you're hip . . . If you dig Bat-Fun . . .

COME TO UCLA

UCLA Satyr

The Classes

1891

FRANK T. WITHERINGTON, *Secretary*
112 Main St., Council Bluffs, N. D.

I rejoiced in the passing of George Penultimate as it leaves me the oldest living Amherst alumnus.

1894

PETER POND, *Secretary*
51 Kerry Lane, Chappaqua, N. Y.

The surviving members of the class are saddened at the passing of Dr. Rudolph Enovid who was strangled when his dog tripped his walker and he fell into his granddaughter's outstretched jump rope. The jump rope is doing fine.

We regret the passing of Sigmund Williams, who was slowly brought to death by his grandson, William Williams, Williams '67, who fed him Williams shaving soap intravenously until Williams was lost in a rest home bubble bath, and soon flushed out of sight.

1897

N. JOY FILLING, *Secretary*
11 So. Pleasant St., Amherst, Mass.

It is my pleasure to announce that all four members of my class are still surviving by the skins of their collective store-bought teeth.

"How was the test?"

Alabama's Farrago

1910

HARRY WINKLEPICKER, *Secretary*
69 Snow Lane, Aspen, Colo.

Hubert Humbent, Chi Psi, who fractured a hip in a skiing accident a year ago, reports that he is erect some of the time, and that his three-month old son is definitely Amherst material.

Rinky Spinokalski seems weakened in his faculties, and we missed him at the last alumni gathering. He showed up at Williams instead.

1911

I. M. MORBID, *Secretary*
11 Lily-Putz Lane, Cut Rate, Cal.

Rosie Bernetsson reports an interesting item: He nearly lost the thing in a pay toilet seat. Even tugged with both hands didn't help. He finally needed two attendants to cut the tip off, although it pained him some. "It was my very favorite necktie" whimpered Rosie.

Merrill Lynch Pierce has been awarded the Superior Achievement Award (SAA) of the Small Business Investment Corporation Program (SBICP).

1920

DICK SKIBISKI, *Secretary*
81 Lessey St., Amherst, Mass.

We regret the passing of Arman Arukian, the only Armenian to have ever attended Amherst College. He died of starvation in a Holyoke garret.

We hear that Pete Gronostalski, Northampton onion grower, has lost his wife, who ran away with a garbage man, whom she subsequently married for security. And just after Pete had bought her a new undershirt. "One man's garbage is another man's lifeblood," said she.

Harlowe Botts is leading a small band of guerillas and is planning to take over California.

Joe Richards is a nothing.

John Envy died of shock when his wife Penelope Isabell Envy, Smith '08, suggested that they have a child.

1928

MARK SILVERSTEIN, *Secretary*
11 Avenue J, Brooklyn, N. Y.

There's nothing you can say about the Jews because they are so good.

Taylor Harold died of shock when his wife denied that Harold Taylor was the father of her child on grounds that Amherst men came first.

We are sad to report that Theodore Baird dissolved in a metaphor.

Captain of Squash Team, Tennis Team, Phi Beta

Kappa, Col. Black, celebrated his wedding to Mary Ann Livingston Delafield Sux, Smith '65 of New York, Bermuda and Capri, Italy. The wedding was held in Winnetka, Illinois. It was attended by the bride and bridegroom.

I. M. Lush attended a gathering of Deke classes from 1923-42. They met in Cal Plimpton's liquor cabinet, as Shea Stadium was not available.

1932

RABBIT ALUM, *Secretary*
84 Futile Point Rd., Jamaica, N. Y.

We've just received word that Stanley "Hash" Thompson—our class wonder who became vice president of General Electric only two years after graduation—has just been fired from his job of 30 years for no apparent reason. Tough luck, "Hash!"

A tragedy marred our weekend last month, when Homer Ratfink wrote to tell us that he's still alive and well. Homer, as you remember, was one of the cruds who didn't contribute anything to the Alumni Fund.

Finally, word has it that Al Greenbaum is presently in Cairo, Egypt heading some Zionist movement. Al went a little haywire, you remember, in 1933 after he was refused admission at 26 medical schools.

1939

REV. MILTON KATZ, *Secretary*
200 Park Ave., New York, N. Y.

Fred Nietzsche '39 (rhymes with Pietzsche) announces that God '39 is dead. We lost sight of him after graduation, although C. H. Plimpton reported treating him for schlerosis of the liver in a Lebanese hospital.

Nobody expressed it better than Lewis S. Mudge who intoned at a service in his honor "Hallowed be Thy Name."

Ken Howard '66 is pleased to announce the marriage of his parents Rhonda Winkeltoe, Smith '16, and Putzram Howard '19.

Lewis Schuartza, along with all Negro alumni from 1923 to 1953 met on May 1 at a table in the Lord Jeff.

CHRISTMAS POEM

Christmas season,
Oh invention wise!
Spearhead for
Free enterprise!

'Tis time of year
For profit making,
Booming sales
And money taking.

There's shopping, shoving,
Screaming, yelling,
Rushing, pushing,
Buying, selling.

Grab it,
Buy it,
Wrap it,
Tie it,
Lick it,
Paste it,
Send it,
Waste it,
Like it?
Swap it,
Stop it,
STOP IT!!

Christmas season?
It's black and bluish;
Jesus Christ—
I'm glad I'm Jewish.

Yale Record

"But everybody loves a lover."

Texas Ranger

1948

MOE ABNITZ, *Secretary*
Main St., U. S. A.

Chi Psi has lost his wife, who died of shock when he bought a pair of Bostonians after the tape gave way on his Weejuns.

1955

DAVID CHRYSTAL, *Secretary*
Council Bluffs, S. D.

I'll be perfectly frank. I realize that I was elected class secretary so that you could continue dumping on me even after graduation. But I haven't heard from anyone in over five years. I'm not really such a bad guy.

Remember when I agreed to shower once a day, but you guys got annoyed when I used the same underwear? You never told me.

And the time I turned in the fraternity next door for violating social hours. I thought that charging your long distance calls to my number would end with graduation. But ten years . . .

And I thought that making a speech at Smith in favor of Platonic relationships would get me a friend instead of a date, which I never had and never wanted.

And I only sat with the faculty in Chapel because no one else would.

And I thought those were only alumni magazines I was burning in the fraternity parking lot.

So you see, I make mistakes, but I'm really not a bad guy. So write. Tell me about your marriages, regional sales managerships, diseases. I'll listen.

1958

I. M. SVACKED, *Secretary*
20 Appletree Close, Upper Montclair,
New Jersey

One of the members of our class recently underwent surgery. Beaten in a New York alley. The operation was successful, and in regards to the June 7th marriage, it looks like all will come out all right.

Amherst Sabrina

I KEEP MY FINGERNAILS LONG

I keep my fingernails long so they'll click when I play the piano,
I keep my fingernails long so they'll click when I play the piano,
And I'll keep 'em that way till the swallows return to Capistrano.

Christopher B. Cerf/*Harvard Lampoon*

Per Wickstrom/Yale Record

If you cross a rabbit with a snake, you get an adder that multiplies.

California Pelican

Columbia Jester

Here we have
a column inch
This poem is
what happens
when you're in
such a pinch.

Carolyn Goldberg/Columbia Jester

Reader's Dijest

One family's happy solution to the pet problem.

Our Friend, the Clam

By Ollie Freeman

Most everyone would call me a man experienced with all sorts of animals. As I grew up, I was privileged to share my various homes, not only with the usual assortment of human beings, but also with a grand parade of dogs, cats, parakeets, hamsters, turtles, goldfish, salamanders, and the like. But all this experience could not prepare me for the entrance of the most unique member of all families to which I have belonged . . . for one happy, gray clam.

It all started one day when Lucy, our youngest child, came running inside, shivering uncontrollably. At first, my wife and I thought it was due to the winter weather outside. (She had forgotten to put on her mittens!) But there was a more important reason for her shivering: she was crying. Between tears, she managed to choke out the fact that her favorite playmate, our pet cat Skippy, had mysteriously disappeared.

Experienced Wife. Both my wife and I had gone through this experience many times before. Calmly we assured Lucy that cats are wont to explore their little world from time to time, and that presently Skippy would return. Still whimpering a little, she was sent off to watch television.

When Skippy did not come home that night, we placed an ad in the local gazette, but to no avail. Weeks passed; Skippy had not put in an appearance at our home, or

any place we could imagine. Regretfully, we had to tell the children that our beloved cat was lost. Our son Tommy accepted the sad news stoically, but poor Lucy was disconsolate. Finally, in an attempt to cheer her, we announced that we would all go together to the pet shop, and buy her a new pet.

The pet shop had a veritable menagerie of cats and dogs, and my wife and I, after careful deliberation, picked out a frisky little terrier for the children. Tommy seemed reasonably pleased with the selection, but Lucy, still whimpering a little, could think only of Skippy. We left the store without a replacement.

The happy hand of fate took its grasp on the way home. We stopped off at a fish market to buy some haddock for dinner. As the man at the counter wrapped up the meal, we heard a tiny "Eureka!" from the back of the store. In came Lucy, beaming as she hadn't since that fateful January day. In her chubby little mittened hand was a tiny object. "What are you holding?" I implored her.

Slowly she opened her hand. "It's a clam, Daddy!" she replied. "I'm going to take it home and not let anyone eat it. It will be my new pet!"

Unhealthy Environment. Needless to say, we knew that the clam's brief stay at the fish market had taken its toll. I began to explain that Skippy (for that was what Lucy had already named it) would not survive in an environment so different from its native home, but my wife, sensing that Lucy needed this new pet to a degree which I could never imagine, quietly signaled me to say nothing. So Skippy, wrapped up in a piece of waxed paper and floating in a bucket of water from the fish market, accompanied us to his new home.

We installed Skippy in an old aquarium in the basement, and returned to normal life, or so we thought! For, as everyone knows, life is just not normal when there are pets around. When our cat was a member of the family, life was full of little surprises; now, with our friend the clam, whole myriads of new experiences awaited us. With Lucy waiting on it hand and foot (if I may use the expression), Skippy promptly recovered its health. Soon the whole family, even the usually stoic Tommy, began to find excuses to go down to the basement to sneak a look at our clam.

And Skippy would not let us down. When it sensed us coming, it would open its shell a bit and send out a stream of jolly bubbles, which seemed to tell us that it appreciated, in its own way, what we had done for it. Life was wonderful until disaster struck again.

Trouble. I was working in my basement woodshop one day late in April when I snuck a peek at the aquarium. There were no bubbles rising to the top . . . but, adult as I

am, I dismissed it, thinking that Skippy was probably oversleeping. Then it struck me . . . in all the months that we had known and loved him, *Skippy had not once overslept!* Feverishly I rushed to the aquarium . . . No Skippy!

Now (as I have said before) I have kept any number of pets since my boyhood days, and the times that they have chanced to go astray for a few days have been many. But what had happened to our cat had taught me a lesson . . . never take anything for granted. Besides, with the cat, it was a different story. It had roved around our house many times, and knew the neighbors and neighborhood well. If the cat could lose its bearings, what would happen to Skippy, who had never been outside the house at all? I dreaded the thought of what might come to pass.

For two days the whole family went without sleep, worrying over what had become of our lovable Skippy. Finally, my wife and I decided that the cause was lost. Stealthily, we crept down to the basement to dispose of the aquarium, so that the children would not be reminded continuously of their grief at having lost their friend Skippy. We turned on the cellar light and what to our incredulous eyes should appear — but a cascade of tiny bubbles, looking for all the world like a string of jewels! Skippy had returned!

Why? Why? People often wonder about why things happen; as for me, whenever a small miracle such as this crosses my life, I just accept it. Some say that dogs can find their way home from hundreds of miles away, traveling doggedly (and this must be where the word comes from) through unfamiliar terrain until they have reached their destination.

My wife has her own theory about Skippy's strange disappearance and reappearance. On the night before our pet's return, we entertained a few guests in the recroom. My wife guesses that Skippy overheard my brother jokingly suggest that we ought to prepare a clam dip in honor of our Skippy. Perhaps Skippy felt the clam-world equivalent of fright, and hid underneath the sofa until the party was over. Who can tell? Much is known about the animal world, but much is yet to be discovered. But in any case, Skippy was back, and everyone was happy and relieved.

Toil and Trouble. A few months later, we began to notice that Skippy had become rather lax in his bubbling; instead of the tankful of bubbles with which he had greeted us before, there were now only a few tiny ones floating lazily to the top of the aquarium. Lucy was alarmed; I was ready to call for the veterinarian. My wife, however, had a feeling as to what was really wrong with Skippy.

"For all his lovable qualities, Skippy still is a wild beast at heart, and not an ordinary domestic animal," she reminded us. She con-

tinued to say that wild animals in a zoo are usually provided, not only with a suitable environment, but also with companionship — usually another member of their species.

"Of course," we agreed, and quickly I returned to the fish market to select a suitable companion for the lonely Skippy.

But the new clam did not seem to do any good; Skippy scarcely revived; his bubblings were as lackadaisical as ever. Now the time I had always dreaded had at last come. Skippy loved us all, yet he still had a yearning to return to the sea — to be among the creatures and places in which he had spent his younger days. Sadly, I informed the family that it was our duty to permit Skippy his return to the sea.

Subhead. The reaction of the children was as I expected. Against their better judgment, they wanted to keep Skippy to try to nurse him back to health. But my wife and I knew better, and felt that this would be a good lesson in life for both Lucy and Tommy. The next day, we motored to the seashore. Sick at heart, I cast our pet clam into the roaring waves. From the depths of the seas there came a great cascade of bubbles, more bubbles than we had ever seen before. Skippy was bubbling good-bye!

Poor Lucy seemed heartbroken for weeks. We discussed buying another pet to take her mind off her beloved clam, but decided that if she really needed a substitute, she would find one somehow.

There is a strange concord between children and nature.

Sure enough, one sunny day in August she came home from a hike in the country, beaming happily. In her dimpled hand she held a new pet — a fine asparagus plant. We call it Skippy!

Yale Record

Fromm the Terrace

by Susan Savage

IT IS EARLY afternoon of a pleasant autumn day. The setting is the Terrace of the University of California at Berkeley.

Tables of various shapes and sizes are scattered around onstage. Newspapers, paper cups, and empty brown paper bags litter the tables, chairs, and ground.

ANOMIE KAPLAN sits at a table near the center. She is dressed in the Terrace uniform: a simply cut dress of a dark color (dark green or dark red), textured black stockings, and grotesque shoes with too many straps. On her left shoulder she wears a large, interesting turquoise and bronze pin. Her hair is long and dark and fastened at the nape of her neck with a tortoise shell barrette. She stares ahead into space.

TORQUE THORDAHL enters stage left. He is tall and thin. He wears a pin-striped button-down shirt which has been professionally ironed and starched, a sweatshirt which is turned wrong side out and pewter-colored Levi's. He carries a clipboard and a paperback book under his left arm and a cup of coffee in his right. He looks around for a place to sit down, spots Anomie, and sits next to her. She glances at him swiftly, then stares straight ahead again. He stares at her. She looks at him out of the corner of her eye, sees that he is looking at her, and quickly looks ahead again. He continues to stare at her. He pushes his chair out from the table, looks at her legs, back at her face, her hair, then the rest of her body. His glance rests on the pin she wears on her shoulder. She looks at him again, sees that he is staring at her chest. He sees that she sees that he is staring at her chest.

TORQUE: That's a very interesting pin you have.
ANOMIE: Thank you.
TORQUE: May I ask where it's from? Etruscan, isn't it?
ANOMIE: No, it's from—listen, do you mind if we speed this up? I have a two o'clock class.
TORQUE (*is obviously relieved; smiles*): Fine. Shall I begin, or do you want to?
ANOMIE: You go ahead.
TORQUE: Name?
ANOMIE: Anomie Kaplan.
TORQUE: Jewish?
ANOMIE: Yes. But only to the extent that I have Jewishness. I mean, I'm not a practicing Jew.
TORQUE: Socio-economic background?
ANOMIE: Upper middle class. Second generation American.
TORQUE: Major?
ANOMIE: History.
TORQUE: Status?
ANOMIE: Non-virgin. But I really loved him.
TORQUE (*very rapid-fire*): Are you socially conscious?
ANOMIE: I'm frightened and concerned about America and the world.
TORQUE (*grunts. To the set of questions immediately following, Anomie either nods or shakes her head*): Do you use Fybates? No-Doz? Lavoris? Crest? Do you cry when you get shots? Did you wear braces? Is there a great deal of sibling rivalry in your family? Are you happy when you wake up in the morning?
ANOMIE: No!
TORQUE: What's your stand on civil rights, free speech, Post Toasties—
ANOMIE: I hate breakfast!
TORQUE: —the HUAC, the ACLU, the DAR, College Boards, Franchot Tone, Enrico Banducci? Milk, beer? Rock and Roll?

What would you say if I told you to strap a pack on your back and climb Founder's Rock with me?
ANOMIE: Probably "The hell with you."
TORQUE: Are you a Leninist, Trotskyite, a Maoist?
ANOMIE: A Norman Thomas socialist.
TORQUE: Blagghh. That doesn't mean a damn thing. *Everybody's* a Norman Thomas socialist.
ANOMIE (*defensively*): Listen. I'll admit I haven't done much reading. But I'm frightened and concerned about America and the world.
TORQUE: All right. Let's get down to it. Do you wear a girdle?
ANOMIE: God, no!
TORQUE: Have you ever been in love? I mean, I know you said you *loved* someone, but have you ever been in *love*? They aren't the same, you know.
ANOMIE: God, yes! I know. I was a freshman; he was a Sigma Chi. (*Torque grimaces; in response to his move, Anomie quickly repeats:*) I was a *fresh*man! I thought he loved me, but he cast me off so quickly . . . .
TORQUE: Why?
ANOMIE: I called his fraternity pin a fraternity *pin* instead of a fraternity *badge*.
TORQUE (*reflecting*): God . . . All right. I've finished. You go ahead.
ANOMIE: All right. (*The following question sequence is very rapidly spoken. Torque makes some kind of gesture or grunt after each phrase; it does not matter whether or not his responses can be distinguished as affirmative or negative*) Do you break crackers with your soup? Do you like children? Are you altruistic? Aimez-vous Brahms? Aimez-vous *vous*? Is Ad Hoc really coming? What do you think of organized religion, love, television, Republicans, George Washington Carver, San Francisco? Aimez-vous Beethoven? Aimez-vous Allen Ginsberg, John Lennon, Dryden, Erasmus? Potrero Hill, Judy Mac, St. Francis of Assisi? Giovanni Bellini, Andy Warhol, Walt Disney? Wolfgang Amadeus Mozart, Benjamin Britten, Irving Berlin? Apple pie? Raisins? Cottage cheese? Paste, the Bible, John Gielgud? Rory Calhoun? Melina Mercouri? Annette Funicello? The Pancake House? Formica tabletops? Marshmallow malteds? Baked chicken marinated in wine marinated in scotch instead? Leon Uris? Leo Tolstoy? Do you know what finger bowls are for?

(She is breathless. They look at each other. Their faces are only inches apart. Together, as if pulled by strings, they rise and continue to look at each other.

Smiles spread on their faces. They laugh. They hug each other.)
TORQUE: Anomie, my darling! Listen, I'll start looking for an apartment right away!
ANOMIE: Yes, yes. No. No. *(She disengages herself, sinks down into her chair.)*
TORQUE: But–What's wrong? Your parents? Well, we'll keep separate apartments then. Or tell them you're married.
ANOMIE: No, no. It's not that. It's just . . . .
TORQUE: What? What could it possibly be? We've questioned each other exhaustively. We *know* we're right for each other. . . .
ANOMIE: But we haven't been so exhaustive. There's one thing you forgot to ask.
TORQUE: Nothing could matter to me now, Anomie! I'm sure that you're the one I've been looking for. I–
ANOMIE: Torque, darling. You forgot to ask where I'm from.
TORQUE: Oh, yes, I did. Well? New York, Chicago, Milpitas. What the hell difference does it make? Unless–
ANOMIE: Yes. I'm from Los Angeles.
TORQUE *(blanches, clutches his throat. He moves his chair away a little)*: Jesus. Look, I . . . listen . . . I mean . . . you must . . . you know . . . It's not that I'm prejudiced or anything . . . You *must* realize I'm not prejudiced or anything. Some of my best friends . . . But I can't . . . I just could *not* . . .
ANOMIE: I understand. Perhaps one day my people will win acceptance. But I understand your position. I really do.
TORQUE: Yeah, well look . . . I mean, I'll always say hello to you if I see you on the street or something.
ANOMIE *(Smiles reassuringly, places her hand on top of his hand, which he draws back)*: I know you will. Listen, I have to get to my two o'clock. Goodbye. *(They both rise.)*
TORQUE: Goodbye, Anomie.

Curtain.

Susannah McCorkle/*California Pelican*

Duke Peer

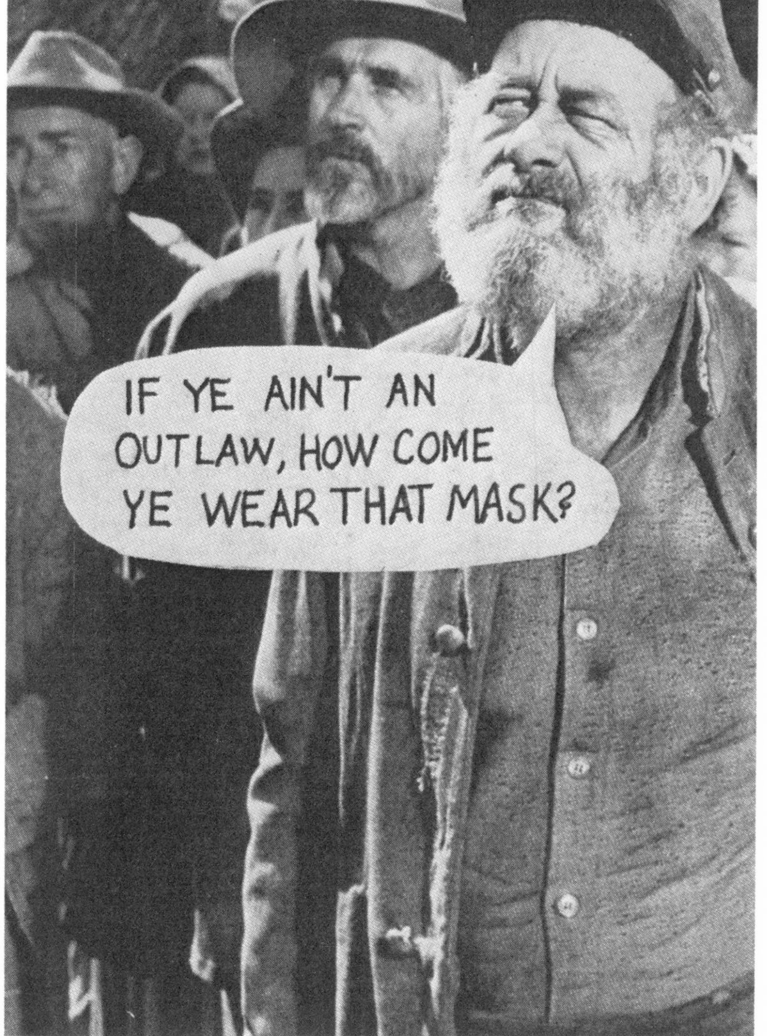

Dick Cortén/*California Pelican*

SMOKEY
STOP! MYSELF AND ALL THE WOODLAND CREATURES HAVE OUR LIVES IN YOUR HANDS

SMOKEY
LAST YEAR OVER 1,000,000,000 ACRES OF FOREST LANDS WERE DESTROYED BY FIRE!

SMOKEY
AND THAT MEANS THOUSANDS OF TINY WOODLAND CREATURES WERE EITHER KILLED OR HOMELESS... AND ALL BECAUSE OF CARELESS PEOPLE.

Uncle Sam's Soft Sell

The thrill is gone, apparently, from the once-glamorous Military Life—probably thanks to peacetime draft and the ROTC. But while traditional image of the American Fighting Patriot (that chesty, cleareyed combat hero with dented helmet and three belts of machinegun bullets) fades in the light of less romantic reality, the Armed Forces are busy reconstructing it in a more fashionable myth. Madison Avenue and BBD&O have been called in to construct an image that will sell to the eager collegiate mind, and so the Ranger as a public service hereby exposes the military's psychological warfare against civilians. Remember: Keep Your Guard Up!

HI, FELLOWS!

Gee, it's good to see the gang every Thursday night out at the National Guard Club House. And you can, too, if you join the troop to defend your country. Really, it's fun—you get to block schools, ride in tanks, shoot guns, and still be home for suppertime and mom's apple pie. Remember:

"THE NATIONAL GUARD IS KIND OF READY, MORE OR LESS"

Ho, Matey!

If it's adventure yer a'seekin, then you'll find it in the Navy! See exotic Treasure Island, Great Lakes, Duluth, Des Moines, or maybe Adack! Girls everywhere, and well within a sailor's generous budget. Acquire skills for civilian life later, like deck swabbing, paint scraping, life raft paddling . . . and don't forget you have a warm, clean hammock and three square beans a day. Remember:

"THE NAVY: A SINKING MAN'S SERVICE"

SMOKEY
SO! BREAK THOSE MATCHES! CRUSH THOSE SMOKES OUT! DROWN ALL CAMPFIRES!
SMOKEY
PLEASE HELP SAVE THE HOMES AND LIVES OF ALL OUR WOODLAND CREATURES... PLEASE... HUH? PLEASE..
SMOKEY
CAUSE THEN I CAN EAT THEM

Tom Mills/*Ohio State Sundial*

LOOK, BUDDY.

It's this way. I mean if you're not looking for a gung-ho outfit and just want to get it over with, its the Army for you. Figure it like this—two years is better than four. And remember:

"YOU'D WALK A MILE FOR THE ARMY"

Hey, Tiger!

Fight! Kill! Slug 'em in the teeth! How would you like to be a hired gun? Kill a man 54 different ways with your bare hands? You would, eh? Then, Attila, you're MARINE material. Here's your chance to storm beaches, crawl through barbed wire, bayonet 'em in the throat, and *actually get paid for it!* The Marine Corps builds men, and we also—–a few women. Remember:

"FOR THE ONE MAN IN FOUR WHO HATES A LITTLE BIT MORE"

SAY, MAN:

It's like the Air Force is a swinging outfit, see? Just dig the cool, blue rags and the crazy medals. Promotions? Man, only a square won't make his first star in six months with the Air Force. So get your kicks in a hot jet, bomb hell out of Cincinnati, and still keep your duck-tails. Remember:

"LIKE THE AIR FORCE BLUES ARE THE THREADS FOR YOU."

Lynn Ashby and Tony Bell/*Tulane Urchin*

JOHNSTON'S INDIAN LACROSSTICS
This Month: "The Nose On Your Face"

Across
1. Ah!
3. Mechanicals
11. Nyssa
16. Rex
18. Whines
19. Insulae
21. EI
22. Tu
23. In
24. Toupees
25. Norm.
26. I'm . . .
27. D. L. O.
28. S. Morse
30. I.S.S.
32. 'Be'
34. AP
35. Po
36. Ralph's Remains
41. Ali's
45. "Every . . ."
46. E. E. C. Fog
47. Llama
49. Sy.
51. Era
53. "I'm dizzy . . ."
56. Ce
57. Bei Hut
60. Pak
62. Toes
63. Ha!
64. Piscine
65. Crete (e.g.)
68. O.P.
69. Mail
71. "Oon"
72. ATTEND!
73. Up
74. S. Bellow
77. Has
78. N/A
80. Miaow
82. Vacuum
85. Model
87. Seat
89. "——gathers no moss"
91. i.e.
92. Ur
93. D.P.
94. Bays
95. Ratify
96. Imp
98. "er"
99. Emit
100. Diorama
105. "Ah ——"
106. U.E.
107. Ca ——
109. Enlarge
110. 'Pram it'
112. Mss.
114. Steep
115. Charismatic
116. Oh!

Down
1. Arf!
2. He
4. —— Ewers
5. Chime
6. Hi!
7. Antifreeze
8. —— neum
9. 'Is'
10. Sit . . .
11. N.S.U.
12. 'Yup'
13. Sled
14. Saelang
15. Aesop's ——
20. No
23. "I'm spry . . ."
28. Spa
29. Moll ——
30. Iles
31. Shy
32. —— Bee
33. Emcees
37. A.V.
38. re:
39. "—— Afric"
40. "Io! Ah, Io! Woe!"
42. 'I Like That!'
43. Sam
44. 'Baited'
48. M.D.
50. We
52. SPCA
54. —— zog.
55. Ysop
56. Cams
57. —— bill me
58. UNO
59. Tent
61. Art.
64. Pie
66. Teach
67. Ensued
70. Abel's dream
73. UN
75. Li
76. O.A.S.
78. "—— no myth!"
79. Ado's
81. Waif
82. Varmint
83. Urp!
84. Ms.
85. Moa
86. E. S.
88. Tey
90. N. B.
95. Recit
97. —— pole
98. Eur.'s
101. Rae ——
102. Arp!
103. M.G.
104. A.E.C.
108. Ash
110. Pi ——
111. M.A.
113. So

J. Jeremy Johnston/Harvard Lampoon

"He likes children."

Ohio State Sundial

Advertising for the recent pun contest attributed the following statement to George Stade: "Puns are corn. The lowest form of wheat." Now we are willing to admit that Professor Stade is a clover fellow with a rye sense of humor, but he has barley touched the subject. Because his outlook is countrified (no grassness intended), the theory is an offshoot. Puns are not low forms; rather they are whole wheat—a type which knead not be cerealized. They must never be shrubbed off with a hoe, hoe. Thus, we are amaized to see Professor Stade shaft puns. In general, it goes against our grain to harrow a member of the faculty. Yet when this quote cropped up we felt, rice or wrong, that we oat to make our views known. If, however, George had stade in his own field, we would not have cut him down. Sow there!

Columbia Jester

"LBJ Is A Scum-Sucking Capitalist Pig."

See? You already know some Activist.

And in a matter of weeks you could be speaking it fluently.

Because the Berlitz method is the fastest and most effective way to learn any language.

Just as we did here, you start right in haranguing. Loud. Your instructor won't speak a word of sensible English to you.

He starts right out with "Screw-you" and, through a process as natural as an infant learning to speak, you'll soon know the difference between a fascist-mechanist tool of mass murder and a button. In fact, within five minutes you'll be shouting a sentence as complicated as "In the coming Revolution, both the fascist-mechanist tool of mass murder and the button will be efficacious against bourgeois-elitist factions."

With the aid of objects, pictures, written Marx, and a lot of English bodies, your instructor will have you speaking fluent Activist before you can say Staughton Lynd.

Just reserve your judgment and listen to the *real* facts, baby: Zealous and card-carrying proletarian-liberals strive always to make love, not war. In the documented pictorial evidence presented at the (New) Left, however, the impersonality of the multiversity and the self-seeking intellectual brutality of the Establishment have impeded the momentum of the Great Leap Onto. Hey, hey, LBJ, how many lies did you tell today? And if you read this once again, you should be committed to every word.

We can have you arguing fluently in five weeks if you're not in jail or in a hyper-bourgeois ecos, or in three or four months if you can only spare a few hours away from draft appeal hearings. (Or in ten to fifteen days, if you refuse to even pay lip service to the running dogs of Wall Street.*)

We guarantee our method if you guarantee your soul, baby.

Now all you need to do is sit in on the New School of Berlitz Research and make an appointment.

You've already started your first lesson.

*The 10-15 day program is called Total Undeclared War and it really works.
In Manhattan: The Sundial; EVO Office; Floating Pot Parties, 674-0808; Chase Manhattan Bank Restrooms; the Times Square IRT station john without the peephole; in Great Neck: Temple Beth-El; Floating Bar Mitzvahs. Also in Antioch, Reed, Oberlin, Haverford, and Chicago. For other areas, write, heckle, or defend with your life the Berlitz Field Manager, 2547 Fuerst Avenue, New York 10023, (212) 521-8779.

James Casimir Wisniewski/Columbia Jester

A FILLER

If placed end to end, it would take 3,783,225,606 lemmings to span the distance from the earth to the moon.

Amherst Sabrina

A tomahawk is what if you go to sleep and suddenly wake up without your hair, there is an Indian with.

Texas (El Paso) El Burro

HE: Pardon me, miss, but would you be amenable to some copulation?
SHE: OK, smooth-talker.

Dartmouth Jack O'Lantern

MANAGING EDITOR: Let's not have any more jokes about sex, drinking, or profanity.
EDITOR: OK, I'm tired of putting out this magazine, too.

Yale Record

Fashion note: They are wearing the same thing in brassieres this year.

Dartmouth Jack O'Lantern

"Did you hear about the illegitimate Rice Krispie?"
"No, what about it?"
"It had snap and crackle, but no pop."

Annapolis Log

Harris and Leveque The Crisis of Modern Man

by Lionel Swilling*

Only because Harris and Leveque's *Basic Conversational French* has for so long been valued essentially for the refreshing powers of its classical simplicity and seemingly serene outlook do I hesitate to suggest what became increasingly apparent to me in my last perusal of the work: Harris and Leveque, to an even greater extent than McGuffey in his *Fourth Eclectic Reader* (and this is surely the only justifiable comparison), are poets of terror. I suspect a short examination of the way Harris and Leveque handle the techniques of dialogue will make this perception abundantly clear.

Let us first note the settings for these conversations: it is no accident that so many scenes take place in hotel lobbies, restaurants, stations, and stores. The situations are, quite intentionally, always public. We are forced to deal only with externals. The primary mode of interpersonal relationship is commercial; never emotional, never intimate. The characters are always asking for prices and rates. What do they really want? we wonder.

"Here, Kitty, Kitty, Kitty!"

Alabama's Farrago

Many of the figures who participate in these dialogues are identified only by occupation—concierge, hôtelier, employé, vendeur. Even when someone has a name, we seldom learn more than his job. "Who is Charles Du Pont?" one character asks. "A chemical engineer," another answers. Nothing more. (There is, by the way, a preponderance of chemical engineers.) The frequency with which this situation occurs suggests nothing less than a devastating critique of industrialized society, a society where one's identity is irrevocably bound to a title, often trivial or functionless.

I cannot emphasize too much that apparent externality must never be construed as unconsidered externality. The simplicity of the settings, the characters, and the syntax is merely a veil covering a wealth of anxieties, frustrations, and dark thoughts. It is, in fact, an aspect of the success of these very good conversations that the authors contrive to bring so many jabberers into their own linguistic mode.

No more conclusive proof is needed for the way in which simple prose serves as an ingenious mask than the celebrated storm scene. The weather appearing fine ("The sky is blue and the sun is shining"), John asks Marie to take a walk with him and assures her it is unnecessary to carry a raincoat. One hour later:

MARIE: Il pleut; il pleut à verse.
Je suis mouillée jusqu'aux os.
C'est votre faute.
JOHN: Ma faute? Comment cela?
MARIE: Vous savez bien. Je n'ai plus confiance en vous.

MARIE: It is raining; it is pouring. I am wet to the skin. It is your fault.
JOHN: My fault? How that?
MARIE: You know well. I no longer have confidence in you.

Needless to say, Marie's savagery and John's pathos defy adequate translation. The idyllic world of one hour earlier has been turned, by means of the fertile image of the rainstorm, to an inimical, sardonic universe. John's remarks are admittedly ineffectual, but, in the face of such a cosmos, how, we must ask ourselves, can they be otherwise? Sensing how painful it is for him to be discredited in public by Marie, we recognize the extraordinary dramatic skill of the authors in conveying this outburst in only three lines of insipid prose.

It is in characterization that the authors reveal their full powers. Consider, for example, their artistic treat-

"What I like about Darwin is that he tells it like it is."

Texas (El Paso) El Burro

ment of Louise Bedel. When she is mentioned in Conversation 10, John is unable to remember meeting her. He cannot recall whether she is a tall blonde or a short brunette. The reader, however, is not permitted to take such an uncommitted view of this haunting figure. Though she leaves the world of John and his friends after her marriage to Charles Du Pont, she reappears again and again in the grammar exercises. Through this unique literary device, the cryptic Louise Bedel is saved from the anonymity imposed by her society. We are not only asked questions about her, but also directed how to answer. The authors have exploited every means available to make this ignored soul a vital part of our life-experience. Their ingenuity deserves comparison with Shakespeare's in his broadly farcical line, "Enter, with Sennett" Henry VI, I, i).

The heart of the work, I believe, lies in the depiction of the protagonist, John Hughes. First of all, he is the only character with much of a revealed past—we sense a certain poignancy in the way he tells the man preparing his identification card—"Mon père habite à Philadelphie . . . ma mère est morte." As in all great works of art, what is left unsaid is of the highest eloquence. Secondly, in situation after situation, the resolution of the conflict in the dialogue involves an acquiescence on John's part: in the hotel, at the tobacco shop, in the restaurant, and at the ticket window at the Eastern Railway Station, John doesn't select; he settles for. Lastly, we soon note that, apart from his duties as a chemical engineer, he is most frequently engaged in finding a room. In only sixteen conversations, he moves no less than three times. At one point he admits he spends "October and November in Marseilles; December, January and February in Paris; March and April in Lyon; May, June, July and August in Paris."

Clearly, the authors have created a startling image of modern man, exploited, restless, unable to find a center upon which to construct a meaningful existence, drifting, lonely. It tears our hearts out.

I can only hope this cursory examination will assure Harris and Leveque of the critical respect they have long deserved and that this study will provide inspiration for a good share of preceptors, associates, lecturers, and others potentially unemployed.

*LIONEL SWILLING, *himself quite a fundamental, is world-famous for his incisive criticisms. He is the last of the so-called "whole" critics, and knows everything. Swilling (no relation to the meat people) graduated from Columbia* Mirabile Dictu, *and resides in a tower, as it were, with stately, plump Buck Mulligan.*

Columbia Jester

THE INCOMPLETE REPORT

Good Doctor Kinsey is a whiz
Who studies sex by giant quiz.
He's probed within our private lives,
Knows husbands' habits and their wives'.
He's hep to all the quips and quirks
That motivate both squares and jerks,
Reveals the strange narcissine elves
Who limit play unto themselves,
Describes the queer, and who ticks
Performing quite irregular tricks.
He's catalogued the frigid quail
Who finds no pleasure in her tail,
The oversexed, the undersexed,
The long frustrated and perplexed,
The sneaks who keep desires hidden,
But always dream of things forbidden,
And wolves who can't control their urges,
In whom insanity verges.
Now all these types he writes about,
But he neglects entirely
A matter that much interests me:
With all this knowledge at his touch,
Is Doctor Kinsey getting much?

CCNY Mercury

Let's see, that's 1500 students at $700 apiece . . .

Occidental Fang

EXOTIC ADVERTISERS
INC.
Present...
the Fang Little Players in.....
QUICK, HENRY,
THE FLIT!!
or
...BUG BOMBS REVISITED
by
Gilliam

1

gilliam '62

8

7

Terry Gilliam/*Occidental Fang*

"I've got the feeling I'm in the wrong foxhole." Florida State Smoke Signals

And then there was the ex-Nazi who became a hired gun in Tucson after a short respite in Argentina. He became famous for practicing his trade dressed in the latest three-piece suit. In fact, he was known as the fascist gun in the vest.

Emory Phoenix

WAGNERIAN FRAGMENT

Siegmund said to Siegelinde,
"Let us have some lovely kinder."
Said Siegelinde that night,
"All right."

Paul D. Gewirtz/Columbia Jester

Then there's the one about the thrifty cat. Every week he puts a little into the kitty.

Texas (El Paso) El Burro

A young housewife was shocked by some language used by her little daughter. When asked about it, the daughter said she learned it from a little girl she played with in Prospect Park.

The next day the mother sought out the little girl in the park, and asked:

"Are you the little girl who uses bad language?"

"Who told you?" was the reply.

"A little bird," said the woman.

"I like that!" exclaimed the little girl. "To think that I've been feeding the little bastards!"

Georgia Tech Rambler

HISTORICAL NOTE

Thus spake Mohammed the prophet,
"Killing women has got to be stopet.
If you don't change your attitude, Muslim,
We soon won't be Islam but Waslam."

OUR MIDDLE EAST POLICY

We are loyal
To the ones with oyal.

THE SITUATION IN PALESTINE

The poor old Egyptians
Are having conyptians,
And so are Iran and Iraq;
They'd have nothing to lews
By killing the Jews
If the Jews would stop killing them baq.

Nancy Ellen Kemp/Emory Phoenix

One day two soldiers were arguing over a dead animal. One of them said it was a mule, and the other insisted it was a donkey. In a little while, an officer came by and they asked his opinion. He said curtly, "It's an ass; bury it!"

While they were digging a grave for the animal, a WAC came by. She asked, "What are you digging? A fox hole?" To which they wryly answered, "No!"

Tulane Urchin

"I CAN GIVE YOU A REALISTIC TOWNEE® VOCABULARY AND APPEARANCE!"

Don't be maimed by mushy, misguided mastery over English. Do the "guys" on corners all over New Brunswick laugh when they see you walk down the street? Are you unable to answer them in their own language? Well fella, I've got a book for you that will end all of your problems!! (and I got a book on English too).

Are you handicapped by a college education? Man, erase all of that intellectual background by reading my book. Learn proper intonation and inflection of the major contemporary obscene idioms in use by the lower socio-economic classes. No longer will you be ostracized by the "black leather jacket set". You, yes YOU, will be able to freely interact, and perhaps some day become a member of "The Other America". Live in slums, have sex – oodles and oodles of sex –dirt, filth, poverty and degeneracy can ALL be yours!!

Now, I'm going to tell you how to become a Townee® through the following questions and answers:

QUESTION: What do you mean by a command of poor English?

ANSWER: Speak in garbled tones, using only one or two syllable words. Most important – get in as many four letter words as possible.

QUESTION: What are some other advantages of speaking poor English?

ANSWER: Language is the method by which we learn to think. By learning to speak poorly, you can overcome thought! Problems, worries, etc. will be gone forever!

QUESTION: Does your book really work?

ANSWER: Yes. Any more questions?

J.B. writes:
"Man, like thanks a $%–&'* lot. I got kicked outa Rutgers, the $%–&'* University."

R.F. writes:
"The greatest! I'm the head'a my street corner gang."

S.K. writes:
"Su$%–& th *'&–% rx &'$%* /)"''$%–wz to be $%–&'* and $%–&'&–%$."

BLENCH DRATFORD – TOWNEE® Inc.
35 Union St., New Brunswick (Zebra), N.J.

Throw me the paper dad. I'll get the coins in when I go on Relief, or pull my first stick up.

HEAD ______________________

TURF ______________________

favorite weapon __________

(check your choice) lower lower class ☐ middle lower class ☐

BEFORE

"Darling, we could travel down the path to Nirvana, engaging in the great tradition of Mill's Ethical Hedonism. Mental and physical pleasures will be ours, my love. Forsake the drudgery of sexual frustration. Let us become enjoined in the empathy of amour."

AFTER

"Got my *$%?/&' wheels baby. Wanna get %–'$? I mean, like I ain't been %–&/*¢%'* since the fuzz got my ¢*$%–&'& old lady. I got a $%–&'*? bottle, so let's shag outa here and %$–&'¢*?."

Rutgers Rut

If you are between the ages of 18 and 26

American Airforce Will fly you to Southeast Asia Absolutely Free!

Sound incredible? Not really. Anytime we take a jet up, there are almost always left-over seats.

So it occurred to us that we might be able to fill a few of them and give our young men a chance to see the world at the same time by giving them a break on the fare.

The American Youth Plan

We call it the American Youth Plan, and what it means is this:

The American Airforce will pay the entire jet coach fare to Southeast Asia for any physically fit young man 18 through 26.

It's that simple.

All you have to do is prove your age (a birth certificate or any other legal document will do) and enlist in the United States Army.

We think it's a simply marvelous idea. Not only do you get to see this very interesting part of the world, but some of our planes are greeted with a 21 gun salute — sometimes even before the airplane lands!

Just complete this coupon and send it to:
Lt. Gen. Lewis Hershey
Selective Service System
Washington, D.C.

Name ______________________

Address ______________________

City __________ State ______ Zip ______

Birth date ______ Signature ______________

Color hair ________ Color eyes __________

Next of kin ______________________

American Airforce

UCLA Satyr

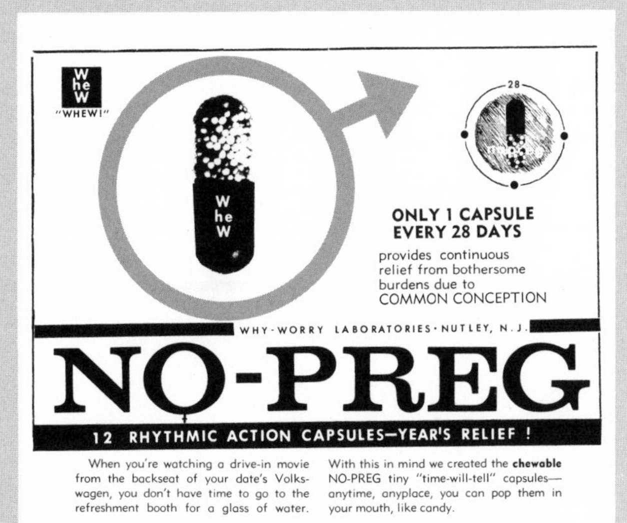

When you're watching a drive-in movie from the backseat of your date's Volkswagen, you don't have time to go to the refreshment booth for a glass of water. With this in mind we created the **chewable** NO-PREG tiny "time-will-tell" capsules—anytime, anyplace, you can pop them in your mouth, like candy.

When taken as directed in a conscientiously applied program of moral hygiene NO-PREG capsules

——Rush decongestants to swollen cavities and shrink them without surgery
——drain naval passages with powerful antihistimines
——Make "my brother was an only child" a reality
——keep you cool, calm and dry
——dissolve slowly, putting just enough LSD and caffeine in your blood to keep you alert and flying
——relieve nausea and depression accompanying unexpected parasites
——reach areas coat hangers cannot
——are fun to use and they taste good too

Play it safe with **NO-PREG**

MIT Voo Doo

The Department of Philosophy and Religion announces a contest open to all students and faculty of the American University and the Wesley Seminary. Write in twenty-five words or less;

I want to go to heaven because.....

THE PRIZES:

–Two reserved seats in the Observation Car of the Glory Train.
–Some Grapes of Wrath.
–One adulteress.
–Two tickets to that Great Movie Show In The Sky.
–A copy of a brass pin engraved on the Lord's Prayer.
–Book: *Celestial Jurisprudence* or *You and Judgment Day*.
–Sheaves, suitable for Bringing In.
–One pillar of salt.
–The Truth: suitable for setting Ye free.
–One cup that hath runneth over.
–One Year's supply of Honest Job's Sure-Fire Boil Oil.

Tear off the top of Paul Tillich and mail with the Official Entry Blank and thirty pieces of silver. All entries must be received by midnight of the Millenium. Decision of the judges will be transitory.

Official Entry Blank

Name ....

Address ....

"I want to go to Heaven because ....

....

....

....

American University Bald Eagle

The Mother Goose

MOTHER GOOSE: Good morning, Socrates. How happy I am to meet you here, for I would like to show you my new rhyme.
SOCRATES: Are you sure that this morning is good? What makes this morning different from all other mornings? And are you really happy to show me your poem? Is anybody happy? But these are inscrutable questions to which only I, in my inscrutable way, know the equally inscrutable answers. Pray read your poem.
M. G.: Er . . . of course. *(she reads)*

Humpty Dumpty sat on a wall.
Humpty Dumpty had a great fall.
All the king's horses and all the king's men
Couldn't put Humpty Dumpty together again.

SOC: Very interesting, on the surface. But now let me ask you some penetrating questions to make you realize how insipid you really are. Taking the last part first: it admits, does it not, that the king's men are unable to accomplish a simple task, i.e., putting Mr. Dumpty together again?
M. G.: Well, now that you put it that way, yes.
SOC.: Good. Now, since I assume (and therefore it must be true) that all poetry is idealized, the king here must be the philosopher king, is he not? Of course he is. Therefore, the "king's men" must then be the guardians, 2nd class, or in the language of the vulgar, the soldiers, and not a group of barber shop quartet rejects, as is commonly supposed.
M. G.: I must admit that originally I hadn't seen it that way, but . . .
SOC.: Now, this failure on the part of the guardians would inspire fear and cowardice in their hearts if they read it, would it not?
M. G.: Well, if you say so.
SOC.: Then obviously we must eliminate the last two lines.
M. G.: But, Socrates, I only intended this to amuse little girls and boys . . .
SOC.: Little boys? You must introduce me to them. Now for the first part. We see that Mr. Dumpty sits on a wall. But Athens also sits on a great wall, the so called "Long Walls" leading to the port. In our recent war, Athens also had a "great fall." Hence it must be obvious to you that these two lines discuss the fall of Athens.
M. G.: I must grant that.
SOC.: But Athens is the home of myself and Plato, in that order. Hence (and don't ask me whence this hence) this is an implied slur upon us, the archetypes of the philosopher king, who is mentioned in the last two lines. I shall not tolerate this, even though I am an understanding man. The first two lines must go.
M. G.: I meant no offense.
SOC.: Of course not. But we are faced with a new problem. We have eliminated the entire poem. Thus, we have turned something into nothing. This is contrary to the Law of Conservation of Matter, is it not?
M. G.: Surely.
SOC.: Therefore, we must reconstruct the poem, which I shall now proceed to do, brilliantly. Since poetry must be sung, we must set this poem to a martial and manly aire.
M. G.: How about "Rock Around the Clock?"
SOC.: I was thinking of "Glory, Glory Hallelujah."
M. G.: "Glory, Glory Hallelujah" to be sure. How could I have not realized?
SOC.: The poem should now read thus:

Humpty Dumpty sat upon the center of a tripod.
Humpty Dumpty thought about the goodness of the gods.
Humpty Dumpty descended down to the land of Nod.
His soul goes marching on.
Glory, Glory to the contemplative king.
Dorian and Phrygian scales we sing.
Educational art is the coming thing.
To Er our souls go on.

Jack Auspitz/Columbia Jester

I have heard that earthlings were filthy bastards but I wasn't prepared for that!
Georgia Tech Rambler

I don't think this is any ordinary omen, Captain.
Richard Bassein/Columbia Jester

What did you expect?

This is not one of those sneaky little German cars that are being used by the communists to corrupt the minds of the American people.

This car was made right here, in the good old United States.

Those damn foreign cars are a menace, and people buying them ought to have their heads examined. Or maybe they ought to be investigated.

Or both.

The way we're losing the cold war (and our gold supply,) it's a shame Congress doesn't pass a law making it illegal to buy anything that doesn't have Made In USA stamped on it.

That way we'd be helping our own.

To hell with the German economy, after what they tried to do to us in World War Two.

The biggest single menace to our country today (outside of atheistic communism) is the drivers of those foreign cars.

They come racing down the highways like bats out of hell, scaring innocent women and children.

And with the extra gas mileage they get, they're putting American oil companies out of business.

So we say, Keep 'em off our roads.

The driver of the car pictured above would say so, too, but he got in an argument with one of the dirty foreign cars. And you can see what happened.

Top crushed in, hood smashed, fenders bent, doors jammed. The radio and heater went out. Two high-speed hubcaps flew off into a ditch. They were never found.

The little foreign car, sneaky as they are, didn't have a scratch. It just drove off.

The whole disgusting, materialistic, communist plot is disgusting.

And something ought to be done about it.

Don Wegars/California Pelican

The Ninety-Nine Most Repeated (& Probably the Worst) College Jokes of the Century

STUDE: Is this ice cream pure?
DRUGGIST: As pure as the girl of your dreams.
STUDE: Gimme a pack of cigarettes.

I've never seen a purple cow,
My eyes with tears are full.
I've never seen a purple cow,
And I'm a purple bull.

PROFESSOR (pointing to the cigarette butt on the floor): Is this yours?
STUDENT (pleasantly): Not at all, sir. You saw it first.

1ST BURGLAR: Where ya been?
2ND BURGLAR: In a fraternity house.
1ST BURGLAR: Lose anything?

"Charlie! Answer the door!"
"Hello, door."

"Do you dance?"
"Oh, yes. I love to."
"Great—that's even better than dancing."

The professor rapped on his desk and yelled, "Order!"
Voice from the rear: "Beer!"

The nurse entered the professor's study and said softly, "It's a boy, sir."

The professor looked up from his book: "Well, ask him what he wants."

Did you hear what the rug said to the floor? . . .
"Don't move, I've got you covered."
Did you hear what the ceiling said to the wall? . . .
"Hold me up, I'm plastered."

My new girl doesn't have much of a face, but you oughtta see her neck.

ECONOMIC PROBLEM: Why is it that women without principle draw the highest rate of interest?

It was dark and quiet, and most romantic. He leaned in close and whispered into her ear, "What are you thinking about, honey?"

"The same thing you are, darling," she whispered back.

"Then let's go!" he shouted. "I'll race you to the icebox!"

"Honey," she asked, "you don't mind if I wear velvet instead of silk, do you?"

"No, darling," he answered, "I'll love you through thick and thin."

Jimmie was assigned by his teacher to write a composition about his origin.

He questioned his mother: "Mom, where did Grandma come from?"

"The stork brought her."

"Well, where did you come from?"

"The stork brought me, and you too, dear."

The small, modern lad then began his composition: "There have been no natural births in our family for three generations."

There was a little girl
Who had a little curl
Right in the middle of her forehead.
And when she was good
She was very, very good;
And when she was bad
She was marvellous.

One Sabbath evening the mother suddenly opened the door to the parlor and started to enter. There she saw her daughter and her daughter's beau.

"Why," gasped the befuddled mother, "I never . . . !"

"But, Mother, you must have!" replied the daughter.

The fraternity man's parents were paying a surprise late-night visit to college. In front of the Greek house, the father called out, "Is this where Robert Jones lives?"

Voice from on high: "Yes—bring him in."

Worst Jokes of the Century

A fellow you'd rather not know sauntered into our office the other day and told us the following tale:

"A little province in Tibet was having a lot of trouble with this bear because he had foot-prints like a boy. Naturally they couldn't track the bear because there were so many boys in the village. So they called in this star bear-catcher from Lhasa named Chan, who had traps made of teak, so that even the strongest bear couldn't smash them. Well, sir, Chan caught the bear without further ado and shipped him off to the Imperial House of Natural Curiosities, and went home."

Our raconteur extraordinaire paused for air and dramatic effect. "And that, gentlemen," he said, "is how they caught the boy-foot bear with teak of Chan."

Of all the fishes in the sea
The queerest is the bass—
He climbs up into seaweed trees
And slides down on his hands and knees.

A divinity student named Tweedle
Refused to accept his degree.
"It's tough enough being Tweedle," he said,
"Without being Tweedle, D.D."

Mary had a little lamb,
The lamb had halitosis,
And everywhere that Mary went
The people held their nosis.

A college boy boarded the train, entered a sleeper, and tipped the six-foot porter liberally to wake him and put him off at Atlanta.

"I'm a very sound sleeper," said the young man, "and you must take no notice of my protests. Seize me and put me out on the platform."

The next morning he woke up to find himself still on the train, steaming into Athens, Georgia. Raging with fury, he found the porter and began to bawl him out in strong language.

"I say, suh," replied the great porter, calmly, "you've got a bit o' temper, but it ain't nothin' compared with the young feller I put out of the train at Atlanta."

"Goodness, George, this isn't our baby!"
"Shut up! It's a better carriage."

The good Dean of Women at we-cannot-say-which institution was lecturing the coeds on the topic of sex.

"In moments of temptation," the Dean said, "ask yourself just one question: Is an hour of pleasure worth a lifetime of shame?"

A shapely miss put her hand in the air, was called on, and asked innocently, "Tell me, Dean, how do you make it last an hour?"

SHE: **Oh, look, the bridesmaid!**
HE: **My gosh, so soon?**

"Are you a fraternity man?"
"No, I tore my pants climbing over a fence. . . . Are you a sorority girl?"
"No, I got caught in the rain and my dress shrank."

A young man and his date pulled over to the side of the road.
SHE: **You're not gonna pull that 'out of gas' routine, are you?**
HE: **Naw, I use the 'hereafter' routine.**
SHE: **The 'hereafter' routine?**
HE: **Yah. If you're not here after what I'm here after, then you'll be here after I'm gone.**

Are you sure this motel is university-approved?

The Phys Ed teacher was discussing water safety. "Now," she said, "what is the safest piece of clothing to have on in case you're drowning? Miss Twillingham?"

"A blouse," replied the young thing.

"Why a blouse?" continued the teacher.

"Because," replied the coed, "air gets under it and acts like a buoy."

Class dismissed.

She was only a contractor's daughter, but was she well built!
She was only a hash-slinger's daughter, but how she could dish it out!
She was only a sergeant's daughter, but she knew when to call a halt.
She was only a lawyer's daughter, but what a will to break!
She was only an artist's daughter, but what a crowd she could draw!
She was only a shoemaker's daughter, but she gave the boys her awl.
She was only a censor's daughter, but she knew when to cut it out.

SHE: **I'm perfect.**
HE: **I'm practice.**

Some girls are built like this one.

Others are built more like this.

But they usually end up like this.

"How can you keep eating at the dining hall?"
"Easy. I just take a tablespoon of Drano three times a day."

A musician and a bunch of his buddies were whooping it up late one night when the landlord came in.

"Do you know there's a little old lady sick upstairs?" he demanded.

"No, man," answered the pianist, "but hum the first few bars and we'll fake the rest."

Noah once said, as the animals were boarding the ark, "Now I herd everything."

Mary had a pair of skates;
On ice she used to frisk.
Now wasn't she a silly girl
Her little *.

An Englishman was conversing with the clerk in the Ambassador Hotel. "Here's a riddle," said the clerk. "My mother gave birth to a child. It was neither my brother nor my sister. Who was it?"

"I can't guess," said the Englishman.

"It was I."

"Ha, ha. Very clever. I must remember that."

The Englishman then told the story at his club. Said he: "Here's a riddle, old top. My mother gave birth to a child. It was neither my brother nor my sister. Who was it? . . . What? You can't guess? Do you give up? Ha! It was the clerk back at the Ambassador!"

"So your boy's at college, eh? What's he going to be when he graduates?"

"Senile."

Once upon a time a boy penguin and a girl penguin met at the equator. After a brief but passionate interlude the boy penguin went away to the North Pole, and the girl penguin went in the opposite direction, to the South Pole.

A few months later, a telegram arrived at the North Pole, saying: "Come quick—am with Byrd."

It is rumored that one professor recently became aware that his class had drowsed off on him, and he decided that he would catch everyone off guard. He suddenly dropped into double-talk.

"You then take the loose sections of feather sniggs and gweld them—being careful not to overheat the broughtabs. Then extract and wampt them gently for about a time and a half. Fwengle each one twice, then swiftly dip them in blinger, if handy. Otherwise, discriminate the entire instrument in twetchels. Are there any questions?"

"Yeah," came a sleepy voice from the back of the room. "What are twetchels?"

"I've found the best way to start the day is to exercise for five minutes, take a deep breath, and finish with a cold shower. Then I feel rosy all over."

"Tell us more about Rosie."

Did you hear about the coed who was so thin that when she swallowed an olive three men left school?

A girl was telling a boy friend that she realized she was very popular, but she didn't know why.

"Do you suppose it's my complexion?" she asked.

"No."

"My figure?"

"No."

"My personality?"

"No."

"I give up."

"That's it."

HUSBAND (answering telephone): What? . . . How should I know? Why don't you call the Coast Guard? Good-bye.

WIFE: Who on earth was that?

HUSBAND: I haven't the faintest idea. Some idiot wanted to know if the coast was clear.

The guy took his doll to an open-air play one summer eve, and during the first act found it necessary to excuse himself. Asking the usher for the men's room, he was told to "turn left by that big oak tree, then right for twenty yards."

Some time later, he returned to his seat.

"Is the second act over?" he asked the girl.

"You should know," she said airily. "You were in it."

HUCKINMIRE: Heard you buried your wife yesterday. Terribly sorry.

VANDERCLEAVE: Had to. Dead, you know.

PAW: Shore too bad about our two daughters laying up in that there cemetery.

MAW: Shore is, Paw. Sometimes I wisht they was daid.

CURIOUS OLD LADY: I see you've lost your leg, haven't you?

CRIPPLED WAR VET: Well, damned if I haven't!

Worst Jokes of the Century

Did you hear about the moron who was practicing to be a magician? He walked down the street and turned into a drugstore.

A farmer was driving past the insane asylum with a truckload of fertilizer. An inmate called out:
"What are you hauling there?"
"Fertilizer," replied the farmer.
"What are you going to do with it?"
"Put it on my strawberries."
"You ought to live here—we get cream and sugar on ours."

STUDENT: Are you the man who cut my hair last?
BARBER: I couldn't be, sir. I've only been here a year.

BEGGAR: Have you enough money for a cup of coffee?
STUDENT: Oh, I'll manage somehow, thank you.

PROFESSOR: I won't begin today's lecture until the room settles down.
VOICE FROM THE REAR: Go home and sleep it off, old man!

Drunken fratman, staggering back to the house, bumps into a telephone pole. Feels way around it several times, then mutters, "S'no use. Walled in."

SAL: I said some very foolish words to my boy friend last night.
GAL: Yes?
SAL: That was one of them.

"Shay, lishen, lady, you're the homeliest woman I ever saw."
"Well, you're the drunkest man I ever saw."
"I know, lady, but I won't be in the morning."

GENTLEMAN (at the door): Is May in?
MAID (haughtily): May who?
GENTLEMAN (peeved): Mayonnaise!
MAID (shutting the door): Mayonnaise is dressing!

"Mother, are there any skyscrapers in heaven?"
"Oh, no, son. *Engineers* build skyscrapers."

TEACHER: Now, Johnny, if I lay two eggs here and three over there, how many will there be altogether?
JOHNNY: Personally, I don't think you can do it.

Two little German boys were walking through the mountains with their mother. As they stopped to admire the scenery, one of them suddenly pushed the little lady off a cliff. Watching her fall, he chortled to his brother, "Look, Hans, no Ma!"

It happened in Tibet. The family had been without meat for weeks and when the father came home one day dragging a yak he had killed, there was great rejoicing.

The mother carefully prepared the animal and placed it inside the crude opening that served as an oven.

The whole family then set out to round up the neighbors for a great feast. This took longer than they had expected, and as they were returning, they saw billows of smoke clouds coming from the hut.

The mother ran toward it, shouting in great anguish: "Oh, my baking yak!"

And then there is the story about the freshman who, on his first visit to the bank, was asked to endorse his check, and wrote: "I heartily endorse this check."

He was a rather undersized freshman at his first college dance, but despite his smallness and bashfulness he was sure of himself in his own way. He walked over to a beautiful and over-sophisticated sorority girl and asked, "Pardon me, Miss, but may I have this dance?"

She looked down at his puny size and lack of fraternity pin and said, "I'm sorry, but I never dance with a child."

The freshman bowed deeply. "I'm sorry," he answered, "I didn't know your condition."

GUIDE: We are now passing the largest brewery in the state.
STUDENT: Why?

JAY: Don't you want to spoon?
MAE: What's spooning?
JAY: What that couple over there are doing.
MAE: Well, let's shovel!

Earlier that day an elephant had escaped from the Barnum and Bailey circus as it passed through town.

That evening, a foreign-born old woman, who did not know what an elephant even looked like, telephoned the police station, very much excited.

"Come over right soon!" she gasped. "One big animal is in my garden, pulling up cabbages with the tail."

"What's he doing with them?" the amused policeman asked.

"If I am to tell you," she answered, "you will not to believe me!"

Then there was the absent-minded prof who forgot to write a $5 textbook and sell it to his class.

Worst Jokes of the Century

"Mrs. Clancy, I'm afraid your son is badly spoiled."
"Gowan—I resent your sayin' such a thing."
"Well, have it your way, but come outside and see what the steamroller did to him."

HE (leering): Do you know what virgins eat for breakfast?
SHE (coy): No, what?
HE (quick): Aha! Just as I thought!

SHE: Will you join me in a cup of tea?
HE: You get in first.

"Robinson?"
"Here."
"Rosenthal?"
"Present."
"Mary Smith?"
"Here, sir."
"Wanamaker?"
Chorus: "YES!"

I'd like to be a could-be
If I could not be an are.
For a could-be is a may-be
With a chance of touching par.
I'd rather be a has-been
Than a might-have-been by far,
For a might-have-been has never been,
But a has-been was an are.

The hospital patients, bored and unable to secure playing cards, filched the diagnoses from a nurse's pocket as she went by. A game of draw poker was started, and on the first hand they bid high and over-raised each other until all their money was on the table.

"Well, I guess I win," said one, reaching out for the money. "I've got three appendices and two gallstones."

"Just a minute," spoke up another. "Not so fast. I got four enemas."

"OK," said the first, "you win the pot."

PROF: Do you like Kipling?
STUDE: I don't know. How do you kipple?

There was a young man from St. Dee
Who was stung on the arm by a wasp.
When asked, "Does it hurt?"
He replied, "No, it doesn't,
But I'm sure glad it wasn't a hornet."

SHE: You bow so English, Cousin Tommie.
TOMMY: I bow 'ow?
SMALL DOG: So do I.

1ST DRUNK: Say, know what time it is?
2ND DRUNK: Yeah.
1ST DRUNK: Thanks.

The mother of triplets was being congratulated by a friend. "Isn't it wonderful," gushed the mother. "And think—it only happens once out of 15,875 times!"

"Well, that *is* remarkable," her friend replied, "but I don't see how you found time to do your housework."

A flea and a fly in a flue
Were caught, so what could they do?
Said the fly, "Let us flee."
"Let us fly," said the flea.
So they flew through a flaw in the flue.

MARK ANTONY: I want to see Cleopatra.
SERVANT: She's in bed with laryngitis.
MARK ANTONY: Damn those Greeks!

"So you want to become my son-in-law?"
"No, sir, but if I marry your daughter, I don't see how I can get out of it."

HE (like a dirty old man): Aren't you afraid of the big bad wolf?
BLIND DATE: No, why?
HE: That's funny, the other pigs were.

FROSH: I want a girl who cooks, sews, keeps house, and doesn't smoke, drink, or pet.
SENIOR: Why don't you go down to the graveyard and dig one up?

"Do you know what good clean fun is?"
"No, what good is it?"

"Will you marry me?"
"I can't—it's Lent."
"Well, when you get it back will you marry me?"

The scene was the reading room of the college library. A studious sophomore was reading birth and death statistics in a large almanac. Amazed by something he read, he turned to the fellow next to him and said, "Do you realize that every time I breathe a man dies!"

"Very interesting," replied the stranger. "Why don't you try Listerine?"

Knock, knock, knock.
ST. PETER: Who's there?
VOICE OUTSIDE THE PEARLY GATES: It is I.
ST. PETER: Go to hell! We have enough English instructors here now.

Worst Jokes of the Century

A sweet young college teacher who had always been virtuous was invited to go for a ride in the country by a handsome, young assistant prof. Under a tree on the bank of a lake, she finally gave in. Later, sobbing uncontrollably, she asked her seducer, "How can I ever face my students again, knowing I have sinned twice?"

"Twice?" asked the young professor, confused.

"Why, yes," said the sweet young thing, wiping a tear from her eye. "You're going to do it again, aren't you?"

The Sunday gospel shouter was in great form.

"Everything God has made is perfect," he preached.

A small, gnarled hunchback rose in the rear of the auditorium: "What about me?"

"Why," responded the preacher, "you're the most perfect hunchback I ever saw."

"No," said the centipede, crossing her legs, "a hundred times, no!"

SMYTHE: Father has given my brother and me a cattle ranch; can you suggest a name for it?

MISS BROWN: Call it 'The Horizon,' because it is there the sons raise meat.

1ST POPPA: Do you think your son will soon forget all he learned at college?

2ND POPPA: I hope so—he can't make a living necking.

HE: Dearie, I must marry you.

SHE: Have you seen my father?

HE: Sure, but I love you just the same.

She took off her shoes and nylons. He took off his shoes, socks and pants. She took off her dress, panties and brassiere. He took off his shirt and shorts. She put on a wisp of a silk nightie. He put on his red striped pajamas. He climbed into the right side of the bed. She climbed into the left side. He faced toward the left. She faced toward the right. He reached and turned out the lamp. She pulled the cord on the table light.

He was in the Waldorf in New York. She was in the Statler in St. Louis. So they both turned over and went to sleep.

Two very cute nurses coming in late met two interns. "Shh!" one nurse said. "We're slipping in after hours."

"That's OK," answered one of the interns. "We're slipping out after ours."

A new inmate checked in at the local asylum. Whereas most of the new arrivals have a sullen attitude, this fellow was all smiles. In fact, he was laughing uproariously.

"Nearest kin?" asked the examining physician.

"Twin brother," responded the fellow. "We were identical twins. Couldn't tell us apart. In school he'd throw a spitball and the teacher would blame me. Once he was arrested for speeding and the judge fined me. I had a girl; he ran off with her."

"Then why are you laughing?"

"Cuz last week I got even with him."

"What happened?"

"I died and they buried him."

St. Peter was interviewing a fair damsel at the pearly gates.

"Did you, while on earth, indulge in drinking, necking, petting, smoking, or dancing?" he asked.

"Never!" she retorted emphatically.

"Then why haven't you reported here sooner? You've been dead a long time."

"Now what should a polite little boy say to a lady who has given him a penny for carrying her parcel?"

"I'm too polite to say it, Ma'am."

"What's the difference between a horse and a girl?"

"I don't know."

"I'll bet you have some swell dates."

INDEX

THE CULPRITS

ALLEN, OLIVER E.: 125
ANTHONY, LOUIS: 155
ANTRIM, MONK: 76
ARNO, PETER: 81, 83
ASHBY, LYNN: 200
AUSPITZ, JACK: 185, 210
BANKS, WILLIAM B.: 6, 7, 71
BARKENTIN, GEORGE: 15
BARTLETT, PAUL: 42
BASSEIN, RICHARD: 210
BAYRD, NED: 179
BECK, JOEL: 180
BELL, TONY: 200
BENCHLEY, NATHANIEL: 100, 103, 117
BENCHLEY, ROBERT: 42, 43, 49
BENET, STEPHEN VINCENT: 38
BERENDT, JOHN: 179
BERGER, H.: 135
BERNSTEIN, THEODORE M.: 67
BIGGERS, EARL DERR: 55
BRECK, JOSEPH: 5
BROWNTON, PAGE: 151
BUCHWALD, ART: 126, 128
BURNS AND LOVING: 195
CANIFF, MILTON: 86
CASE, WILLIAM S.: 32
CATNIP, JOE: 67
CERF, BENNETT: 40, 54
CERF, CHRISTOPHER B.: 186, 196
COCHRAN, CLIVE: 180
COOLIDGE, CHARLES A.: 28
CORNELIUS, TOM: 185
CORTEN, DICK: 199
CRAWFORD, ALLAN RUDYARD: 82
CROPP, RICHARD: 7
DANA, RICHARD HENRY, JR.: 38
DARROW, WHITNEY, JR.: 111
DEDMAN, J. JULIEN: 136
DEEMS, PAUL S.: 98
DE, TOLEDANO, RALPH: 109
DRUCKERMAN, ERVIN: 96
EBEL, HENRY: 156
EPSTEIN, JASON: 123
FAIRFIELD, FLASH: 127
FITZGERALD, F. SCOTT: 42
FORD, COREY: 70
FRAZER, JOHN: 165
FREEDLEY, DURR: 6
FRENI, AL: 15
FRIEDLANDER, MARK: 162
FRITH, MICHAEL K.: 186
FULLER, GEORGE: 13
GATTEN, REX: 162
GEISEL, THEODOR S.: 79, 84
GELLERMAN, SAUL: 127
GEWIRTZ, PAUL D.: 208
GILLIAM, TERRY: 206
GINSBERG, ALLEN: 131
GIST, GILMAN, JR.: 118
GOLD, IVAN: 155
GOLDBERG, CAROLYN: 196
GOLDBERG, RUBE: 39
GOLDBERG, TOM: 133
GRUBER, MITCHELL: 168
HALLOWELL, ROBERT C.: 5
HAVERSON, CAPTAIN JIMMY: 76
HEDGEPETH, WILLIAM: 184
HEMMINGER, G. L.: 39
HIX, AL: 135
HOLMGREN, R. J.: 6
HUMPHRIES, RICHARD: 114
INGRAM, GORDON: 12
IVINS, PERRY: 70
JACOBSON, HERBERT L.: 113
JOHNSTON, J. JEREMY: 202
JOY, J. R.: 24, 25
KEMP, NANCY ELLEN: 208
KENT, ROCKWELL: 4
KLEES, FREDERICK S.: 6
KOREN, ED: 170
KRAEMER, WALT: 164, 171
LAX, ROBERT: 111, 113
LEFER, HENRY: 96
LOPHAUSER, SIGMUND: 146
MACMULLEN, C. F.: 77
MARQUAND, JOHN P.: 55
MAX, ALAN M.: 86
MCCORKLE, SUSANNAH: 198
MEEKS, GIRARD: 7
MERTON, THOMAS: 116
MILLS, TOM: 200
MOORE, WESLEY F.: 14
MORGENTHAL, J. STANLEY: 104
MUELLER, T. C.: 70
NAGANO, PAUL T.: 165
NICKLAUS, CAROL: 14
OSBORNE, MORRIS M.: 53
OSBORNE, R. C.: 65
OVIATT, E. S.: 21
PADAN, WILEY: 66
PERELMAN, S. J.: 85
PERSON, ELAINE S.: 190
PETERS, CURTIS A.: 81, 83
PETERSON, DON: 164
PHINIZY, COLES H.: 131
QUIRK, BRYAN: 7
REINHARDT, AD F.: 94
ROBERTS, D.: 151
ROBERTS, TOM: 172
ROBINS, TED: 163
ROCKWELL, NORMAN: 2
ROSAND, DAVID A.: 156
RUARK, ROBERT C., JR.: 95, 117
RUSSELL, BRUCE: 86
SALA, EDWARD R.: 14
SANTAYANA, GEORGE: 25, 31
SELLERS, FRED: 164
SEUSS, DR.: 79, 84
SHAW, FRANK: 66
SHELTON, GILBERT: 164, 165
SHERWOOD, ROBERT E.: 48
SHULMAN, MAX: 132, 134
SIEGEL, "SPARKS": 154
SIMPSON, LOUIS: 122
SMITH, ANDRE: 58
SMITH, FIELDING K.: 64
SMITH, ROBERT PAUL: 112
SNEE, H.: 152
STEVENSON, J. S.: 160
STRAIGHT, WILLARD DICKERMAN: 58
SULLIVAN, JOHN J.: 114
SYMONS, BOB: 129
TARKINGTON, BOOTH: 22, 26, 30
TERRIBERRY, WILLIAM STOUTENBOROUGH: 18
THURBER, JAMES: 46
TILSON, BARNARD: 166
UMMINGER, FREDERICK W., JR.: 172
WALKER, MORT: 146
WEAVER, DOODLES: 115
WEGARS, DON: 211
WEST, BILL: 173
WICKSTROM, PER: 196
WIEDER, BOB: 188
WILBUR, BOB: 136

WILSON, ROWLAND: 160, 161
WINTER, JACK M.: 186
WISNIEWSKI, JAMES CASIMIR: 203
WOLFE, THOMAS: 52
WOOD, WAYNE: 12
WOUK, HERMAN: 93

THE MAGAZINES

ALABAMA'S FARRAGO: 194, 204
ALABAMA RAMMER JAMMER: 136
AMERICAN UNIVERSITY BALD EAGLE: 151, 164, 171, 209
AMHERST LORD JEFF: 119
AMHERST SABRINA: 194, 203
ANNAPOLIS LOG: 76, 190, 192, 203
ARIZONA KITTY-KAT: 67, 114, 172
BOWDOIN BEAR-SKIN: 6, 62, 81
BREVARD ENGINEERING COLLEGE PELICAN: 180
BRIGHAM YOUNG Y'S GUY: 82
BROWN JUG: 13, 67, 77, 80, 82, 85, 88, 111, 116, 117
CALIFORNIA PELICAN: 13, 39, 77, 82, 86, 119, 164, 172, 180, 188, 196, 198, 199, 211
CARNEGIE TECH PUPPET: 85
CCNY MERCURY: 96, 114, 205
COLGATE BANTER: 82, 117
COLORADO DODO: 102, 131
COLORADO FLATIRON: 136, 153, 170
COLUMBIA JESTER: 4, 6, 7, 15, 40, 44, 54, 67, 70, 78, 80, 86, 93, 94, 99, 104, 109, 111, 112, 113, 116, 122, 123, 131, 137, 138, 153, 155, 156, 160, 161, 165, 168, 170, 178, 185, 193, 196, 202, 203, 204, 208, 210
CORNELL WIDOW: 37, 39, 40, 58, 81, 111, 117, 144, 161, 166
DARTMOUTH JACK O'LANTERN: 53, 73, 79, 80, 81, 84, 146, 179, 203
DENVER PARRAKEET: 86
DENISON FLAMINGO: 86
DUKE PEER: 199
EMORY PHOENIX 12, 29, 184, 208
FLORIDA STATE SMOKE SIGNALS: 153, 163, 164, 172, 190, 208
GEORGE WASHINGTON UNIVERSITY GHOST: 66
GEORGIA TECH RAMBLER: 190, 208, 210
GEORGIA TECH YELLOW JACKET: 81, 117, 130
GRINNELL MALTEASER: 82
HAMILTON ROYAL GABOON: 79, 81
HARVARD LAMPOON: 5, 6, 14, 15, 20, 23, 24, 25, 27, 28, 29, 31, 38, 39, 41, 42, 43, 48, 49, 53, 55, 66, 80, 85, 100, 103, 105, 106, 108, 110, 117, 119, 125, 129, 131, 179, 186, 196, 202
HARVARD-RADCLIFFE GARGOYLE: 185
ILLINOIS SHAFT: 154
IOWA STATE GREEN GANDER: 170
JOHNS HOPKINS BLACK & BLUE JAY: 6, 7, 63, 71, 77
LAFAYETTE LYRE: 116
LAFAYETTE MARQUIS: 124
LEHIGH BURR: 95
MAINE MAINIAC: 76, 80
MASSACHUSETTS YAHOO: 174, 178, 182
MICHIGAN GARGOYLE: 114, 133
MICHIGAN STATE SPARTAN: 134, 142
MIDDLEBURY BLUE BABOON: 66, 81, 84
MINNESOTA SKI-U-MAH: 79, 132, 134
MISSOURI SHOWME: 127, 130, 143, 145, 146, 155
MIT VOO DOO: 12, 14, 80, 144, 190, 209
MONTCLAIR STATE GALUMPH: 190
MOUNT HOLYOKE RAVIN': 77
NEBRASKA AWGWAN: 40
NEW MEXICO JUGGLER: 183
NORTH CAROLINA BOLL WEEVIL: 79
NORTH CAROLINA BUCCANEER: 95, 114, 117
NORTH CAROLINA TAR BABY: 52
NORTHWESTERN PURPLE PARROT: 117
NOTRE DAME JUGGLER: 82
NOTRE DAME LEPRECHAUN: 181
NYU MEDLEY: 5, 82, 114
OCCIDENTAL FANG: 172, 178, 205, 206
OHIO GREEN GOAT: 117
OHIO OHIOAN: 119
OHIO STATE SUNDIAL 14, 46, 76, 79, 80, 86, 140, 192, 200, 202
OKLAHOMA COVERED WAGON: 136
OKLAHOMA WHIRLWIND: 66, 84, 117
OREGON STATE ORANGE OWL: 76, 81
PENN STATE FROTH: 39, 86, 99, 130, 143, 144, 145
PENNSYLVANIA PUNCH BOWL: 40, 80
PITTSBURGH PANTHER: 39, 42, 79, 80, 98, 111, 143, 151, 153
POMONA NEW SAGE HEN: 169
POMONA SAGE HEN: 12, 133, 153, 170
PRINCETON TIGER: 5, 13, 19, 20, 22, 24, 25, 26, 30, 31, 37, 39, 42, 45, 53, 56, 57, 68, 74, 82, 111, 113, 130, 131, 143, 144, 153, 154, 155, 164, 165, 174
PURDUE RIVET: 8, 130, 131
RANDOLPH-MACON WOMAN'S COLLEGE OLD MAID: 143
RICE OWL: 77
ROANOKE EXPRESSION: 14
RPI BACHELOR: 184
RUTGERS RUT: 209
ST. JOHN'S ANALYST: 119
SAN DIEGO STATE CACTI: 113
SAN JOSE STATE LYKE: 151
SEWANEE MOUNTAIN GOAT: 95
STANFORD CHAPARRAL: 31, 42, 66, 75, 76, 102, 115, 118, 129, 170
TEMPLE OWL: 111
TEXAS RANGER: 145, 151, 153, 160, 161, 164, 165, 172, 173, 180, 195
TEXAS (EL PASO) EL BURRO: 180, 203, 205, 208
TORONTO GOBLIN: 76, 82
TULANE URCHIN: 200, 208
UCLA SATYR: 191, 192, 209
UCLA SCOP: 153
USC WAMPUS: 117, 126, 128, 135
UTAH HUMBUG: 7, 64, 66, 67
UTAH UNIQUE: 134, 143
VIRGINIA SPECTATOR: 162
VIRGINIA POLYTECHNIC INSTITUTE SKIPPER: 119
WASHINGTON & LEE SOUTHERN COLLEGIAN: 135, 136
WASHINGTON STATE COUGAR'S PAW: 95
WEST POINT POINTER: 93, 98
WILLIAMS PURPLE COW: 43, 104, 117
WISCONSIN OCTOPUS: 67, 116, 117, 119, 145
YALE QUIP: 32
YALE RECORD: 18, 20, 21, 24, 25, 26, 28, 38, 39, 42, 43, 58, 65, 76, 81, 83, 114, 135, 136, 144, 145, 152, 159, 160, 167, 168, 172, 180, 195, 196, 197, 203

THANKS

Well over a hundred students, professors, librarians, college administrators, and alumni courteously helped in the unhumorous task of gathering material and securing permissions for this anthology. All of them deserve a word of gratitude.

Several friends and helpers deserve special thanks for unusual kindness and patience: Susan Alexion; Lounsbury Bates; Christopher B. Cerf; Dick Corten; John Goodwillie; Ken Hurwitz; Paula Matta; Leon Rosenstein; Max Shulman; Peter Shulman; David Heim and Elizabeth Van Siclen Townsend, who served as semi-willing sounding boards for every two-liner in this book, some of which they laughed at; Sally Kovalchick and Charles Schmalz, of Random House, who gave and received headaches with equal good cheer; and my mother, Ethel Mag Carlinsky, who unashamedly tells people I inherited my sense of humor from her.

D.C.

ABOUT THE EDITOR

DAN CARLINSKY never wrote for a college humor magazine. At Columbia, where he earned two degrees in the long-gone decade of the sixties, he spent his witticisms on the daily newspaper, weekly football band shows, and occasional passers-by. Thus he learned pity for those whose task it is to amuse. This is his fifth book; his articles and humorous writings have appeared in many publications, including *Esquire, Look, Sports Illustrated, The Sunday New York Times,* and *TV Guide.*